Fundamentals of Accounting

Fundamentals of Accounting

Chloe Hill

MURPHY & MOORE
www.murphy-moorepublishing.com

Published by Murphy & Moore Publishing,
1 Rockefeller Plaza,
New York City, NY 10020, USA

ISBN: 978-1-63987-241-1

Cataloging-in-Publication Data

Fundamentals of accounting / Chloe Hill.
p. cm.
Includes bibliographical references and index.
ISBN 978-1-63987-241-1
1. Accounting. 2. Bookkeeping. 3. Financial statements. I. Hill, Chloe.
HF5625 .F86 2022
657--dc23

For information on all Murphy & Moore Publications
visit our website at www.murphy-moorepublishing.com

MURPHY & MOORE

Contents

Preface

The process of recording financial transactions which are related to business is known as accounting. It measures the results of economic activities of an organization and conveys the information to different types of users such as investors, management, regulators and creditors. The subject of accounting is divided into four branches, namely, management accounting, tax accounting, financial accounting and cost accounting. Management accounting deals with measurement, analysis and reporting of information for internal use by the management. Tax accounting refers to accounting for tax purposes. Financial accounting is concerned with preparation of financial statements for the use of external users such as regulators, suppliers and investors. Cost accounting refers to the set of procedures used to record and report cost of manufacturing goods and services. This book is compiled in such a manner, that it will provide in-depth knowledge about the theory and practice of accounting. It unfolds the innovative aspects of accounting which will be crucial for the holistic understanding of the subject matter. Through this book, we attempt to further enlighten the readers about the new concepts in this field.

A short introduction to every chapter is written below to provide an overview of the content of the book:

Chapter 1 - The process of systematic recordation of financial transactions along with storing, sorting, analyzing, reporting, summarizing and presenting the results in reports is known as accounting. It is a necessary function which facilitates decision-making, cost planning and assessing performance of a business. This chapter serves as an introduction to the world of accounting, its branches and terms such as orientation, cash book, etc; **Chapter 2 -** Accounting has its own rules and guidelines that must be followed by businesses while reporting their financial data, which all fall under accounting principles. While dealing with accounting situations, another set of general conventions known as accounting concepts is strictly observed. This chapter deals with the basic accounting principles, concepts, conventions, their inherent differences along with traditional and modern accounting systems in an easy-to-understand manner; **Chapter 3 -** The easiest and most basic way to record a transaction is to use a journal entry. Journals and ledgers are the commonly used methods to record financial transactions. Mercantilism, the systems of accounting, share capital, debenture, etc. are a few aspects which come under financial transactions and the methods used to document them. This chapter has been carefully written to provide the reader with a clearer understanding of the subject matter. **Chapter 4 -** A financial statement is a written report or record which conveys the business activities and financial performance of a company and includes a summary of the financial results, position and cash flow. Balance sheets, liabilities, income statements, equities, etc. are a few types of financial statements. This chapter covers these financial statements and its types in a clear and concise manner. **Chapter 5 -** Auditing refers to the independent examination or inspection of financial information of an organization in order to ascertain the accuracy of its financial statements and can be either internal or external. Financial audit, internal audit, cost auditing, continuous auditing, etc. are different types of auditing. This chapter discusses auditing and it's various aspects in a comprehensive manner.

Finally, I would like to thank my fellow scholars who gave constructive feedback and my family members who supported me at every step.

Chloe Hill

1

Introduction to Accounting

The process of systematic recordation of financial transactions along with storing, sorting, analyzing, reporting, summarizing and presenting the results in reports is known as accounting. This chapter serves as an introduction to the world of accounting, its branches and terms such as orientation, cash book, etc.

Earning adequate profits is the basic necessity for the smooth functioning and long term survival of any business. Without profits no firm can think of running its functions smoothly. For the purpose of earning profits, business houses deals with the monetary transactions either by selling the goods (manufactured on its own or purchased) or by purchasing the items (on cash or credit). This sale and purchase of products in the market leads to either profits or losses, which needs to be carefully recorded in the books of accounts, so as to keep a record of the same for communication purposes, both to the insiders and the outsiders. This recorded information is used up by the management in taking financial decisions, controlling and deciding upon the budgets. And it will be available only when recorded properly by following a set devised system. This system is known as Book Keeping and Accounting.

Book keeping merely deals with the process of recording, classifying and summarizing business transactions, which are measurable in terms of money. Accounting on the other hand is concerned with the interpretation of the recorded transactions, for the use of the management as well as the outside users. Accounting is not only used in the field of business but has spread its wings to various other fields, and has gained importance for providing adequate, accurate and timely information to the users of the financial data.

Book Keeping, as the name suggests is the art of keeping a record of transactions in the books. It is the process of recording, classifying and summarizing the monetary transactions in the books of accounts, in a systematic manner, so as at the end of accounting year a clear picture of the profits earned and the losses incurred throughout the year, are portrayed in front of the management.

Accounting, is not confined only to the recording of transactions in the books, but extends far beyond, and analyses, interprets the information for the benefit of management. Accounting is not a new system; its existence is believed as early as 4500 B.C., in the civilizations of Babylonia and Assyria, where the transactions were recorded for the payment of wages and taxes on clay tablets. Accounting has evolved since ages and now with the advancement in social and economic environment, its use has been expanded and new dimensions are added up to the accounting discipline.

In simple terms, accounting refers to the science of classifying the business transactions and events with a main purpose of communicating the results to persons who are involved in decision making process. It deals with presenting the accounting information in simpler terms, so as to help the management and the outside users in making judgments. Accounting is considered as a language of business, which is understandable by everyone. Basically the main aim of accounting is to ascertain the profit and loss of the business for an accounting year, to disclose the financial position of the business, measuring income of the firm and communicating the summarized information, so that it can be used up by the managers, owners and other related parties.

Accounting is considered as an important part for any business house. The entire structure of business is based on the concept of accounting, as without accounting the business will not survive. Accounting has several definitions by different authors and books. However, certain definitions are mentioned below:

> "Accounting may be defined as the art of recording, classifying and summarizing in a significant manner and in terms of money, transactions and events, which are in part, at least of financial character, and interpreting the results thereof."

This definition is widely accepted by majority of accounting professionals and organisations worldwide. Other definitions are as follows:

> "Accounting is the science of recording, classifying and summarizing transactions so that relation with outsiders is exactly determined and result of operation during a particular period can be calculated, and the financial position as the end of the period may be shown."

"Accounting may be defi ned as the art and science of recording business transactions in a methodological manner", so as to show:

- The true state of affairs of a business of a particular period of time.
- The surplus or deficiency which has accrued during a specified period.

"Accounting is an information system that provides reports to stakeholders about the economic activities and conditions of a business." From the above definitions, following points are highlighted:

- Accounting discloses the nature and amount of incomes.
- Only the transactions of financial character are disclosed.
- It is the art of summarizing the business transactions.
- The economic activities carried out by business are disclosed, along with the financial condition.
- Importance is laid on the communication of information to the persons who are to make the important decisions.

Methods of Accounting

Accounting deals with the recording, analyzing and interpreting the accounting information to the interested users (both inside and outside). Business transactions can be recorded in the books, by two ways:

- Single Entry: Business Organisations if follow this system, prepare only cash book and personal accounts of debtors/creditors. Therefore complete record maintenance is not possible and trial balance cannot be prepared.

- Double Entry: It maintains a two-fold effect of benefit giving and receiving aspects. It means that the record of equal debit and equal credit is maintained. In India, business transactions are recorded by the way of double entry system, hence depicting the debit and credit of every transaction.

Objectives of Accounting

The main objectives of accounting include:

- To depict the profit/loss for a particular period: Accounting tells about the efficiency of the business. Every businessman is keen to depict the net profit or loss for its business, which can be calculated with the help of income and expenses by preparing profit and loss account.
- To maintain record of Business Transactions: It is very difficult for the businessman to summarize the numerous amount of different transactions, so in order to avoid this, proper record of transactions is kept in the books of accounts. The recorded information verifies the information so recorded and acts as an evidence for the financial transactions.
- To depict true financial position: One of the objective of accounting is to find the correct financial position of business in the form of assets and liabilities, presented in a balance sheet, prepared at the end of every accounting year.
- To disclose the liquidity position: Financial reporting provides information about the liquidity position of an enterprise, and how it spends the cash, how much cash it borrows and other resource distributions, and factors that may affect the liquidity and solvency of an enterprise.
- To help making rational decision making: Accounting records provide a well record of financial information which help the businessman in making proper decisions about the business, by the help of the presented information.
- To fulfill the requirement of Law: All the Companies, societies, public trusts etc are required to maintain accounts as per the law, such as Companies Act, Societies Act, Income Tax Act etc. Hence, business houses keep a record of the financial transactions by the way of accounting records.
- To provide accounting information to its users: The accounting process is involved in generating the accounting information, which is communicated to the interested users, belonging to different users such as investors, management, suppliers and creditors etc. it is prepared in such a way, so as to help the users for taking important decisions regarding the business.
- To disclose the creditworthiness of business: Business houses operate through the finances which they generate by different means. One of the ways is by the way of investments made by investors in the business. Investors will invest only if they are satisfied by the working of the business and have an assurance that it will generate enough profits. This assurance is gained by looking at the past accounting records, which help in building trust upon the management.

Accounting as an Information Source

The main objective of accounting is to provide information to the interested users, for making useful decisions. The main aim of accountants is usually to enhance the quality of the financial data and make it understandable and useful for its users. In order to make sure that the accounting information is useful in decision making, following characteristics must be possessed in the accounting information:

- Reliable: Reliable information is one which is true and correct, and the users can blindly depend upon the information. The information should be free from biasness, error and truly represent what it is supposed to depict about the financial position.
- Relevance: It refers to the importance of the information communicated. It means that the information must be available on time, and help in proper predictions and decision making.
- Comparable: Accounting information is said to be comparable when the users can easily compare various aspects of information over different time periods as well as with other entities. It should be noted that the accounting information must belong to a common period.
- Understandable: Information is said to be understandable when the decision makers are able to interpret it in the same sense, as the information was prepared and conveyed to them. It is the duty of the accountants to present the information in the most accurate, clear and understandable manner without any biasness and error.

Accounting Functions

Accounting functions are termed as those set of financial systems that help in the bookkeeping of financial information in the organization, financial analysis, summary creation, reporting of transactions and act as the backbone for almost any business. The accounting as a system tries to identify, assess and record the transactions of financial nature in a very systematic approach.

Functions of Accounting

- The accounting helps in the maintenance of bookkeeping and record keeping.
- Accounting helps in the collection and storage of the financial information, transactions happening within the organization, and financial activities happening in the organization.
- It helps in the tracking the several information on daily or a monthly basis.
- It helps in the creation and documentation of financial history from day to the latest period.
- It helps in the formulation of comprehensive financial policy for the business.
- It is also utilized in the preparation of budgets and financial projections.
- It also helps in the reconciliation of information between two sources of financial systems.

- The accounted information can be shared with the external stakeholders with the intent for business planning and growth.
- Accounting does not focus on the activities about the capital budgeting.
- It also helps in audit functions and curbs the internal weakness as it makes the systems accountable.
- A business or an organization can prepare and work on several journals to maintain different accounts.
- A comprehensive accounting system ensures that the accounts of corporates expenses do not get mixed with the personal accounts of vice presidents or managers. Such instances are generally referred to as red flags.

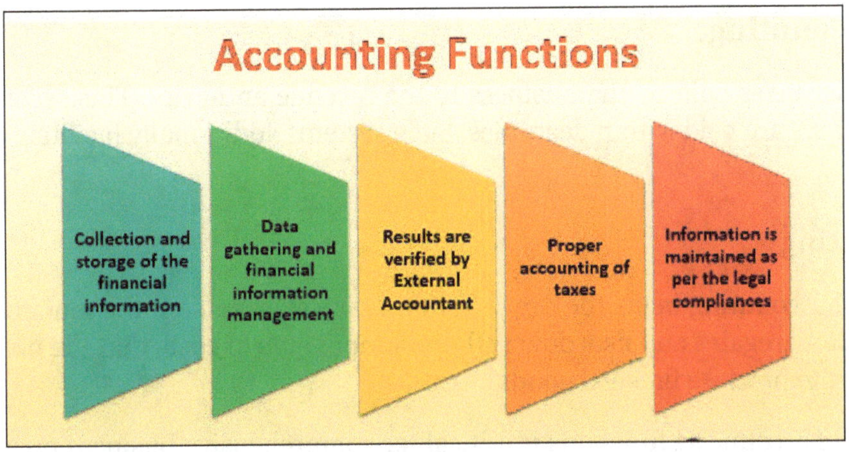

Types of Accounting Functions

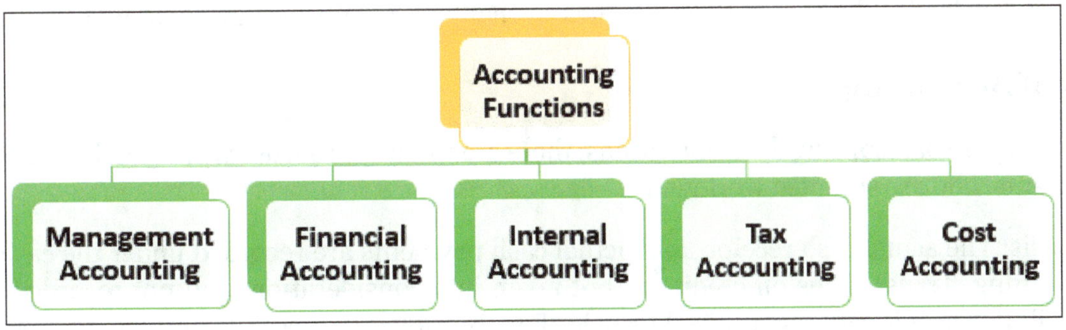

Management Accounting

- This type of accounting observes the performance of a business and identifies the opportunities to improve the entity's financial health. Such a system or function recommends the management with a price that it should set to make the business profitable.
- The management helps in the preparation of internal management reports. It looks into trends, expectations on sales, and corresponding costs. It also helps the management in comprehensive workforce planning.

- In short, it could be inferred that it helps the organization to make decisions on the management.

Financial Accounting

This type of accounting utilizes accounting transactions and transforms them into consolidated financial statements. These systems also help in historical analysis. The users of the results presented by the financial accounting functions can be utilized by creditors and lenders.

Internal Accounting

Internal accounting monitors and examines the controls and processes implemented within the organization to detect fraud and weakness within the management and teams.

Taxation Accounting

These account for taxes paid by the business to the revenue authority. This system ensures that the returns on taxes are paid within deadlines. Such systems additionally facilitate the planning of taxes.

Cost Accounting

This function of accounting helps the organization make decisions on the amounts and types of costs it incurs. It segregates and lists down all the components of costs that the business incurs to render service or to produce finished goods.

The knowledge of accounting functions is critical for comprehensive business management. They additionally play a crucial role in daily pursuits of life. It helps in tactful record-keeping of resources of the organization, which in turn ensures compliance in the organization. The lenders and investors only lend and invest in those businesses that have sound accounting practices.

Basis of Accounting

For the purpose of recording the transactions, there are three approaches which can be used by the accountants, and are accepted worldwide:

Cash Basis: The actual cash receipts and actual cash payments are recorded under the cash basis of accounting. Transactions on credit are not taken into consideration, and not recorded in the books, till the cash is actually received or paid. For Example: the Receipts and Payment Account prepared by the Non- Profitable Institutes (schools, hospitals, charitable houses etc.).

Advantages:

- It is realistic in nature.
- It is simple to use and verifiable.

Demerits:

- It does not depict the true profit and loss of the enterprise.

- It does not follow the matching principle of accounting.
- It ignores the credit transactions, hence incomplete results.

Accrual Basis: The drawbacks of cash basis of accounting paved the way for the development of accrual basis by the accountants. Under this system the costs and revenue are recognised in the same accounting year in which they occur, rather than when they are actually paid. This does not violate the matching concept of accounting. For example: the raw materials consumed are matched against the cost of goods sold.

Advantages:

- It is more scientific as compared to the cash basis of accounting.
- It gives a complete picture of the financial transactions of the business.
- It does not violate the matching concept of accounting.

Demerits:

- It is not as simple as cash basis.
- The net profit or loss cannot be reached at quickly, as lots of adjustments are required.

Hybrid/Mixed Basis: The accountant tried to club in both the basis of accounting and come up with one, where the advantages of both the basis are used up. Under hybrid system, Incomes are recorded on cash basis, whereas expenses are taken on accrual basis of accounting.

Advantages of Acounting

Accounting is the language of the business, it means it acts as a means of communication with the outside world and discloses the financial activities to the users. The accounting information so presented serves various benefits to the organisation:

- Acts as a memory replacement: Accounting information is a replacement of the human memory, as it is quite difficult to remember each and every transaction by the businessman, therefore accounting has served as a replacement to the human memory.
- Comparative Study: Accounting helps the owners to judge the profits, sales, expenses of the company in one accounting year, as compared to that of the previous year. And also, helps in finding any kind of differences or changes between the two period figures.
- Provides assistance to different parties: Accounting information provides the information to different classes of users and helps them in taking the decisions concerning the business affairs.
- Complete Record: Accounting is a process of recording, classifying, summarizing and communicating the business transactions to the interested users, who are directly or indirectly related to the business. Therefore accounting provides a complete set/ record of the business transactions in a systematic manner.

- Supplying information about financial activities: Accounting provides information about the financial activities i.e. the profits earned and losses incurred are disclosed by the accounting information. Moreover, the basic function of accounting is also to reveal the financial activities to the owners and managers of the business.
- Complying legal formalities: Tax assessment is made easy with the help of accounting information; means accounting information helps the owners of the business in deciding the amount of taxes to be paid and also helps in fulfilling other formalities of income tax and sales tax returns.
- Evidence in Court: If the accounts are maintained properly, they will act as proper evidence in the court, in case of any disputes. It is because the transactions when recorded are entered in with proper proof and in a systematic order.

Uses of Accounting Information

Accounting information is presented by the accountants, so that it is used by different users. It is utilized by the interested parties, who are directly or indirectly related to the business, for their own benefit respectively. The way how different parties utilize the accounting information is stated below:

- Owners: Owners use up the accounting information to judge the financial position of its concern, and find out if profits were earned or losses were incurred in the previous year. Owners need information for the study of past performance and considering the future prospects.
- Investors: Before putting their money in the business, investors access the financial efficiency, profit earning capacity, dividend paying capacity and solvency of the firm. The investors are interested to know that whether the firm is growing steadily, and whether the value of its shares is increasing.
- Government: Government utilizes the accounting information for studying the performance of a particular unit, income, and expenditure in order to impose tax and excise duty on the company.
- Creditors/Suppliers: Banks, suppliers and financial institutions use accounting information to judge the credit paying capacity of the enterprise, interest paying capacity. By judging so, they are able to actually decide whether to grant loans/credit to the institute.
- Managers: The managers of the enterprise use accounting information to plan, control, evaluate the performance and for decision making regarding the affairs of business.
- Employees: Employees are the assets of an organisation, they are concerned with the profits of the business because they are paid salaries, bonus etc. from the profits. And the profits of the organisation are judged from the accounting information.
- Research Scholars: Students involved in the research work, often use up the published accounting information for the purpose of analyzing the financial position and hence proving their thesis.

Limitations of Accounting

Following are some of the limitations affecting accounting:

- Only monetary transactions are recorded: Accounting records only the transactions that are capable of being presented in terms of money, and does not include the events of non-monetary nature, even though it is of great importance to the business. Example: Strikes by the labour, efficiency of the R&D department.
- Personal biasness involved: Accountants are involved in the process of recording the accounting information, it may be affected by his personal biasness, such as, he may select any way of depreciating the machinery, valuing the stock and treating deferred revenue expenditure. The judgment of accountant will definitely affect the preparation and presentation of accounting information.
- Historical in Nature: The information supplied is on the basis of the already prepared Profit and Loss account and Balance Sheet. This means that only the information about already happened events is disclosed and no information about future is presented. Hence, accounting is historic in nature.
- Allows different treatments: Accounting allows different treatments within Generally Accepted Accounting Concepts (GAAP). An accountant for example, can either use the LIFO (last in first out) method or FIFO (first in first out) method in order to value the closing stock. Applying different methods might lead to different results and as a result the comparable quality of information might get lost. 5) Changes in price are not considered: Accounting transactions are recorded in the books of accounts at cost basis, whereas the effect of changes in price level is not considered and not recorded in the books. As a result comparing the data of various years becomes quite difficult.

Accounting Systems

The financial transactions of any accounting system can be grouped into four major accounting cycles: Revenue, Purchase, Payroll, and General Journal.

Accounting system transactions in the form of sales invoices, receipts, purchase invoices, checks, and payroll entries are posted to the appropriate journals. Simultaneously — as a form of internal control — these postings are recorded in the general ledger, or "GL". The GL is an important part of an accounting system because it accumulates all transaction activity, where it is organized by account class.

Various reports, including financial statements, can be prepared from the data collected in the GL. Corrections or necessary adjustments can be made to the general ledger by creating adjusting journal entries, posted to the general journal.

Accounting System Cycles

There are four main accounting cycles within all accounting systems: the Revenue Cycle, Purchase Cycle, Payroll Cycle, and the General Journal Cycle.

Revenue Cycle

- Order Entry: Invoices entered through direct entry, sales orders, or point-of-sale (POS) systems, such as a cash register, are posted to the sales journal. These entries also accumulate on the accounts receivable ledger, organized by customer. If the business maintains an inventory, the posting of sales also affects the inventory ledger. Finally, all sales journal activity is also posted to the GL. A discussion of your revenue cycle should be covered in your revenue procedures.
- Cash Receipts/Deposits: Receipts on sales and other bank deposits are posted to the cash receipts journal. Sales receipt information also accumulates on the accounts receivable ledger, organized by customer. These postings are also entered on the bank account ledger. Finally, all cash receipts journal activity is also posted to the GL.
- Accounts Receivable: Accounts Receivable, and important part of any accounting system, is a separate journal that records both sales and cash receipt data by customer. The data comes from the postings to the cash receipts journal and the sales invoice journal.

Purchase Cycle

- Purchase Orders/Purchasing: Invoices entered through direct entry, or through purchase orders, are posted to the purchase journal. These entries also accumulate on the accounts payable ledger, organized by vendor. If the business maintains an inventory, the posting of purchases also affects the inventory ledger. Finally, all purchase journal activity is posted to the general ledger.
- Cash Disbursements/Checks: Payments on account or for expenses are posted to the cash disbursement journal. Payment on account information also accumulates on the accounts payable ledger, organized by vendor; these postings are also entered on the bank account ledger. Finally, during this cycle of an accounting system, cash disbursement journal activity is posted to the general ledger.
- Accounts Payable: Accounts Payable is a separate journal that records both sales and cash receipt data by vendor. The data comes from the postings to the cash disbursement journal and the purchase journal.

Payroll Cycle

During this part of an accounting system, payroll data by employees are entered into the payroll journal. These postings are also entered in the cash disbursements journal and the payroll ledger. Finally, all payroll journal activity is also posted to the GL.

General Journal Cycle

Corrections or adjustments to the above major transaction cycles can be made through adjusting journal entries, posted directly to the general ledger. These are also compiled in a separate journal, known as the "general journal".

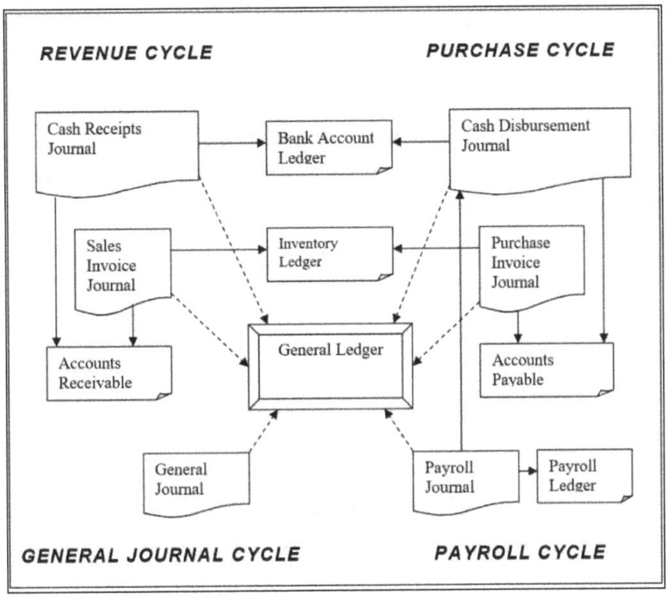

Posting Process

The specific postings, as outlined in the cycles above, do not necessarily take place as separate steps, especially in computerized accounting software systems. There are only two basic posting methods in computerized accounting systems: *real-time* and *batch* posting.

In real-time posting, the source transaction (check, bill, payment, receipt, etc.) is posted to the specific journal and any related subsidiary ledger (e.g., accounts receivable, accounts payable, inventory) and is simultaneously posted to the general ledger.

In batch posting, the journals and subsidiary ledgers are posted, but entries are not yet posted to the general ledger. Posting these journals to the general ledger is done separately. Typically, a group of transactions (often a full day's worth) is entered. Later, after the journals are reviewed for accuracy, this entire day's group, or "batch", is posted to the general ledger.

To understand this posting process of an accounting system better, it would be helpful to follow specific transactions through a sample company. First, however, we need to define various accounting terms and concepts.

Accounting Ratios

Financial ratios can be calculated by dividing one number by another, and are usually expressed in the form of percentage (%). Ratio analysis enables business owners to examine the relationships between seemingly unrelated items which help in decision-making. Financial ratios are simple to calculate, easy to use, easily understandable by the layman and provide a wealth of information that cannot be gotten anywhere else. Ratios are tools that aid judgment and cannot take the place of experience. They do not replace good management, but they can make a good manager better. Virtually any financial statistics can be compared with another by using the concept of ratio analysis. Small business owners and managers only need to be concerned with a small set of ratios in order to identify where improvements are needed. Different organizations require different types of ratio depends upon the scale of business operation, the age of the business, the point in the business cycle, and any particular information sought. In simple words "Different ratios are used for different problems". As, some ratios indicate the trend or progress or downfall of the business firm. However, ratio analysis is not an end in itself. It is only a means of better understanding of financial strengths and weaknesses of the financial position of the concern. Thus, the ratio of two figures 200 and 100 may be expressed in any of the following ways:

- 2:1
- 2/1
- 2 to 1
- 200%

In all these cases the inference is that the first figure is double, 200% or 2 times than that of the second. Ratios provide clues to the financial position of the concern. These are the pointers of financial soundness of enterprises.

Objectives of Ratio Analysis in a Concern

For purpose of analysis, accounting ratios are indispensable. A meaningful analysis of the financial situation and performance is the first great advantage of accounting ratios. This requires ratios and their comparison which may be:

- Within the same firm over a period of years.
- The comparison of one firm with another.
- One firm against the industry as a whole or against predetermined standards.
- For one division or department of a firm against other divisions or departments of the same firm.

Inter-firm comparison and intra-firm comparison are, thus possible on the basis of accounting ratios; this can also be attempted in other ways but accounting ratios are indispensible in this respect. Example: To judge which firm has the best overall efficiency, one should compare the rate of profit on capital employed for the firms concerned- the size of the profit as such is not relevant.

Accounting ratios not only indicate the present position, they also indicate the causes leading up to the position to a large extent. For instance, accounting ratios may indicate not only that financial position is precarious but also the past policies or actions which have caused it. Best results are obtained when ratios for a number of years are put in a tabular form so that the figures for one year can be easily compared with those of other years. Some other significance is as follows:

- Ratio analysis is an aid to measure general efficiency.
- Ratio analysis is an aid in comparison of financial data.
- Ratio analysis helps in planning and forecasting various issues.

- Ratio analysis is an aid in Intra firm comparison.
- Ratio analysis helps in facilitating decision making.
- Ratio analysis used to test profitability.
- Ratio analysis to test solvency position.
- Ratio analysis is an effective tool for management.

Expressional Form of Ratio

Accounting ratios express the relationship between two financial variables of the financial statements. They are expressed in any one of the following forms:

- Pure: It is expressed as a quotient.
- Percentage: It is expressed in percentage.
- Times: It is expressed in a number of times a particular figure is compared to another figure.
- Fraction: It is expressed in fraction.

Steps in the Ratio Analysis

Step-1: Relevant data is to be selected from the financial statements depending upon the objectives of the concern.

Step-2: Calculation of appropriate ratios from the above data (Step-1).

Step-3: Comparison of the calculated ratios with the ratios of the same firm in the past, or the ratios developed from projected financial statements or the ratios of some other firms.

Step-4: Interpretation of the calculated ratios.

Ratios Interpretation

Interpretation of the Ratio is an important factor as it requires skill, intelligence and foresightedness. The impact of various factors like price level changes, change in accounting policies, window dressing etc., should keep in mind while interpreting the financial statement through this tool i.e. Ratio Analysis. A single ratio in itself does not convey much of the sense. To make ratios useful, they have to be further interpreted. The interpretation can be done in the various ways few of them are as follows:

- Single Absolute Ratio: When single is considered in isolation one cannot draw any meaningful conclusion but single ratios may be studied in relation to certain rules of thumb which are based upon well proven conventions.
- Number of Ratios: Ratio can be interpreted by calculating number of related ratios because when a single ratio supported by other related additional ratios, becomes more understandable and meaningful.

- Comparison: The simple and best method of evaluating the performance of the firm is to compare its present ratios with the past ratios as it gives an indication of the direction of change and reflects whether the firm's performance and financial position has improved, deteriorated or remained constant over a period of time.
- Projected Ratios: Ratios can be calculated for future standards based upon the projected or Performa financial statements. These future ratios may be taken as standard for comparison and the ratios calculated on actual financial statement can be compared with the standard ratios to find out variances, if any. Such variances help in interpretation.
- Inter Firm Comparisons: Ratio of one firm can be compare with the ratios of another firm at the same point of time. This type of comparison helps in evaluating relative financial position of the firm. It is consider as inter- firm comparison.

Guiding Principles for use of Ratios

The calculation of ratios may not be difficult task but their use is not easy. The information on which they are based is important which influence the use of ratios. Following guiding principles need to be followed while interpreting different ratios:

- Data available in financial statements: The ratios are calculated from the data available in financial statements. The reliability of ratios is linked to the accuracy of information in these statements. Before calculating ratios one should see whether proper concepts and conventions have been used for preparing financial statements or not.
- Objective of Analysis: The type of ratios is to be calculated will depend upon the purpose for which these are required. The purpose of user is also important for the analysis of the ratio. Different objectives may require the study of different types of ratios.
- Choice of Ratios: The proper choice of appropriate ratios is also one of the important factors. The ratio should match the purpose for which these are required and only those ratios should be selected which can throw proper light on the matter to be discussed then only relevant conclusion can be come.
- Following Standards: The ratios will give an indication of financial statements only when discussed with reference to certain standards. These standards can be considered as rule of thumb. The comparison of calculated ratios with the standards will help the analyst in forming his opinion about financial health of the concern.
- Caliber of the Analyst: The ratios are only the tools of analysis and their interpretation will depend upon the caliber and competence of the analyst. He should be familiar with various financial statements as wrong interpretation may create havoc for the concern since wrong conclusions may lead to wrong decisions.

Importance of Ratio Analysis

The interrelationship that exists among the different items in the Financial Statement are revealed by accounting ratios. Thus, they are equally useful to the internal management, prospective investors, creditors and outsiders etc.

Besides, ratios are the best tool for measuring liquidity, solvency, profitability and management efficiency of a firm. That is why the role of accounting ratios is very significant to increase the efficiency of the management, to reduce the expenditure arid to increase the rate of profit etc.

The Importance of Ratio Analysis is Discussed Hereunder

- Analysis and Scrutiny of the Past Result: It helps to analyse the probable causal relation among different items after analyzing and scrutinizing the past result.
- Preparation of Budgets: The ratios that are derived after analyzing and scrutinizing the past result helps the management to prepare budgets and estimates, to formulate policy, and to prepare the future plan of action and, thus, helps as a guide to harmonize among different items for preparing budgets.
- Time Dimension by Trend Analysis: It helps to take time dimension into account by trend analysis, i.e. whether the firm is improving or deteriorating over a number of years that can easily be studied by the trend analysis. So, comparison can be made without difficulty by the analyst and to see whether the said ratio is high or low in comparison with the Standard or Normal Ratio.
- Measurement of Degree of Efficiency: It throws light on the degree of efficiency of the management and utilization of the assets and that is why it is called surveyor of efficiency.

Inter-Firm Comparison: It helps to make an inter-firm comparison, either between the different departments of a firm or between two firms employed in the identical types of business, or between the same firms on two different dates. Thus, the comparative analysis can be made possible between the industry average ratio and the ratio of each business unit.

- Testing Short-term Liquidity: Short-term liquidity position, i.e. whether the firm is able to maintain its short-term maturing obligations or not that can be easily known by applying liquidity ratios. At the same time, long-term solvency position can also be measured by the application of leverage or profitability ratios. Thus, the ratio is an invaluable aid to the users of Financial Statements.
- Communication: With the help of ratio analysis, meaningful information can be communicated to the users of accounting information and as a result the analyst can draw right decisions.
- Formulating Govt. Polices: Since ratios are the tools to measure industrial efficiency and performance the Governments takes various financial policy on the basis of the results of various related ratio analysis.
- Measuring Corporate Sickness: Undoubtedly, ratio analysis helps us to measure the corporate sickness well in advance so that the management, shareholders and other interested parties may take proper steps to avoid such a situation.
- Testing Long-Term Solvency Position: Long-term solvency position can be tested with the help of ratio analysis e.g. Debt-Equity ratio, Capital Gearing Ratio etc. These ratios help the analyst to assess the long-term debt paying capacity of the firm. Prospective investors, long-term creditors etc. are interested to measure the long-term solvency position before taking investment decisions.

Limitations of Ratio Analysis

Even the ratio analysis is not free from snags. There are certain limitations, such as:

- Proper Comparison not Possible: Comparison between two variables proves worthwhile provided their basis of valuation is identical. But, in reality, it is not possible, such as methods of valuation of Stock-in-Trade or charging different methods of depreciation on Fixed Assets etc. That is, if different methods are followed by different firms for their valuation, then comparison will practically be of no vise.
- Unreliable Data: Ratio depends on figures of the Financial Statements. But, in most cases, the figures are window-dressed. As a result, the correct picture cannot be drawn up by the ratio analysis, although certain structural defects can be detected. Moreover, manipulation made through time of reporting which may lead to manipulate the ratio analysis as well.
- Trend Analysis not Always Possible: Ratio analysis becomes more meaningful and significant if trend analysis (i.e. the analysis over a number of years) is possible instead of analyzing the result of a particular year. But, in practice, it is not always possible.
- Not Helpful for Preparing Budgets: Ratios are computed on the basis of past result. It does not help properly to predict the future, to prepare budgets and estimates since the business policies are constantly changing.
- Difficult to Ascertain Normal or Standard Ratio: It is very difficult to ascertain the Normal or Standard ratio in order to make proper comparison. Because, it differs from firm to firm, industry to industry, and even between different seasons of the same industry. Besides, it may happen that in one firm, a current ratio of 1: 1 is found to be quite satisfactory, whereas, in another firm, even 2.5: 1 may be found unsatisfactory.

Changes in Price-level: Ratios do not present true information in case of changing price-level of the variables. In that case, ratios will present distorted figure or misleading information.

- Not Possible to Solve the Problems: Analysis and interpretation of ratios helps us to locate the problems relating to the variables but cannot help us to solve such problems.
- Historical: Since ratios are computed form the past data which are contained in the financial statements they cannot predict future and as such they are not the real tool to make proper comparison.
- Fails to Detect the Role of Negative Number: Ratio-fails to detect the role of negative number—Arithmetical calculations gives wrong information and ratios cannot detect them.

Branches of Accounting

Financial Accounting

Financial accounting refers to collecting, summarizing and presentation of the financial information resulting from business transactions. It reports the operating profit and the value of the business to the stakeholders. In other words, financial accounting is used for reporting financial transactions to the stakeholders in a format that is acceptable and adaptable by all businesses. Accounting Concepts that form the basis of financial accounting are:

Accrual Concept

Financial accounting can be done on an accrual basis or cash basis. Accrual basis is highly accepted. An organization may also use a combination of both. Cash basis of accounting requires transactions to be recorded only when the transaction results in a flow of cash. However, under accrual basis, a transaction is recorded when the transaction occurs and revenue is recognized.

Once an organization selects the method, cash or accrual, it should consistently use the same:

- Economic entity concept: This concept assumes that the owners are separate from the business and there are no personal transactions recorded in business.
- Going concern concept: Under this concept, it is assumed that the organization will remain in business for a long time and hence the revenue can be deferred to a different period.
- Matching concept: This concept stresses that the expenses relating to a particular income must be recorded in the same period. This ensures that a transaction is fully accounted for.
- Materiality Concept: Reporting of all material transactions should be the aim of reporting. Material transactions are those transactions if omitted can alter an investors analysis of the business.
- Conservatism: Revenue must be recorded only when it is reasonably certain that it will be realized in the near future.

The heart of financial accounting is the Double entry system of bookkeeping. Double entry system refers to recording two aspects of the same transaction. The recording of the aspects will be as per the Golden Rules for Accounting.

Preparing Financial Statements

The financial statements of all businesses in a particular country/region will follow a standard format and standard accounting principles. This enables consistency and helps in effective comparison of the financial statements and financial position of different companies. The accounting principles that an organization follows depends on the regulatory and reporting requirements of the region and audience to which a business caters. Companies with international exposure follow International Financial Reporting Standards (IFRS).

The standards issued by the various boards, not only assist an organization in reporting the transactions correctly but also give clarifications for complex transactions faced by businesses. The standards ensure uniform accounting. These standards issued are amended from time to time keeping in mind the nuances of business.

Presentation of Financial Statements

Financial accounting is the reporting of transactions that have occurred during the financial period. A financial period can be any period. However, year-end financial statements are usually prepared for 12 months. Some companies follow the calendar year for reporting. At the end of the said period, the organizations will present its financial statements also known as financial reporting.

The financial statements report on five main aspects of a business:

- Revenue.
- Expense.
- Asset.
- Liabilities.
- Equity.

The revenue and expenses are accounted for in the income statement and the asset, liabilities, and equity are reported for in the balance sheet.

Income Statement

The income statement records the revenue and expenses for the financial period. It records all the revenue earned and expenses incurred for that period. It shows the operating wellness of the organization; this statement also provides the necessary information for tax computation.

Balance Sheet

The balance sheet is a parameter to check the financial health of the business. It records assets, liabilities, and equity of an organization. The balance sheet analysis enables an investor to derive at the worth of the company. It is also used to gauge the credibility of the organization.

Cash Flow Statement

In addition to the statements above, an organization also prepares the cash flow statement which shows the movement of cash; this is presented under the following three categories:

- Cash Flow from operating activities.
- Cash Flow from investing activities.
- Cash Flows from financing activities.

Shareholders Equity Statement

This statement shows the changes in shareholders' equity for the accounting period. It also depicts the changes in ownership if any.

Accounting is a vast function; it varies depending on the purpose it is used for. Financial accounting is used for business analysis, by parties external to the organization. While managerial accounting is used for reporting to the management and assist in decision making. On the other hand cost accounting is used by management to effectively manage costs.

Management Accounting

Management accounting is the presentation of analysis of business activities to the internal management to facilitate decision making. The Institute of Cost and Management Accountants, London, has defined Management Accounting as: "The application of professional knowledge and skill in the preparation of accounting information *in such a way as to assist management in the formulation of policies and in the planning and control of the operation of the undertakings.*

Similarly, according to American Accounting Association:

> "It includes the methods and concepts necessary for effective planning for choosing among alternative business actions and for control through the evaluation and interpretation of performances."

Difference between Management Accounting and Financial Accounting

Financial accounting and management accounting have some inherent differences. They are:

Basis for Comparison	Management accounting	Financial accounting
Purpose	It is used for internal purpose.	It is used for external reporting primarily, although the management also reviews it.
Regulation	It is not regulated by any law.	It has to be presented as per standards.
Users	Its users are the management of an organization.	Its users are shareholders, investors and regulators.
Objective	It aids in internal decision making.	It aids in investment decision by outsiders and monitoring by regulators.
Mandatory	Preparation and presentation of financial statements is not mandatory.	Preparation and presentation is mandatory.
Audit	It is not subject to audit.	Financial statements must be audited.
Frequency	There is no defined frequency for preparation and presentation of the statements	Financial statements must be prepared for the financial year and presented.
Contents	Management accounts include both monetary and non-monetary information.	Financial accounts include only monetary information.

Benefits of Managerial Accounting

Management accounting is very beneficial and hence is being used widely now. The benefits are as follows:

Planning

In management accounting, the financial information and non-financial information is presented at regular intervals say weekly, fortnightly to the management. This presentation includes forecasts, budgets and in-depth analysis. Hence it assists the management in planning the business activities.

Decision Making

Since management accounting presents various charts, forecasts and analysis the management uses it for decision making.

Identify Early Signs of Problems

If a product is not performing well the management can identify it early on as the accounts are presented at regular intervals. This will aid in overcoming the constraints early on and avoiding future losses.

Strategic Management

Based on the information presented in management accounting, the management can take decisions about continuing a product or modifying the sale strategy. Since management accounting is not regulated by any law, the management can decide the areas that require more analysis, investigation and accordingly draw up strategies.

Functions of Managerial Accounting

Managerial accounting performs the following functions in general:

- Profitability: Management accounting determines the profit from a particular product, project or line of business.
- Break even analysis: It determines the number of units at which the organization will attain a no profit, no loss situation.
- Forecasting: It determines the bottlenecks in the organization and their impact on the organization.
- New product analysis: It prepares analysis for the new product in terms of standard costs, actual cost and reasons for deviations.
- Stock valuation: Determine the direct and indirect costs of stock in hand and presenting it to management.
- Variance analysis: Performing trend analysis for various costs incurred and understanding the causes for the variances.
- Capital budgeting analysis: Understanding the need for acquiring fixed assets and the costs involved and allocation of finances to the best available option.
- Aids in Financial accounting: Management accounting presents financial information at regular intervals and hence it aids in the preparation of financial statements at year-end.

Just as automation has touched every aspect of business so also ERP systems enable reporting under management accounting. The various functions of management accounting like capital budgeting, variance analysis, profitability are performed by ERP systems and reports are generated. The management accountant has to ensure correctness of the information inputted and reports generated.

Management accounting provides the management with better control of the business. Although not regulated by any law it provides the management an assurance. It provides the management the confidence to face auditors and regulators. It aids in better management.

Cost Accounting

Cost Accounting is a formal system of accounting for costs in the books *of accounts by means of which cost of products and services are ascertained and controlled.*

According to definition given by CIMA, London "Cost Accounting is the process of accounting for cost from the point at which expenditure is incurred to the establishment of its ultimate relationship with cost centers and cost units".

This definition is authoritative. In simple words we can say cost accounting is the classifying, recording and appropriate allocation of expenditure for the determination of the costs of products or services and the presentation of arranged data for the purpose of control and guidance of management.

Costing, Cost Accounting and Cost Accountancy

In practice, the terms 'costing' and 'cost accounting' are used interchangeably. However, costing should not be confused with cost accounting. Costing refers to the technique and process of ascertaining costs. The technique consists of the principles and rules for determining the cost of products and services.

The technique is, however, dynamic and changes with the change of time. The process of costing is the day-to-day routine of ascertaining costs. Cost accounting, on the other hand, is defined as the process of accounting for cost from the point at which expenditure is incurred or committed.

The process continues till the establishment of its ultimate relationship with cost centre or cost unit. It is that specialised branch, of accounting which involves classification, accumulation, allocation, absorption and control of costs. Costing can be carried out by the process of arithmetic, by means of memorandum statements or by the methods of integral accounts.

But cost accounting denotes the formal mechanism by means of which costs are ascertained and data are provided for various purposes of management. Cost accountancy is a wide term which includes several subjects such as costing, cost accounting, cost control, budgetary control and cost audit.

The Chartered Institute of Management Accountants, London, defines cost accountancy as "the application of costing and cost accounting principles, methods and techniques to the science, art and practice of cost control. It includes the presentation of information derived therefrom for the purposes of managerial decision-making."

Here, science includes the body of systematic knowledge a cost accountant should possess for proper discharge of his responsibilities. Art includes the ability and skill with which a cost accountant applies his cost accountancy background and knowledge to the problems of cost ascertainment, cost control and ascertainment of profitability.

Practice includes the continuous efforts of a cost accountant in the field of cost accountancy. Such efforts also include the presentation of information for the purpose of managerial decision-making and keeping statistical records.

Financial accounting is largely concerned with financial statements for external use by investors, creditors, labour unions, financial analysts, government agencies, and other interest groups.

It involves recording, classification, and analysis of business transactions in a subjective manner according to nature of expenditure so as to facilitate preparation of profit and loss account and balance sheet for showing the results of the business operations as a whole. It is these published financial statements which are generally the basis for investment decisions by the shareholders, lending decisions by banks and financial institutions and credit decisions by vendors.

The requirements of management may be summarized as follows:

- Measurement of Performance and Efficiency: To face severe competition in the business world, a management always needs to maintain their customers. Therefore, to evaluate the present product and market it, it is necessary to measure the performance and business efficiency. Financial accounts cannot serve this purpose at all. In normal times, we can say that profit or loss shown by Profit and Loss account is an indicator of overall efficiency or inefficiency.
- But in the periods of inflation or depression this may not be true. So the management would be well advised to ascertain the profit or loss of each product separately. Besides this, management must also try to see that in producing each unit of product there is no unnecessary wastage or loss as regards materials, labour and other expenses.
- This information is available to the management only under Cost Accounting System. Again a management can know the exact reason of profit or loss by making proper cost analysis which is possible only in cost accounts.
- Pricing: For fixing prices of products or services, it is necessary to have information regarding each product or unit of service rather than total expenditure. Only, Cost Accounting system can provide this information to the management.
- Control: To maximize profit by minimizing costs, it is necessary to set up standards and then compare actual costs with these standards. The reason for the discrepancy may be ascertained and then only possible action can be taken to rectify the situation. Such action is possible only in Cost Accounting.
- Forecasting: For planning in future, preparations of budgets are necessary. Budgets are prepared on the basis of forecasts of future costs and revenue. In this field also, Cost Accounting is more capable of helping management than Financial Accounting.
- Day-to-Day Decisions: Besides price fixing decisions, various other decisions have to be taken continuously such as make or buy, whether an old machine should be replaced by a new one, when operational activities be stopped or started, whether an order at concessional rate should be accepted or not etc. Cost accounting is able to provide the necessary information for such decisions.

Thus, the need for Cost Accounting arises because of the management's requirement to know the cost of various activities in various circumstances. Costing has a vital role to play in almost any activity which involves expenditure of money, whether it is a business house or a charitable concern or whether it is a Government Department.

The nature of cost accounting can be discussed under the following headings:

- Cost Accounting is a Branch of Knowledge: Though cost accounting is considered as a branch of financial accounting, it is one of the important branches of knowledge. It is an organised body of knowledge consisting of its own principles, concepts and conventions. These principles and rules vary from industry to industry.
- Cost Accounting is a Science: Cost accounting is considered as a science because it is a body of systematic knowledge relating to not only cost accounting but relating to a wide variety of subjects such as law, office practice and procedure, data processing, production and material control, etc. It is necessary for a cost accountant to have intimate knowledge of all these field of study in order to carry on day-to-day activities. But it is to be admitted that it is not a perfect science as in the case of natural science.
- Cost Accounting is an Art: Cost accounting is an art in the sense it requires the ability and skill on the part of cost accountant in applying the principles methods and techniques of cost accountancy to various management problems. These problems include the ascertainment of cost control of costs, ascertainment of profitability etc.
- Cost Accounting is a Profession: In recent years cost accounting has become one of the important professions which have become more challenging. This view is evident from two facts. First, the setting up of various professional bodies such as National Association of Accountants (NAA), the Institute of Cost and Management Accountant U.K., and such other professional bodies both in developed and developing countries have increased the growing awareness of costing profession among the people. Secondly, a large number of students have enrolled in these institutes to obtain costing degrees and membership for earning their livelihood.

Main Objectives

The main objectives of cost accounting are as follows:

- Ascertainment of cost: This is the primary objective of cost accounting. For cost ascertainment different techniques and systems of costing are used under different circumstances.
- Control of cost: Cost control aims at improving efficiency by controlling and reducing cost. This objective is becoming increasingly important because of growing competition.
- Guide to business policy: Cost accounting aims at serving the needs of management in conducting the business with utmost efficiency. Cost data provide guidelines for various managerial decisions like make or buy, selling below cost, utilization of idle plant capacity, introduction of a new product, etc.
- Determination of selling price: Cost accounting provides cost information on the basis of

which selling prices of products or services may be fixed. In periods of depression, cost accounting guides in deciding the extent to which the selling prices may be reduced to meet the special situation.

Need of Cost Accounting

Cost accounting provides valuable help to the management. It is not easy to quantify the need and importance since it cannot be concluded about where the work of a cost accountant comes to an end. The following points can be taken under the concept of "need". The same points are also the main advantages of cost accounting:

- Helps to ascertain cost.
- Helps in price fixation.
- Helps to eliminate wastages.
- Helps to identify and eliminate unprofitable activities.
- Helps to check statement accuracy.
- Helps in inventory control.
- Helps for cost and revenue estimation.
- Helps to increase productivity and earning capacity.
- Helps investor's, moneylenders and other financial institutions to know about the business.
- Helps in formulating efficient policy for day-to-day business activities.
- Helps cost control.

11 Major Functions

Cost Accounting is to serve management in the execution of policies and in the comparison of actual and estimated results in order that the value of each policy may be appraised and changed to meet the future conditions.

To elaborate the statement, the functions of cost accounting can be enumerated as follows:

- To calculate the cost per unit of the various products manufactured by the firm.
- To prepare a correct cost analysis of both by process or operations, and by the different elements of cost.
- To ascertain the wastage in each process of manufacture and to prepare reports, this can assist to wastage control.
- To provide the necessary information for the determination of selling prices.
- To compute product-wise profit, and advise the management for the enhancement of profit.

- To serve the management in the valuation of goods-in-process and finished goods, so that the minimum capital is blocked up in the stocks.
- To install and implement cost control systems (budgetary control or standard cost system) for the control of material, labour, and overhead expenses.
- To advise the management for the formulation of future expansion policies and proposed capital outlays.
- To establish an effective reporting system. This will help the different levels of management to receive the necessary cost data in time in order to enable them to fulfill their individual responsibilities in an efficient manner.
- To guide the management in the preparation and implementation of incentive schemes based on productivity and cost savings.
- To advise the management on the profitability of present or new lines of products, the comparative advantages and disadvantages of different types of production methods, the replacement of manual operations by automation, and other such policy matters which have a direct impact on the development of the company.

The additional functions can be briefly listed as under:

- To supervise punched card accounting or data processing division operations.
- To organize internal audit system so that the effective working of the accounting control and production control methods can be introduced from time to time and be well ensured.
- To coordinate with the industrial engineers for the introduction and implementation of methods suggested for improvement and or redundancy of programmes and data.
- To provide the Government or other public bodies with the specialized service of cost audit.

Importances: Cost Accounting and Management, Cost Accounting and Employees, Cost Accounting and Creditors and a Few others

The limitations of financial accounting have made the management to realize the importance of cost accounting. Whatever may be the type of business, it involves expenditure on labour, materials, and other items required for manufacturing and disposing of the product. Moreover, big business requires delegation of responsibility, division of labour and specialization.

Management has to avoid the possibility of waste at each stage. It has to see that no machine remains idle, efficient labour gets due initiative, proper utilization of byproducts is made and costs are properly ascertained. Besides management, creditors and employees are also benefited in numerous ways by installation of a good costing system in an industrial organisation. Cost accounting increases the overall productivity of an industrial establishment and, therefore, serves as an important tool in bringing prosperity to the nation.

Thus, the importance of cost accounting in various spheres can be summarized under the following headings:

Cost Accounting and Management

Cost accounting provides invaluable aid to management. It is so closely allied to management that it is difficult to indicate where the work of the cost accountant ends and managerial control begins. Adequate costing data help management in reaching certain important decisions such as, whether hand labour should be replaced by the machinery or not; whether a particular product line should be discontinued or not etc.

Costing checks recklessness and avoids occurrence of mistakes. Cost can be reduced by proper organisation of the plant and executive personnel. As an aid to management it also provides invaluable information to enable management to maintain effective control over stores and inventory, to increase efficiency of the business and to check wastage and losses. It facilitates delegation of responsibility for important tasks and rating of employees. However, for all this, it is necessary for the management to be capable of using in a proper way the information provided by the cost accounts.

The various advantages derived by management on account of a good costing system can be put as follows:

- Costing helps in periods of trade depression and trade competition – In periods of trade depression the business cannot afford to have leakages which pass unchecked. The management should know where economies may be sought, waste eliminated and efficiency increased. The business has to wage a war for its survival. The management should know the actual cost of their products before embarking on any scheme of reducing the prices or giving tenders. Adequate costing facilitates this.
- Aids in price fixation – Though economic law of supply and demand and activities of the competitors, to a great extent, determine the price of the article, cost to the producer does play an important part. The producer can take necessary guidance from his costing records.
- Helps in estimate – Adequate costing records provide a reliable basis upon which tenders and estimates may be prepared. The chances of losing a contract on account of over-rating or losing in the execution of a contract due to under-rating can be minimized. Thus, "ascertained costs provide a measure for estimates, a guide to policy, and a control over current production."
- Helps in channelizing production on right lines – Costing makes possible for the management to distinguish between profitable and non-profitable activities. Profit can be maximized by concentrating on profitable operations and eliminating non-profitable ones.
- Wastages are eliminated – As it is possible to know the cost of the article at every stage, it becomes possible to check various forms of waste, such as time, expenses etc., or in the use of machine, equipment and tools.
- Costing makes comparison possible – If the costing records are regularly kept, comparative

cost data for different periods and various volumes of production will be available. It will help the management in forming future lines of action.

- Provides data for periodical profit and loss accounts – Adequate costing records supply to the management such data as may be necessary for preparation of profit and loss account and balance sheet, at such intervals as may be desired by the management.
- It also explains in detail the sources of profit or loss revealed by the financial accounts; thus helps in presentation of better information before the management.
- Aids in determining and enhancing efficiency – Losses due to wastage of material, idle time of workers, poor supervision etc. will be disclosed if the various operations involved in manufacturing a product are studied by a cost accountant. The efficiency can be measured and costs controlled and through it various devices can be framed to increase the efficiency.
- Helps in inventory control – Costing furnishes control which management requires in respect of stock of materials, work-in-progress and finished goods.
- Helps in cost reduction – Costs can be reduced in the long-run when alternatives are tried. This is particularly important in the present-day context of global competition. Cost accounting has assumed special significance beyond cost control this way.
- Assists in increasing productivity – Productivity of material and labour is required to be increased to have growth and more profitability in the organisation. Costing renders great assistance in measuring productivity and suggesting ways to improve it.

Cost Accounting and Employees

Workers have a vital interest in their employer's enterprises and the industry in which they are employed. Workers are benefitted by a number of ways by the installation of an efficient costing system in their enterprise. They are benefitted because of systems of incentives, bonus plans etc. They get benefit indirectly through increase in consumer goods and directly through continuous employment and higher remuneration.

Cost Accounting and Creditors

Investors, banks and other moneylenders have a stake in the success of the business concern and, therefore, are benefited immediately by installation of an efficient costing system. They can base their judgment about the profitability and further prospects of the enterprise upon the studies and reports submitted by the cost accountants.

Cost Accounting and National Economy

An efficient costing system brings prosperity to the concerned business enterprises resulting into stepping up of the government revenue. The overall economic development of a country takes place due to increase in efficiency of production. Controlling of costs, elimination of wastages and inefficiencies lead to the progress of the industry and in consequence of the nation as a whole.

Social Accounting

Business is a socio-economic activity and it draws its inputs from the society, hence its objective should be the welfare of the society. It should owe a responsibility towards solving many of the social problems. In the present age of growing technological, economic, cultural and social awareness, the accounting has not only to fulfill its stewardship function for the owners of the enterprise, but also accomplish its social function.

Changing environments and social parameters have compelled business enterprises to account and report information with regard to discharge of their social responsibilities. The boundaries of the principles, practices and skills of conventional accounting have been extended to such areas for social disclosure and attestation with regard to the measures of social programmes.

The concept of 'Social Accounting' has gained importance as a result of high level industrialization which has brought prosperity as well as many problems to the society. It has necessitated the corporate sector, with huge amounts of funds at their disposal, to invest substantial amounts in social activities so as to nullify the adverse effects of industrialization. "In modern times, accounting efforts have been extended to the assessment of the state of society and of the social programmes not for the satisfaction of any individual or group but for the application of evaluative procedures in the allocation of resources towards better social well-being as a whole."

Social accounting is concerned with the study and analysis of accounting practice of those activities of an organisation. The concept of socialistic pattern of society, civil rights movements, environmental protection and ecological conservation groups, increasing awareness of society towards corporate social contribution, etc. have contributed towards the growing importance of Social accounting.

Social Accounting, also known as Social Responsibility Accounting, Socio-Economic Accounting, Social Reporting and Social Audit, aims to measure and inform the general public about the social welfare activities undertaken by the enterprise and their effects on the society.

As per F.F. Perry's Dictionary of banking, social accounting is the reporting of the cost incurred in employing with anti-pollution, safety and health and other societal beneficial requirements and, more generally the impact of business entity on the endeavor to project society its amenities and the environment.

Social accounting is "the measurement and reporting of information concerning the impact of an entity and its activities on society." The National Association of Accountants (NAA) Committee defined social accounting as 'the identification, measurement, monitoring and reporting of the social and economic effects of an institution on society." It is, thus clear that social accounting is concerned with the internal and external reporting of social costs and benefits both in quantitative as well as qualitative terms by a business enterprise.

The term 'social audit' has in the past been mostly linked with 'social accounting' and the two terms have been used interchangeably in the literature. However, some writers on the subject use the term social accounting as distinct from the term social audit. Social audit is an objective assessment of a business enterprise as to how it has been able to discharge its social obligations in the course of its operations. The concept of social audit is a new emerging dimension in the audit literature. It is neither a statutory audit nor a performance audit, but a mixture of both.

Features of Social Accounting

- Social accounting is an expression of a company's social responsibilities.
- Social accounting is related to the use of social resources.
- Social accounting emphasize on relationship between firm and society.
- Social accounting determines desirability of the firm in society.
- Social accounting is application of accounting on social sciences.
- Social accounting emphasizes on social costs as well as social benefits.

"The technology of an economic system imposes a structure on its society which not only determines its economic activities but also influences its social relationship and well-being. Therefore a measure limited to economic consequences is inadequate as an appraisal of the cause and effect relationships of the total system, it neglects the social effects."

The True blood committee report on the objectives of traditional financial statements in 1973 broke with traditional orientation of them toward stewardship reporting and instead added new dimensions of socio economic to the scope of accounting literature.

An objective of financial statements is to report on those activities of the enterprise affecting society which can be determined and described or measured and which are important to the role of the enterprise in its social environment.

Need/Benefits of Social Accounting

The important benefits of social accounting are as follows:

- A firm fulfills its social obligations and informs its members, the government and the general public to enables everybody to form correct opinion.
- It counters the adverse publicity or criticism leveled by hostile media and voluntary social Organisations.
- It assists management in formulating appropriate policies and programmes.
- Through social accounting the firm proves that it is not socially unethical in view of moral cultures and environmental degradation.
- It acts as an evidence of social commitment.
- It improves employee motivation.
- Social accounting is necessary from the view point of public interest groups, social Organisations investors and government.
- It improves the image of the firm.
- Through social accounting, the management gets feedback on its policies aimed at the welfare of the society.

- It helps in marketing through greater customer support.
- It improves the confidence of shareholders of the firm.

Project Accounting

Project accounting focuses on the financial transactions related to managing a project including costs, billing and revenue. Professionals such as project managers and accountants use this method to integrate key financial tasks on a project-by-project basis and report their progress and success to management.

Project managers rely on project accounting to inform them of the status of direct costs, overhead costs and any revenues in a specific project. Project accountants generate these figures in financial reports. A project manager uses these reports to determine if they need to adjust the project's budget and work breakdown structure (WBS).

Project accountants often develop a project accounting plan to ensure the projects they manage are completed on-budget and on-time. This plan delineates every cost element in the project and includes regular—even daily—checks. Managers can track the expenditure of resources, such as people, via their timesheets and adjust allocated hours, if necessary. A subspecialty of project accounting is production accounting, which is what a film or television project uses. Project accountants turn each production into a unique project accounting opportunity.

Project accounting also includes internal projects such as construction builds, new product launches, advertising campaigns, research or clinical research, long-range purchases and company strategic planning. These are capital projects with discrete beginning and end periods that are not business-as-usual type work.

Project control is another essential accounting procedure. Any deviations from the project plan affect the project's bottom line. Project control can achieve significant cost savings during the planning and design phase, as well as in the advanced stages of the project. Therefore, it is the project manager's main role to help achieve the best setup and development of the project plan. It's the project accountant's role to ensure the project financials such as billing and revenue are set up correctly to match the contract terms for the project. They need to fulfill this plan before they start to identify and mitigate changes later.

Project Cost Accounting

Although project cost accounting principles have a different intent and scale than standard financial or management accounting in business accounting, they are the same concepts. Project accounting (project cost accounting) tracks costs to the project in addition to billing and revenue recognition for project profitability.

Standard business accounting tallies expenses, revenues and budgets across an organization. Business-as-usual accounting focuses on revenue and expenses by department and looks at the revenue stream. The project accounting methods are the same whether they are for business-as-usual or specific projects and whether accountants use an accrual, cash-basis or some hybrid accounting method. Accountants have a wide variety of calculations to choose from to meet the methodological requirements.

Project accounting sets itself apart from standard accounting by using different systems, processes and reporting standards. The method should include:

- Separate System of Accounting: This process is more detailed than overall company finance tracking, and accountants may want to use more granular accounting. In some cases, the company's financial application may let them complete all accounting processes in one program.
- Reporting Frequency: Projects require frequent reporting to ensure they are on track financially and meeting deliverables. Accountants may want to increase their report frequency, especially when the project and its contract are coming to an end.
- Simplified, Specific Reports: Project managers and accountants should determine the key performance indicators (KPIs) specific to the project. For example, when staff is not meeting a KPI such as budget variance, the dashboard could show the figure in red. When the project manager sees the red number, they know quickly they must adjust either the budget projection or their plan to meet it.
- Transaction Identification Processes: Accountants and project managers should work together to set up processes that identify project-specific transactions. This way, they can allocate these transactions to the appropriate cost centers.
- Forecasting: Project managers should forecast the project budget and update this forecast as the project progresses and through completion. Stakeholders are often concerned about the ongoing financial progress and completed cost, as well as the required deliverables. Initially, these project costing activities develop a forecast with a defined scope that completes the overall cost estimate.

Project accounting also focuses on resource management. Every project requires internal resources, external resources and in some cases, third-party material costs. Project managers should track their resources closely to avoid spiraling costs, which is known as time and materials or T&M. Here's what you should consider for each element:

- Typically, the most expensive cost is the labor worked by resources on a project. There are a variety of costs and billing rates based on services provided expertise, location, etc. Materials, such as third-party costs or pass-through expenses, have initial and subsidiary costs. Materials may incur additional costs for a late delivery or if installers miss a scheduled appointment.
- Time relates to labor. Resources must track their time accurately and regularly, identifying when they are either short allotted hours or over the budgeted amount. They should also notify project managers when they complete their work or will use additional hours to complete it, exceeding the budget.

Project accountants break down the project accounting process flow into six main areas: initiation, budget, administration, allocation, maintenance and analytics and reports.

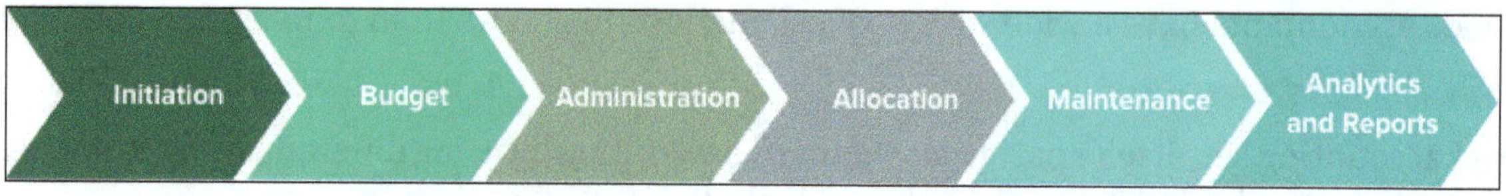

Figure: Project Accounting Process Flow Diagram.

- Initiation: Before starting a project, project managers should decide who is responsible for each task and how those resources will code their time. They can set up roles in their software using different levels of permission, as necessary.
- Budget: Project managers should confirm the overall budget is broken down into categories or groups. A software solution should support defining the budget and offer varying budgets, such as versioning that includes an initial baseline budget. These budgets should be based on the business's required reporting.
- Administration: Project accountants process the transactions by recording and processing costs and revenues as well as tracking financial commitments, running billing and invoicing, recognizing revenue and generating project profitability reports.
- Execution: During this phase, the project managers assign costs, revenues and measurements to activities. Accountants can base allocations on fixed percentages, specified factors, percentage and factor combinations, computations or a list of parameters.
- Maintenance: Project staff should have a process to continually review and validate the data and have a way to identify inconsistencies.
- Analytics and Reports: Regular access to the accounting data on the project helps project accountants and managers create user-defined reports. They can use this information to perform analyses and make accurate and timely business decisions.

Project accounting techniques and processes also support project billing. Many businesses develop standards to bill either by time and materials (hourly, daily, weekly or monthly), by project, by emphasizing the deliverable or by Fixed Fee (as determined by a deliverable or milestone, percent complete or fixed amount). Many companies also charge a set scoping or discovery fee for project inception.

Cost Accounting

Tax accounting refers to the methods and policies used for the preparation of tax returns and other statements needed for tax compliance and therefore, it provides frameworks and guidelines for arriving at a taxable profit.

Also, tax policies in each country differ with Generally Accepted Accounting Principles on various items. This variation leads to the generation of Deferred Tax assets and liabilities. Also, there are separate guidelines for VAT (Value Added Tax) accounting, transfer pricing, and cross border transactions, which all fall under tax accounting.

The reason for doing Income Tax accounting is arriving at taxable profit and tax payable by making adjustments in the book profit arrived by accounting principles. All these working and adjustments form part of the Tax return, and these statements are kept for Tax audits.

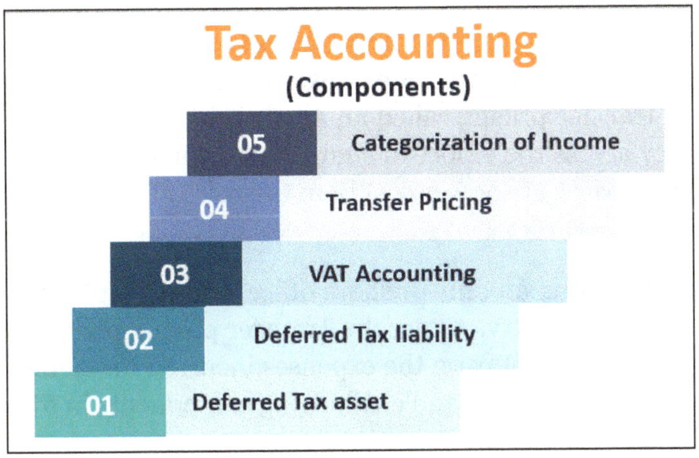

Deferred Tax Asset

Deferred Tax asset is generated when there is a difference in book profit and taxable profit arises due to a timing issue. There are expenses like provision for doubtful debts, which are considered for deduction in accounting in the current year. However, these are allowed for a deduction for taxation only when the amount is declared as bad debt, which can happen in the coming years.

In this case, the taxable profit will be higher compared to accounting profit, and the person or organization will pay more taxes this year, which. The extra amount paid as tax on incremental profit due to rejection of provision amount for deduction is considered as deferred tax, which will be realized in the coming years.

Deferred Tax Liability

Deferred Tax Liability is generated when the person or organization has to pay fewer taxes in the current year due to the timing difference. For example – let's consider that an asset of $10,000 is being depreciated in accounting books under (SLM) straight-line method for 8 years – the depreciation each year will be $1,250 ($10,000/8).

However, if the tax rules state that assets have to be depreciated @20% (WDV) written down value method. The depreciation for taxation purpose in second year will be $1,600 (($10,000 – 2000 i.e. 20% for first-year) = $8,000*20% = $1,600)).

Here the organization will get an extra deduction of $350 ($1,600-$1,250) for taxation purposes. If we consider the tax rate to be 30%, the deferred tax liability here is $105 ($350*30%).

VAT Accounting

Most of the countries a Good & Service Tax (GST) or VAT (value-added tax), which forms part of almost all the invoices issued. Now, this should not be considered as expenses directly because the organizations get an Input Tax credit on the amount already paid. To claim those inputs, the tax authorities lay certain conditions regarding the format of invoice, name, and registration of the company, details of the second part, etc. and all these conditions have to be met by tax accounting team before claiming VAT/GST input credit.

Transfer Pricing

In today's world of globalization, many companies open their branches in various parts of the world. A policy monitor transfer pricing called an Arm's Length transaction pricing, which advocates the fair-trade policy across the globe. In simple words, it says that a related part or person should not avail good or services at a lower cost than the price at which it has been sold to an unrelated third party.

Also, if an organization has set up an only offshore office where people are working and no other business is being done in that country. As per the Transfer pricing policy, the organization has to pay a certain percentage (8-15%) of tax on the expenses incurred in operating the offshore office. Transfer pricing is one of the fast-paced and challenging components in today's world.

Categorization of Income

Accounting considers all the receipts and payments for calculating the accounting profit. However, not all receipts are related to business, and the rate of tax differs depending on the type of receipt it is.

Table: Profit and Loss Account of XYZ Ltd.

Particulars	Amount (Dr.)	Particulars	Amount
To Rent	$5,000	By Gross Profit	$35,000
To Salaries	$12,000	By Interest on Deposits	$4,000
To Other operating Expenses	$8,000	By Profit on sale of Land	$6,000
To net Profit	$20,000		
Total	$45,000	Total	$45,000

Statements of Profit and Loss for Taxation Purpose			
(A) Business		Amount$	Amount$
Gross Profit		$35,000	
Less- All expenses:			
Rent	$5,000		
Salaries	$12,000		
Others	$8,000	$25,000	$10,000
(B) Income from other Sources			$4,000
(C) Long Term Capital Gain			$6,000
Total Income (A+B+C)			$20,000

The extract from accounting books is shown, and in the second table shows how tax accounting has to categorize the type of income as the Income-tax rates differ on types of income.

Advantages

- Categorization of Income for application of correct tax rate.

- Statutory compliance adherence.
- Losses of current and previous years can be set off in future periods by filing Tax returns.
- Tax audit facilitation.
- Self-assessment and tax payments in a timely manner.

Disadvantages

- Needs extra time and resources for the work.
- Tax professionals charge dearly to organizations.
- There are changes in tax policies almost every year.

Non-Profit Accounting

A non-profit is an organization whose primary objective is to fill a need of society (as opposed to a regular business, the priority of which is to maximize revenue for its owners and shareholders). Non-profits *do* generate profit, but that revenue is put back into the non-profit's mission. Non-profits are tax exempt and have different accounting priorities and financial statements.

The most common types of non-profits are:

Charities

Charities rely mainly on contributions to survive, although they can also generate revenue from other sources, such as membership dues, fundraising events and grants.

Charity organizations can be:

- Religious.
- Educational.
- Environmental.
- Research related.
- Health oriented.
- Literary.
- Social Services organizations.
- Sports Clubs.
- Arts Clubs.
- Disaster relief organizations.
- International development initiatives.

- Child sponsorship programs.
- Animal welfare programs.
- Human rights' initiatives.

Private Foundations

Foundations exist to support charities or individuals through grants. They do not fund their own programs or activities. A foundation also does not solicit money, the income comes from the individual or business that started the foundation and that money is invested. The returns on that investment become donations.

Private Operating Foundations

This is a hybrid between a public charity and a foundation. This type of foundation does fund their own programs or activities.

There is some confusion around the definition of "Foundation", as often the word is used in a charity's official name. For instance, the Clinton Foundation, started by former United States president Bill Clinton, is actually a charity that anyone can donate to. However, the Clinton Family Foundation is a foundation that accepts no donations. It is funded by the Clintons themselves, and the return from that money is donated to organizations that the foundation determines to be in need. As such, the Clinton Family Foundation is considered a private foundation.

Purpose of Fund Accounting

Fund Accounting is used by non-profits to measure accountability as opposed to profitability (in other words, to show that the non-profit's money is being spent appropriately).

Fund accounting is a process by which all of a non-profit's accounts must be assigned to one of two categories: Unrestricted or Restricted. This allows a non-profit to know not only how much money it has to work with, but where it can be spent.

Unrestricted Funds

This is money that can be used for any purpose, such as renting or buying a piece of land.

Restricted Funds

This is money that can only be used for a specific purpose, as specified by the donor. This is an important distinction because by law, the restricted fund money must be used as intended. Restricted funds can be temporary or permanent.

Endowments are a good example of a permanently restricted fund. The principle is never spent, but the interest generated is. How that interest is spent is determined by the donor.

Difference between Profit and Non-profit Accounting

The process of accounting is different for non-profits, as these types of organizations are tax-exempt.

As a result, non-profits typically focus their efforts on keeping overhead low so that more money can go into the programs and/or services they offer.

A non-profit organization can choose cash accounting method or an accrual accounting method for recording its expenses and income. Cash accounting method records transaction amounts when the money trades hands. An accrual accounting method records the amounts when a transaction occurs. Many believe an accrual method of accounting gives a more accurate picture of a company's finances.

Some of the financial statements that a non-profit must generate are also different than that of a regular business.

Statement of Activities

A "Statement of Activities" is a financial statement a non-profit organization would generate, instead of an "Income Statement".

An income statement shows a company's profitability during a specific time period, while a statement of activities shows the changes in value in the organization's "assets" instead.

For instance, an income statement for a company would show revenue from the sale of goods, and its expenses would show the cost of goods sold. A statement of activities for a non-profit would show revenue from contributions, and expenses from fundraising.

At the bottom of the document, a statement of activities would show a "Net Assets" total, while an income statement would list a "Net Income" total instead.

Statement of Financial Position

Instead of a "Balance Sheet", a non-profit would issue a "Statement of Financial Position" instead.

On a Balance Sheet:
Assets = Liabilities + Shareholders' Equity

On a Statement of Financial Position:
Assets = Liabilities + Net Assets

The reason for the difference is that non-profit organizations do not have owners, meaning there can't be shareholders' equity.

Public Disclosure

Non-profit organizations are required to submit their financial statements to the IRS. The IRS, or the non-profit organization, must disclose these reports to anyone who asks. In this way, the information is made "public".

Non-profits face heavy scrutiny because of their tax-exempt status. Often, there is an interest by both the public and media on how money is spent by a non-profit, how much, and if it is spent wisely.

Government Accounting

Government Accounting, on the other hand, refers to the Governments (both States and Central). That is, the objectives of this accounting are the financial administration of the activities of the Government to promote maximization of welfare in the form of various services.

The principles of Government Accounting may be summarized as under:

System of Accounting

It has already been explained that the Government usually follows the Single Entry System of Accounting. But, in some cases, (viz., Loans and Borrowings) the system of Double Entry has been followed Because, in order to ascertain this arithmetical accuracy by preparing a Trial Balance and to determine the balance of the account as well, Double Entry System has to be taken into consideration.

Commercial Enterprises under Public Sector

In public sector enterprises, however, Double Entry System has been followed under mercantile basis like commercial accounting. Because, for ascertaining the results of the undertaking, the Profit and Loss Account and the Balance Sheet are to be prepared. But, in some cases, however, various management techniques, Cash Flow Analysis, Funds Flow Analysis, Ratio Analysis etc. and some charts and diagrams with the help of statistical data, are taken into consideration.

Classification of Incomes and Expenditures: According to the requirements of the Government, it is necessary to classify the incomes and expenditures of the services under various heads and sub-heads.

For example, revenue of the Central, Budget is classified into:

- Tax Revenue.
- Non-Tax Revenue.

Tax-Revenue again sub-divided into:

- Taxes on incomes and expenditures.
- Taxes on property and capital transactions.
- Taxes on commodities and services, etc.

Similarly, Non-Tax Revenue is again sub-divided into:

- Interest Receipts.
- Dividend and Profits.
- Others.

At the same time, expenditure in the form of different services are also classified under various heads and sub-heads, as under:

- General Services.
- Social Services.
- Economic Services.
- Grant-in-aid and contribution.

Now, general services are again sub-divided into:

- Administrative services.
- Defence services.
- Servicing of debts.
- Fiscal services etc.

Consolidated Transaction

In Government accounting, although the transactions are recorded primarily under various heads of accounts, later they are consolidated in order to show the combined result for the period concerned.

Forensic Accounting

Forensic Accounting is an art of investigation over accounting records, financial statements, and other related financial records. The result of investigation mostly use for legal support, and resolving conflict. This job requires technical skills in accounting, investigation and legal. These are what drive forensic accounting to become more attractive and highly paid.

The investigation is cover certain areas include fraud, crime, insurance claims as well as a dispute among shareholders. The investigation and verification are normally done to the company's financial statements, management accounts, and other related documents, data, and information related to the subject matter being investigated.

The common procedures would be financial statement analysis, computer assistance, supporting document examination, investigation, and interview. This engagement is engaged with the professional firms that have professional experiences, expertise in accounting standards, and legal background. In general, Forensic Accountants are required to have knowledge and experience in accounting and investigation skills. These are the most important requirements.

Also, to be able to perform its works efficiently and effectiveness, knowledge in those related industries that being investigate also consider to be important. Forensic accounting is very important not only because they have a special skill and trained in the investigation, and expertise in accounting records, but also because of the evidence that found is playing a very important role in judicial decision making. This job is quite different from the auditor and cannot substitute by them.

As we know, the auditor performs its testing in the accounting records against accounting standards like US GAAP or IFRS. Their responsibility is not investigating and quantifying the fraud that happens in the company and also the evidence found in by the auditor might not be used by the court. However, the evidence found by forensic accounting could be used by the court as expert evidence.

For example, the FBI also has a forensic accounting team to work for them in investigating any matter related to accounting.

Provide Litigation Support

So basically, this is the popular service that provides by Forensic Accounting. The Forensic Accounting report is prepared to support the litigation in the court in certain areas. For example:

- Produce the Profit and Loss report of the company. This is simply figuring out how much profit or loss related to the company, project or related subject matter.
- Lost earnings/wages prepare reports related to lost or earn of the employee. The best example for this point is that, for example, there is the employee sue its employer for wrongful dismiss and the court wants to figure out what is the subsequent loss of this dismissed for the employee.
- Investigation of breach of contract of parties. This normally happens in daily business activities. Such examination will study the detail of terms of the contract, and the way how parties in the contract. The report on those who respect, disrespect, and loss as the result of the breach of contract will be calculated and present to the court.
- A wrongful death report is the result of investigation related to death whether it is criminal or civil.
- Patent and copyright violation reports.
- Fraud Investigation report: This report used by court and lawyer to understand and figure out the amount of loss and who are related parties.
- Business diminution report.
- Professional malpractice report.
- Wrongful termination report.
- Others services.

Sometimes it is required by the lawyer or court to have someone who has the special skill in accounting and investigation skills to examine and produce the report on the areas related to accounting.

These people do not only have a special skill in accounting and investigation, but also independence from all parties so that the report will be more reliable and no objection from all the parties.

Because forensic accountants are independence and expert, they are not only preparing the expert report, but they also could be the witness used by the court. So that is the reason why most of the forensic accountant is hired by a lawyer or court to investigate the subject meter and produce the report.

They can be the witness over the areas like profit and loss, fraud, patent and copyright, breach of contract, and many others. For example, the Forensic Accountant is engaged to investigate fraud that happens in the purchasing department of a company and present its report to the court.

In this case, a Forensic Accountant could also be the expert witness testimony on how the fraud is committed, who commit fraud and the amount of loss. Such a witness will be part of the court decision making. They also could be the witness over the accounting records related area on the dispute between shareholders.

Fraud Investigations

Fraud is the major expenses to the company and it is the virus that hardly to investigate and eliminate. The fraud investigation here could be performed in many different types of organizations like corporate, public, or private organizations.

The investigation could also perform in many different areas like fraud over financial reporting and fraud over the entities' assets. Yet, employee fraud investigation is the most popular service.

For example, Fraud over salaries, inventories, fixed assets or cash collects. In this case, forensic accounting could provide the investigation services and figure out how much the loss for those cases.

The investigation report could also include the cause of fraud, who involve with and how the fraud happens.

Such an investigation is also similar to the audit.

Insurance Claims Analysis

The forensic accountant can help both policyholders and insurers to have prepared and reviewed the claim based on the term and conditions that cover the insurance policies.

The claim will prepare based on the deep and detail analysis of the coverage in the policies on behalf of policyholders. In this case, a forensic accountant might work closely with the accounting assurance team that knows clearly about financial loss.

In some cases, this service also provides the insurance company to review the claim that submits by policy's holder to quantify the claim amounts.

Difference between Forensic Accounting and Audit

Forensic accounting and audit have some form of similarity and difference. For example, the purpose of an audit financial statement is to let auditors perform an independence review and then express an opinion. The auditor will only provide reasonable assurance on the financial statements.

However, forensic accounting normally performs an investigation on the financial statements and quantifies the loss that might happen. They will not issue the opinion.

Auditor normally required holding CPA to enable them to sign the audit report. But, forensic accountant normally required both CPA and CFE.

Audit report normally not use for legal support however forensic accounting report is normally used as the expert report to deal with the legal case.

Forensic Accountants: The Bloodhounds of Book-keeping

Comparing with a normal accountant who acts like a watchdog, a forensic accountant acts like a bloodhound. They look behind the facade and do not accept financial records at their face value. These bloodhounds inhale fraud and criminal transactions which may occur in bank, corporate entity or from any other organization's financial records. They hound for the conclusive evidences and find out the misstatements calculatingly. Forensic accountants make use of business information and financial reporting systems, accounting and auditing standards and procedures, evidence gathering and investigative techniques, and litigation processes and procedures to perform their work.

Now-a day's Forensic accountants are playing key role by designing and performing extended procedures as part of the statutory audit, acting as advisers to audit committees, fraud deterrence engagements, and assisting in investment analyst research. Forensic accountant takes a more proactive, skeptical approach in examining the company's books of Accounting and is often asked to serve as an expert witness for a lawsuit or criminal case in a court. A Forensic Accountant must be open to consider all alternatives, scrutinize the fine details and at the same time see the big picture. In addition, a Forensic Accountant must be a good listener and have effective communication skills.

Limitations of Forensic Accounting

Privacy

The privacy of confidential matters as well as financial statements cannot be maintained since the scrutiny of a company's financial records is done by an external forensic accountant. It is true that their code of ethics clearly mentions that forensic accountants and other members involved in the scrutiny must not engage in disclosing confidential data to outsiders, but the possibility of disclosure cannot be stopped.

Coercion and Negative Publicity

If the analysis of a company's financial statements points out the involvement of a particular person in fraudulent activities, there is a significant chance that the person will try to threaten the company to safeguard himself from the trial. Also, any trial that confirms a fraud happening in the company comes under public eye then it may have direct effect on the goodwill of the company and if the goodwill is effected then nobody will be interested to invest in such company's which ultimately led to decrease in the value of share.

Very Expensive

Forensic accounting can be an expensive affair as it involves analyzing of accounts through high-end accounting software. Moreover the fees of the forensic accountants are usually very high. So this can be adopted by only large size organizations and can be a matter for concern for small size organizations.

Losing Employee's Faith

Employees are considered to be assets of any organization because it is the only alive factor among all 5M's (Men , Material, Machine, Method and Money) and they feel offended when they come to know that their job is under scrutiny by a third person. Feeling may arise in the minds of employees that their employer does not have faith in them and lost trust can be difficult to regain.

Possibility of Risk

Forensic accounting involves detection of fraudulent activities and their representation in a court of law. It exposes the forensic accountant to criminal acts like blackmail and threats from the individuals. There are also risks of adverse publicity to the company which restricted the future investments. But despite of all the disadvantages as stated above forensic accounting, will continue to be an important part in the era of competitive business. This is because it helps organizations and individuals to figure out whether their financial accounts are accurate or fabricated to hide illegal activities going on within the organization.

Money Laundering

Money laundering is the common word used to describe the process by which criminals disguise the original ownership and control of the proceeds of criminal conduct. It is an act of laundering in circumstances where a person is engaged in an arrangement (i.e. by providing a service or product) and that arrangement involves the proceeds of crime. These arrangements include a wide variety of business relationships e.g. banking, fiduciary and investment management. The objective of the money laundering is to take the profit out of crime. The rationale for the creation of the offence is that it is wrong for individuals and organizations to make possible the commission of such crimes by providing financial services to them. Such activity damages the financial-sector institutions that are critical to economic growth, reduces productivity in the economy's real sector by diverting resources and encouraging crime and corruption, which slow economic growth.

There are two key elements to a money laundering offence:

- The necessary act of laundering itself i.e. the provision of financial services.
- A requisite degree of knowledge or suspicion (either subjective or objective) relating to the source of the funds or the conduct of a client.

Different Stages of Money Laundering

There are three stages involved in money laundering which are described as follows:

Placement: This is the movement of cash from its original source. Occasionally the source can be easily disguised or misrepresented. This is followed by placing it into circulation through financial institutions, casinos, shops and other businesses, both national and international. The process of placement can be carried out through many processes including:

- Currency Smuggling: The physical illegal movement of currency and monetary instruments from one country to another country.
- Bank involvement: When a financial institution are owned or controlled by unscrupulous individuals or organized crime groups.
- Securities Brokers: Through structuring large deposits of cash in a way that disguises the original source of the funds.
- Asset Purchase: It is a classic money laundering method.

Layering: The purpose of layering is to make it more difficult to detect and uncover a money laundering activity. It is meant to make the trailing of illegal proceeds difficult for the law enforcement agencies. This may involve:

- Cash conversion: This involves the use of banker's drafts and money orders into monetary instruments.
- Material Assets: Purchasing through illicit funds can be resold locally or abroad.

Integration: This is the movement of previously laundered money into the economy mainly through the banking system and these earnings appear to be normal business earnings. This is dissimilar to layering, for in the integration process detection and identification of laundered funds is provided through informants. This may include:

- Property Dealing: The sale of property to integrate laundered money back into the economy.
- Front Companies and False Loans: Criminals lend themselves their own laundered proceeds in an apparently legitimate transaction.
- Foreign Bank Complicity: It represents a higher order of complexity and presents a very difficult target for law enforcement.

Financial Intelligence

Since the mid-1980s, the need for a modern anti-money-laundering strategy has become widely accepted globally. The negotiations of the 1988 United Nations Convention against Illicit Traffic in Narcotic Drugs and Psychotropic substances can be seen as the starting point of financial intelligence. It is the process of receiving data, converting it, and disseminating it, for the purpose of enhancing key decision making Depriving criminal elements of the proceeds of their crimes has increasingly been seen as an important tool to fight against drug trafficking and all serious crimes.

Progress in this area is becoming a critical element in fighting organized crime, corruption, and the financing of terrorism, and maintaining the integrity of financial markets. As countries developed their anti-money-laundering strategies and found that law-enforcement agencies had limited access to relevant financial information, it became clear that the strategy required them to "engage the financial system in the effort to combat laundering while, at the same time, seeking to ensure the retention of the conditions necessary for its efficient operation." Organizations also found that implementation of a system requiring disclosures of suspicious transactions on the part of financial institutions created the need for assessing and processing these disclosures.

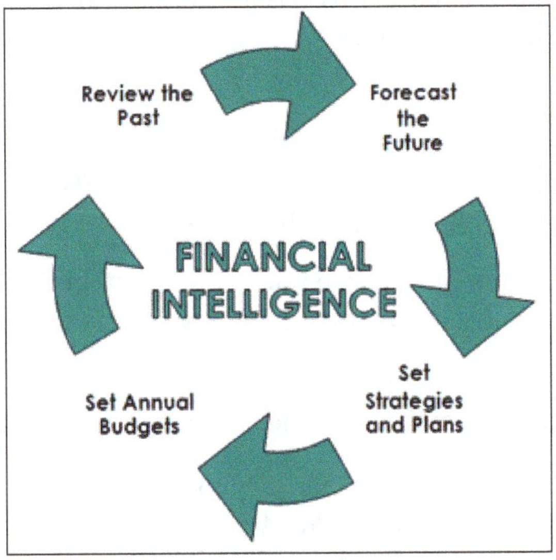

From the above image it can be concluded that Financial Intelligence involves different stages which are described as follows:

- Stage 1. Review the past: The past performance of the company helps the manager to decide what went well, what went wrong and what can be improve.
- Stage 2. Forecast The Future: Forecasts are vital to planning, so for the smooth planning it is im-portant to forecast the future so that various policies can be framed.
- Stage 3. Set Strategies and Plans: Strategic planning is critical to business success and it sits above and informs all other plans in the organization. Strategic planning can provide an overall strategic direction to the management of the organization.
- Stage 4. Set Annual Budgets: Budgets usually represent a detailed analysis of how a company ex-pects to spend money in future time periods. Using an annual budget process restrict the amount of time companies spend creating and managing capital resources.

Characteristics

- Financial intelligence is only one part of the organizational which may include its employees, systems, physical and intellectual property, and customer and supplier relationships.
- It will provide the organization with a competitive advantage on adding worth to customers (who are considered to be a king of the market) by either using less or providing more.

- Financial intelligence is able to reduce uncertainty as well as speed up the feed-back loops to enable better understanding of cause and effect relationships.
- Financial intelligence processes should be considered a key part of the governance framework.
- Sufficient management time and resource should be allocated to planning, establishing, monitoring and interpreting various financial intelligence processes.
- The financial intelligence is an aid to the top management in an organization in understanding tactics in framing strategies.

Functions

- To ensure that professionals fulfilling obligations in respect of double checking, customer identification, book-keeping and reporting obligations.
- To establish and maintain an effective policy and strategies to oversee compliance and to provide high quality, financial intelligence for use in the fight against crime, money laundering and terror finance.
- To protect the integrity and stability of the company's financial systems.
- It strives to develop a strong legal basis to combat money laundering, financing of terrorism activities and other financial crimes to protect the stability of the financial system, by monitoring and supervising the anti-money laundering and anti-financing of terrorism controls.
- To produce intelligence products that incorporates the analysis of relevant classified information.
- Financial intelligence units are agencies that receive reports of suspicious transactions from financial institutions and other persons and entities, analyze them, and disseminate the resulting intelligence to local law-enforcement agencies to combat money laundering.
- It will be only one part of overall organization knowledge and provide the organization with competitive advantage to be associated with overall organization strategy.

Forensic accounting refers to the use of accounting, auditing and investigative knowledge to form a suitable analysis of a business. It can be consider as the private eyes of the corporate culture as it involves the application of special skills in accounting. As forensic accounting helps in SWOT (Strength, Weakness, Opportunity and Weakness) analyzing of a business, it provides a path for interested people to make thoughtful investment decisions. Comparing with a normal accountant who acts like a watchdog, a forensic accountant acts like a bloodhound. They look behind the facade and do not accept financial records at their face value. Money laundering is the common word used to describe the process by which criminals disguise the original ownership and control of the proceeds of criminal conduct. It is an act of laundering in circumstances where a person is engaged in an arrangement (i.e. by providing a service or product) and that arrangement involves the proceeds of crime. Financial intelligence is an important part of overall organization knowledge and one that can provide strong benefits to the bottom line if gathered and used effectively. Financial intelligence must however be treated as a strategic resource, must give the organization a competitive advantage, and needs to be developed in a systematic way to ensure the best use of resources. Financial intelligence has uses in both tactical and strategy areas but organizations need to ensure its use is appropriate for each purpose.

Fiduciary Accounting

Fiduciary accounting involves recording the transactions associated with a trust or estate entity, and issuing periodic reports on the status of the entity. This accounting is dealt with on a cash basis, where cash is recorded when received and disbursements and distributions are recorded when paid.

A large part of the trustee's accounting work involves determining whether receipts and disbursements should be assigned to income or principal. Income is money or property received as a current return from a principal asset, while principal is property held in trust for later distribution to a remainder beneficiary. The rules for how to allocate receipts and disbursements may be contained within the relevant will or trust document; if not, the trustee uses the rules laid out in the Uniform Principal and Income Act (as modified by the applicable state government).

In addition, a will or trust agreement may have a unique distribution scheme that varies from the standard approach of issuing income periodically to the income beneficiary, with the remainder beneficiary receiving the principal at a later date. Thus, the accounting associated with a specific estate or trust could be entirely unique from what is needed for other estates or trusts.

At least once a year, the trustee issues a fiduciary accounting to all trustee beneficiaries. There is no fixed format for this document, but it usually contains the following:

- Cover page and summary of accounts.
- Schedule of receipts.
- Schedule of disbursements.
- Schedule of distributions.
- Schedule of gains and losses.
- Beginning and ending schedules of assets on hand.

Another fiduciary accounting issue is the concept of carrying value. In most accounting frameworks, this simply means the current book value of an asset, but in a fiduciary accounting system, it means that an asset's value has been re-measured after a specific event, such as the start of a trustee's administration, so that subsequent changes in asset value can be ascribed to that specific trustee.

The trustee may also need to account for transfers between income and principal. These transactions may be needed to pay for large expenses, to make significant capital investments, or to pay for trust indebtedness.

Orientation in Accounting

The main aim of business is to earn profit. For earning profit, the businessman will either purchase the goods in one market at certain price and sell it in another market at higher price or will convert the raw materials into finished products and sell it to the different customers at a price which will give him some percentage of profit on cost of production. But this may not be true in all cases. Sometimes it may happen that the goods purchased or produced may go out of fashion and may be unsold simply because of depression in the market or keen competition. Moreover, in big business information is required for planning, control, evaluation of performance and decision making. This information can be provided only when business transactions are recorded, classified and summarized properly. Before recording the transactions in the books it is essential to understand the basic terms which have their special meaning in Accounting. These basic terms are called Accounting Terminology.

1. Accountant: Accountant is a person who is trained to prepare and maintain financial records. An accountant with his education, training, analytical mind and experience is best qualified to provide multiple need-based services to the society. The accountant of today can do full justice not only to matters relating to taxation, costing. Management accounting but they can act in the fields relating to financial policies and even economic policies.

2. Accounting period: It is referred to the period of time over which profits are calculated. Normal accounting periods are months, quarters, and years (fiscal or calendar).

3. Account: It is a statement of the various dealings which occur between a customer and the firm. It can also be expressed as a clear and concise record of the transaction relating to a person or a firm or a property (or assets) or a liability or an expense or an income.

4. Accrued Income: Accrued Income also known as Outstanding Income. Such incomes are accrued during the accounting period but not actually received in cash during that period.

5. Assets: Any physical thing or right owned that has money value is an asset. In other words, an asset is that expenditure which results in acquiring of some property or benefits of a lasting nature. As-sets are properties of business which were acquired at measurable money cost. They are classified on the basis of their nature.

Different types of assets are as under:

- Fixed assets: Fixed assets are the assets which are acquired and held permanently and used in the business with the objective of making profits. Land and building, Plant and machinery, Furniture and Fixtures are examples of fixed assets.
- Current assets: The assets of the business in the form of cash, debtors bank balances, bill receivable and stock are called current assets as they can be realized within an operating cycle of one year to discharge liabilities.
- Tangible assets: Tangible assets have definite physical shape or identity and existence; they can be seen, felt and have volume such as land, cash, stock etc. Thus tangible assets can be both fixed assets and current assets.

- Intangible assets: The assets which have no physical shape which cannot be seen or felt but have value are called intangible assets. Goodwill, patents, trademarks and licenses are examples of intangible assets. They are usually classified under fixed assets.
- Fictitious assets: Fictitious assets are not real assets. Past accumulated losses or expenses which are capitalized for the time being, expenses for promotion of Organisations (preliminary expenses), discount on issue of shares, debit balance of profit and loss account etc. are the examples of fictitious assets.
- Wasting assets: These assets are also called depleting assets. Assets such as mines, Timber forests, quarries etc. which become exhausted in value by way of excavation of the minerals, cutting of wood etc. are known as wasting assets. Such assets are usually natural resources with physical limitations.
- Contingent assets: Contingent assets are assets, the existence, value possession of which is based on happening or otherwise of specific events. For example, if a business firm has filed a suit for a particular property now in possession of other persons, the firm will get the property if the suit is decided in its favor. Till the suit is decided, it is a contingent asset.

6. Bad debts: Bad debts refer to those amounts owed to a company that are not going to be paid. An account receivable becomes a bad debt when it is recognized that it won't be paid. Sometimes, bad debts are written off when recognized. This is an expense. Sometimes, a reserve is set up to provide for possible bad debts. Creating or adding to a reserve is also an expense.

7. Balance: It is the sum of Debit entries minus the sum of Credit entries in an account. If it is found to be positive, the difference is called a debit balance; if found to be negative it is a credit balance.

8. Balance sheet: It is a statement of the financial position of a company at a single specific time (often it is prepared at the close of business on the last day of the month, quarter, or year.) The balance sheet normally lists all assets on the left side or top while liabilities and capital are listed on the right side or bottom. The total of all numbers on the left side or top must equal or balance the total of all numbers on the right side or bottom. A balance sheet balances according to this equation: Assets = Liabilities + Capital.

9. Capital: It is the part of the wealth which is used for further production and thus capital consists of all current assets and fixed assets. Cash in hand, Cash at bank, Building, plant & machinery, etc are the capital of the business. Capital should not necessarily be in cash, as it may be in kind also. Capital can be classified as: Fixed Capital, Floating Capital and Working capital.

10. Closing stock: Closing stock is the value of goods remaining at the end of the accounting period. It includes closing stock of raw materials, work progress (where manufacturing account is not separately prepared) and finished stock.

11. Cost of sales, cost of goods sold: It is the expense or cost of all items sold during an accounting period. Each unit sold has a cost of sales or cost of the goods sold. In businesses there are many items flowing through, the cost of sales or cost of goods sold is often computed by this formula: Cost of Sales = Beginning Inventory + Purchases During the Period - Ending Inventory.

12. Creditor: A person to whom money owes by the firm is called creditor. These creditors may be creditors for goods and creditors for expenses.

13. Credit: In simplest terms the right side of an account is arbitrarily or traditionally called Credit side.

14. Cast and Carry Forward: When journal entries extend to several pages of the journal, the totals is cast (done) at the end of each page. At the end of each page the words Total C/F are written in the particulars column against the debit and credit totals. On the next page, in the beginning the words Total b/f is written in the column against the debit and credit totals.

15. Compound Journal Entry: If there are two or more transaction of a similar nature are occurring on the same day and either Dr. or Cr. Account is common, such transactions can be conveniently recorded in the form of one journal entry instead of making a separate entry for each transaction. Such entry is known as compound Journal entry.

16. Cash Discount: This discount is allowed by a creditor to a debtor when the latter pays the amount of goods purchased by him either immediately or within a specified period. It is an incentive given to a debtor for making an early payment.

17. Debtor: A person who owes money to the firm mostly on account of credit sales of goods is called a debtor. For example, when goods are sold to a person on credit that person pays the price in future, he is called a debtor because he owes the amount to the firm.

18. Drawings: It is the amount of money or the value of goods which the proprietor takes for his do-mestic or personal use. It is usually subtracted from capital as it is an expense for a company.

19. Discount: When customers are allowed any type of deduction in the prices of goods by the businessman that is called discount. When some discount is allowed in prices of goods on the basis of sales of the items, that is termed as trade discount, but when debtors are allowed some discount in prices of the goods for quick payment, that is termed as cash discount.

20. Depreciation: The term depreciation refers to loss on account of reduced value of assets due to wear and tear, obsolescence, damaged with time or accident. Depreciation is treated as the cost or loss arises.

21. Debit: In simplest terms the left side of an account is arbitrarily or traditionally called Debit side. Usually an increase in assets or a reduction in liabilities. Every debit has a balancing credit.

22. Double Entry: It is a system of accounting in which every transaction is recorded twice, as a debit and as a credit. Each credit has a balancing debit.

23. Expense: The terms “expense” refers to the amount incurred in the process of earning revenue. If the benefit of an expenditure is limited to one year, it is treated as an expense (also know is as revenue expenditure) such as payment of salaries and rent.

24. Goods: It is a general term used for the articles in which the business deals; that is, only those articles which are bought for resale for profit are known as Goods.

25. Gross Profit: If the sales revenue is higher than the cost of goods sold the difference is known as Gross Profit.

26. Gross Loss: If the sales revenue is less than the cost of goods sold the difference is known as Gross Loss.

27. Invoice: While making a sale, the seller prepares a statement giving the particulars such as the quantity, price per unit, the total amount payable, any deductions made and shows the net amount payable by the buyer. Such a statement is called an invoice.

28. Liability: A liability is an amount which a business firm is "liable to pay" legally. All the amounts which are claims by outsiders on the assets of the business are known as liabilities. It means the amount which the firm owes to outsiders that is, accepting the proprietors. In simple terms, debts repayable to outsiders by the business are known as liabilities. They are credit balances in the ledger.

Liabilities = Assets - Capital

Liabilities are classified into further categories as given below:

- Owner's capital: Capital is the amount contributed by the owners of the business. In addition to initial capital introduced, proprietors may introduce additional capital and withdraw some amounts from business over a period of time. Owner's capital is also called "net worth". Net worth is the total fund of proprietors on a particulars date. It consists of capital, profits and interest on capital subject to reduction of drawings and interest on drawings. In case of limited companies, capital refers to capital subscribed by shareholders. Net worth refers to paid up equity capital plus reserves and profits, minus losses.

- Long term Liabilities: Liabilities repayable after specific duration of long period of time are called long term liabilities. They do not become due for payment in the ordinary "operating cycle" of business or within a short period of lime. Examples are long term loans and debentures.

- Current liabilities: Liabilities which are repayable during the operating cycle of business, usually within a year, are called short term liabilities or current liabilities. They are paid out of current assets or by the creation of other current liabilities. Examples of current liabilities are trade creditors, bills payable, outstanding expenses, bank overdraft, taxes payable and dividends payable.

- Contingent liabilities: Contingent liabilities will result into liabilities only if certain events happen. Examples are: Bills discounted and endorsed which may be dishonored, unpaid calls on investments.

29. Losses: Loss in simplest terms means something against which the firm receives no benefit. It represents money given up without any return. It may be noted that expense leads to revenue but losses do not, e.g. loss due to fire, theft and damages payable to others.

30. Purchases: Buying of goods by the trader for selling them to his customers is known as purchases. As the trade is buying and selling of commodities purchase is the main function of a trade. Here, the trader gets possession of the goods which are not for own use but for resale. Purchases can be of two types; viz, cash purchases and credit purchases. If cash is paid immediately for the pur-chase, it is cash purchases. If the payment is postponed, it is credit purchases.

31. Purchase Returns: When purchased goods are returned to the suppliers these are known as purchase returns. Such returns are also termed as "returns outwards".

32. Proprietor: The person who makes the investment and bears all the risks connected with the business is known as proprietor.

33. Revenue: It means the amount which, as a result of operations, is added to the capital. It is defined as the inflow of assets which result in an increase in the owner's equity. It includes all incomes like sales receipts, interest, commission, brokerage etc., However, receipts of capital nature like additional capital, sale of assets etc., are not a part of revenue. Revenue is different from "Income". Amount received from sale of goods is called "Revenue". The Cost of goods sold is called "Expense".

34. Sales: When the goods purchased are sold out, it is known as sales. Here, the possession and the ownership right over the goods are transferred to the buyer. It is known as 'Business Turnover' or sales proceeds. It can be of two types, viz., cash sales and credit sales. If the sale is for immediate cash payment, it is cash sales. If payment for sales is postponed, it is credit sales.

35. Stock: The goods purchased are for selling, if the goods are not sold out fully, a part of the total goods purchased is kept with the trader unlit it is sold out, it is said to be a stock. If there is stock at the end of the accounting year, it is said to be a closing stock. This closing stock at the yearend will be the opening stock for the subsequent year.

36. Solvent: A person who has assets with realizable values which exceeds his liabilities is insolvent.

37. Sale of Shares: If shares or security are sold, the entry should be passed at market value less bro-kerage, if any, paid on such shares.

38. Transaction: "An event the recognition of which gives rise to an entry in accounting records. It is an event which results in change in the balance sheet equation and changes the value of assets and equity. In simple terms, transaction means the exchange of money or money's worth from one account to another account. Events like purchase and sale of goods, receipt and payment of cash for services or on personal accounts, loss or profit in dealings etc., are the transactions". Cash transaction is one where cash receipt or payment is involved in the exchange. Credit transaction, on the other hand, will not have "cash" either received or paid, for something given or received respectively, but gives rise to debtor and creditor relationship. Non-cash transaction is one where the question of receipt or payment of cash does not at all arise, e.g. Depreciation, return of goods etc. Transactions are of four kinds:

- Cash transaction: Cash transactions are those transactions in which cash is involved in the exchange.
- Credit transaction: Credit transactions are those in which cash is not paid immediately. The settlement is postponed to a later date.
- Barter transactions: Barter transactions are those transactions where, no doubt, there is an exchange of goods, but the exchange of benefit is not in terms of money.
- Paper transaction: Paper transactions are those transactions where there is no question of meeting the value of transaction.

39. Trading Account: It is an account prepared for an accounting period to find the trading results or gross margin of the business i.e., the amount of gross profit the concern has made from buying and selling during the accounting period.

40. Opening Stock: The stock at the beginning of an accounting period is called opening stock.

41. Opening Entry: The balances of the previous year are brought forward in the beginning of the year by means of an entry in a going concern. Such entry is made on the basis of accounting equation i.e. by debiting all assets and crediting liabilities and capital account.

42. Interest on Drawings: Any amount charged as interest on drawings made by the proprietors for his personal use during the particular period is treated as interest on drawings. Interest on drawings should be taken as an income for ascertaining the true profit for a period.

43. Non-Operating Income: Non-Operating incomes refer to other than operating income. For exam-ple, interest on investment of outside business, profit on sale of fixed assets and dividend received etc.

44. Provision for Doubtful Debts: Those bad debts of which recovery is doubtful. Thus doubtful debts should not be written off from the books of accounts. Doubtful debts are treated as anticipated loss therefore making suitable provisions for these is required to be made in the books of accounts.

45. Interest on Capital: In order to ascertain true profitability of the business concern, it is essential that profit is determined after deducting interest on the capital provided by proprietor.

46. Income Received in Advance: It is any income received in advance which is not earned during the accounting period. Therefore, if any income received in advance, it should be treated as income for the subsequent year.

47. Outstanding Expenses: Outstanding expenses refer to those expenses incurred and remain unpaid during the accounting period. For example, salary, rent, interest etc. are expenses which are incurred but remain unpaid during the accounting period. In order to ascertain the correct profit and loss made during the year, it is essential that such related expenses are treated as Salary Outstanding, Interest Outstanding and Rent Outstanding etc.

48. Operating Income: It refers to the income earned from the operation of the business excluding Gross Profit and Non-Operating incomes.

49. Voucher: A voucher is a written document in support of a transaction. It is a proof that a particular transaction has taken place for the value stated in the voucher. Voucher is necessary to audit the accounts.

Cash Book

Cash book is the books of original entry which records the cash receipts and cash payments incurred during a particular period. All receipts and payments whether is received through Cheque, Cash, Bank Transfer, Postal order, Bank overdraft are recorded in the cash book.

Though cash book is considering as an original book of entry, it is also considered as an integral part of the ledger. Cash book is the book which serves the purposes of both journal and ledger. The details of every transaction are described in the cash book. Point to be noted that the balance of the cash balance always be a debit balance because a person cannot pay more than he had.

As cash book is another kind of ledger, it has double entry in the cash book. In order to complete recording of other aspect of a cash transaction, only one sided posting is required to be made from the cash book. Payments are recorded in credit side and receipts are recorded in the debit side.

The folio of cash book is written in the ledger and the folio of ledger is mentioned in the cash book for cross reference.

Types of Cash Book

Normally three types of cash book is used in practical field, such as:

- Single Column Cash Book – records only cash transactions in cash column.
- Double Column Cash Book – records both "cash and Cheque" transactions in cash and bank column.
- Treble Column Cash Book – records cash, Bank and discount in cash, bank and discount column.

Single Column Cash Book

In a single column cash book, only cash transactions i.e. cash receipts and cash payments are recorded. Cash received from the several sources are recorded in the Debit side of the cash book and all payments are recorded in the credit side the book. The difference between the received side (Opening balance and received during the period) and cash payments equal ending cash balance of that period.

Example of single column cash book is as follows:

Enter the following transactions in the cash book of Square Limited.

Year -12:

August:

1-Aug: Opening Cash balance of Cash book is $ 1,780

4-Aug: Electricity Bill paid $ 600

5-Aug: Rent received from Mr. X $ 450

8-Aug: Received from Customers $ 1,840

10-Aug: Furniture Purchase $ 1,800

13-Aug: Raw Materials Purchase $ 1,200

14-Aug: Loan paid to Mr. Y $ 3,000

28-Aug: Received from sale of goods $ 1,940

30-Aug: Staff Salaries paid for Aug $ 1,500

Solution:

Table: Square Limited Cash Book.

Date	Receipts	V.No.	L.F	$	Date	Payments	V.No	L.F	$
01	O/B			1,780					
05	Rent Received			450					600
08	Received from Customer			1,840					18,000
28	Received against Goods sale			1,940					1,200
									3,000
									1,500
									2,090
	Total			6,010		Total			6,010

Double Column Cash Book

In Single Cash column cash book only cash column is maintained but in double column cash book both Cash and Bank column are maintained. For bank transactions it not necessary to open a bank account in the ledger.

In a cash column cash receipts and payments are recorded and in a bank column Cheque issued for the payment and money received and deposited into bank account are recorded.

Cash Deposited to Bank Account, or Cash withdrawn from Bank

- When Cash is deposited to into Bank account, Bank balance increases and cash balance decreases. Hence, Bank column is debited and cash column is credited. For example, $ 200 is deposited to Bank account can be shown in the cash book in the following manner:

Date	Particulars	Cash	Bank	Date	Particulars	Cash	Bank
01.08.2011	To Cash		200	01.08.2011	By Cash	200	

- When Cash is withdrawn for office purpose, cash column is required to be debited and the bank column is required to be credited. Example as above.
- Entries for cash deposited to the bank and withdrawn from the bank are called "Contra Entries." and should be indicated by (C) in L.F. Column. As double entry is made for the contra items, no ledger posting in not needed.

Date	Receipts	V.N.	L.F	Cash	Bank	Date	Payments	V.N.	L.F	Cash	Bank

Treble Column Cash Book

Discount Column is added in Treble Column Cash Book. Hence, in addition to the Cash column and Bank Column, the discount column is also added. The Format of the Treble Column is presented below:

Date	Receipts	V.N.	L.F	Discount	Cash	Bank	Date	Payments	V.N.	L.F	Discount	Cash	Bank

Features of Cash Book

A Cash Book has the following features:

- Only Cash transactions are recorded in cash book.
- It plays a twin role as it is both a book of original entry (Journal) as well as a book of final entry.
- All cash transactions are primarily recorded in it as soon as they take place that is why it is considered as a book of original entry. On the other hand, the cash aspect of all cash transactions is finally recorded in the Cash Book.
- A Cash Book is also a Ledger this is one of the reasons to consider it as a book of final entry.
- Only one aspect of cash transaction is posted to the ledger account.
- Since the Cash Book is the substitute for Cash A/c, no Cash A/c is opened in the ledger.
- It has two equal sides one is left hand side, which is called as the debit side and the other side is right hand side (credit side).
- All the cash receipts of the business are recorded on the debit side of cash book and all the payments related items on the credit side of cash book.
- The difference between the total of left hand side and right hand side shows cash in hand.
- The balance of cash book can be verified by accountant by counting actual cash in the cash box.
- Cash book always shows debit balance. It can never show credit balance.
- Unlike any other account, cash book is balanced daily.

Advantages

Generally cash transactions are numerous. "What is credit transaction today will be cash transactions tomorrow". In other words, all credit transactions are finally settled by cash. If like all other transactions cash transactions are also recorded primarily in Journal, the cash aspect of the transactions will be required to be posted to Cash A/C, in the Ledger separately and this becomes time consuming exercise and expensive, this is for the reason company's prefer to record all cash transactions in a separate book named Cash Book. It is time saving and cheap.

Besides this the Cash Book renders the following benefits:

- Daily cash receipts and cash payments are easily ascertained.
- Cash in hand at any time can easily be ascertained through Cash Book balance.
- Any mistake in the book can be easily detected at the time of verification of cash.
- Any defalcation of money can be detected while verifying cash.
- Since cash is verified daily, Cash Book is always kept up-to-date.

Cash Book: A Journal or a Ledger

From the above discussion it appears that the Cash Book is the substitute for the Cash Account. In fact, no separate Cash Account is opened in the Ledger; Cash Book serves the purpose of the Cash Account. In the cash book entries can be regarded as one aspect of the Double Entry System whereas the other aspect is posted to the Ledger in the concerned account.

- Form of cash book resembles with ledger.
- Words To and By are used in the ledger.
- No separate cash and bank account are required in the ledger.
- Cash and bank columns of the cash book are periodically balanced just like ledger accounts.

On the other hand, all cash transactions are primarily recorded in the Cash Book in order of date and thereafter posted to the concerned ledger accounts. Judging from this angle, 'Cash Book is a Journal'. Thus we see that a Cash Book is the 'mixture of Journal and Ledger'.

Similarity of cash book with journal:

- Cash transactions are recorded in the cash book at the time of origin.
- Transactions are recorded date-wise.
- Cash book contains ledger folio as in the journal.
- Narration is given for each entry.

Specimen of simple cash book:

Date	Particulars	V. No.	L.F.	Amount	Date	Particulars	V.No.	Amount

The columns of the cash book are explained below:

- Date: The date on which transaction is occurred is to be written in this column. In the first line, the year and in the second line, the name of the month followed by the actual date.

Particulars: In this column the name of the opposite account is written (the second aspect of cash transaction) along with the narration of the transaction.

- L.F. (Ledger Folio): The page number of the Ledger where the concerned (opposite) account has been opened is written in this column. This will help to locate the account from the Ledger. It may be noted that in a Ledger account J.F. is written as reference, while in a Cash Book L.F. is written. It is so, because cash transactions are not recorded in any Journal.
- Amount: The amount of the transaction is recorded in this column. The amount of cash received is recorded on the debit side in amount column and the amount of cash paid is recorded on the credit side in amount column.
- V. NO. (Voucher Number): The voucher number of each item of receipt and payment is also to be written as voucher number is necessary for each item of receipt and payment. Generally, a voucher has a serial number and this number-is written in this column (V. No.).

Bottom line difference between a Cash Book and a Cash Account:

In fact, Cash Book is a substitute for a Cash Account. Yet there are some differences between the two, which are given below:

Cash Book	Cash Account
1. It is a separate book in which cash transactions are directly recorded.	1. It is an account in a ledger in which posting is made from journal.
2. It serves the purpose of both journal and ledger.	2. It serves the purpose of a Ledger only.
3. Narration is required.	3. Narration is not required.
4. A column for Ledger Folio is provided.	4. A column for Journal Folio is required.

Cash Discounts

A cash discount is an incentive offered by a seller to a buyer for paying an invoice ahead of the scheduled due date. Cash discounts are incentives offered by sellers that reduce the amount that the buyer owes by either a percentage of the total bill or by a fixed amount.

For example: If an invoice is due in 30 days, a seller could offer the buyer a typical cash discount of 2pc if they were to pay the invoice within the first 10 days of receiving it.

Small cash discounts benefit the seller because they increase the likelihood that a buyer will pay quickly, therefore providing the seller with cash in a shorter period of time, as it is better to receive e.g. 95% of an invoice with a few days than wait 30 or more days to receive the full amount.

Having cash sooner means that the seller can in turn put the cash back into the business sooner – a good motivation for any organisation.

How Cash Discounts Work

An example of how a cash discount is applied:

- Net price of goods: £200.00.

- VAT Calculation.
- Goods £200.00.
- Less 10% cash discount (£20.00).
- Goods after cash discount £180.00.
- VAT @ 20% of £180.00 = £36.00.
- Gross Invoice total £216.00.

If, as a supplier, you offer a cash discount on condition the invoice is paid early or within a specific time frame the VAT can be calculated on the basis that the discount will be taken so the VAT will be a percentage of the net amount after discount.

Cash Discounts vs. Trade Discounts

Cash discounts are not reductions in the agreed sales price of the goods or services at the time of the transaction – they are a reduction in the amount to be paid by a credit customer (to whom you have given credit terms) if that customer pays within a specified time period.

A cash discount is intended to persuade credit customers to pay their bills quickly – not an incentive to make the purchase.

Recording Cash Discounts: Net vs. Gross Method

In accounting, there are two different ways that cash discounts can be recorded in the books: the net method and the gross method.

The net method treats sales revenue as the net amount after the given discount, and any discounts that the buyer doesn't take are recorded as interest revenue. The discounts are essentially treated as compensation to the seller for providing credit to the buyer.

The gross method views discounts that aren't taken by the buyer as a portion of total sales revenue – not as separate interest earnings. The gross method is the most common in business practices today.

No matter which recording method is used, a cash discount taken by a buyer will reduce sales revenue.

References

- How-does-an-accounting-system-work, tighten-accounting-controls: bizmanualz.com, Retrieved 25, June 2020
- Accounting-ratios-definition-importance-and-limitations, accounting-ratios, accounting-65812: yourarticlelibrary.com, Retrieved 02, Jan 2020
- What-is-cost-accounting, cost-accounting-17513: accountingnotes.net, Retrieved 15, March 2020
- Social-accounting-concept-definition-features-and-benefits-financial-analysis, social-accounting, accounting-67703: yourarticlelibrary.com, Retrieved 19, August 2020

- Project-accounting-concepts-and-business-calculations, accounting-software: netsuite.com, Retrieved 09, July 2020
- Principles-of-government-accounting, government-accounts, accounting-51846: yourarticlelibrary.com, Retrieved 11, Feb 2020
- What-is-a-cash-book-types-of-cash-book: accountantskills.com, Retrieved 16, May 2020

2

Accounting: Principles and Concepts

A few of the basic principles of accounting are revenue recognition principle, cost principle, matching principle, full disclosure principle, and objective principles. This chapter deals with the basic accounting principles, concepts, conventions, their inherent differences along with traditional and modern accounting systems in an easy-to-understand manner.

Basic Accounting Principles

A number of basic accounting principles have been developed through common usage. They form the basis upon which the complete suite of accounting standards has been built. The best-known of these principles are as follows:

Accrual Principle

This is the concept that accounting transactions should be recorded in the accounting periods when they actually occur, rather than in the periods when there are cash flows associated with them. This is the foundation of the accrual basis of accounting. It is important for the construction of financial statements that show what actually happened in an accounting period, rather than being artificially delayed or accelerated by the associated cash flows. For example, if you ignored the accrual principle, you would record an expense only when you paid for it, which might incorporate a lengthy delay caused by the payment terms for the associated supplier invoice.

Conservatism Principle

This is the concept that you should record expenses and liabilities as soon as possible, but to record revenues and assets only when you are sure that they will occur. This introduces a conservative slant to the financial statements that may yield lower reported profits, since revenue and asset recognition may be delayed for some time. Conversely, this principle tends to encourage the recordation of losses earlier, rather than later. This concept can be taken too far, where a business persistently misstates its results to be worse than is realistically the case.

Consistency Principle

This is the concept that, once you adopt an accounting principle or method, you should continue to use it until a demonstrably better principle or method comes along. Not following the consistency principle means that a business could continually jump between different accounting treatments of its transactions that make its long-term financial results extremely difficult to discern.

Cost Principle

This is the concept that a business should only record its assets, liabilities, and equity investments at their original purchase costs. This principle is becoming less valid, as a host of accounting standards are heading in the direction of adjusting assets and liabilities to their fair values.

Economic Entity Principle

This is the concept that the transactions of a business should be kept separate from those of its owners and other businesses. This prevents intermingling of assets and liabilities among multiple entities, which can cause considerable difficulties when the financial statements of a fledgling business are first audited.

Full Disclosure Principle

This is the concept that you should include in or alongside the financial statements of a business all of the information that may impact a reader's understanding of those statements. The accounting standards have greatly amplified upon this concept in specifying an enormous number of informational disclosures.

Going Concern Principle

This is the concept that a business will remain in operation for the foreseeable future. This means that you would be justified in deferring the recognition of some expenses, such as depreciation, until later periods. Otherwise, you would have to recognize all expenses at once and not defer any of them.

Matching Principle

This is the concept that, when you record revenue, you should record all related expenses at the same time. Thus, you charge inventory to the cost of goods sold at the same time that you record revenue from the sale of those inventory items. This is a cornerstone of the accrual basis of accounting. The cash basis of accounting does not use the matching the principle.

Materiality Principle

This is the concept that you should record a transaction in the accounting records if not doing so might have altered the decision making process of someone reading the company's financial statements. This is quite a vague concept that is difficult to quantify, which has led some of the more picayune controllers to record even the smallest transactions.

Monetary Unit Principle

This is the concept that a business should only record transactions that can be stated in terms of a unit of currency. Thus, it is easy enough to record the purchase of a fixed asset, since it was bought for a specific price, whereas the value of the quality control system of a business is not recorded. This concept keeps a business from engaging in an excessive level of estimation in deriving the value of its assets and liabilities.

Reliability Principle

This is the concept that only those transactions that can be proven should be recorded. For example, a supplier invoice is solid evidence that an expense has been recorded. This concept is of prime interest to auditors, who are constantly in search of the evidence supporting transactions.

Revenue Recognition Principle

This is the concept that you should only recognize revenue when the business has substantially completed the earnings process. So many people have skirted around the fringes of this concept to commit reporting fraud that a variety of standard-setting bodies have developed a massive amount of information about what constitutes proper revenue recognition.

Time Period Principle

This is the concept that a business should report the results of its operations over a standard period of time. This may qualify as the most glaringly obvious of all accounting principles, but is intended to create a standard set of comparable periods, which is useful for trend analysis. These principles are incorporated into a number of accounting frameworks, from which accounting standards govern the treatment and reporting of business transactions.

Importance of Accounting Principles

Accounting principles are important because they establish a consistency that allows for more accurate and efficient viewing of company statements and reports.

Standards

The generally accepted accounting principles represent a complex, important set of accounting definitions, methods and assumptions that create a standard method of reporting the financial details of a business. With the GAAP, a hierarchy exists that dictates which standard should be used and when. FASB statements, accounting research bulletins and Accounting Principle Board opinions from the AICPA must be consulted first, followed by guides from the FASB and AICPA. If a standard is not found in the statements or guides, the questions and answers in FASB and AICPA implementation guides and industry standards must be used. When all companies follow a standard reporting method, greater financial transparency exists because investors know exactly what an "asset" is or that "inflation is ignored." Individual companies may not make their own rules.

Industry Comparisons

Potential investors who want to direct funds to a certain type of industry without a particular company in mind will find accounting principles an important tool as individual businesses are reviewed. Standards allow the investor to compare and contrast companies across a singular industry or multiple industries quickly through balance sheet, income statement and annual report reviews. Lessons in each company's reporting practices are not required when every business uses GAAP.

Company Performance

Even though the principles have become more complex in recent years, the complexity relates to augmenting the principles to include new, complex situations versus heavily altering existing definitions and methods on an annual basis. Because of the long-term consistency in key accounting definitions and methods, standard company performance measures listed on financial statements and annual reports provide a realistic view of the company's growth or lack of growth over a period of years.

Considerations not Covered by GAAP

While the generally accepted accounting principles serve an important purpose, a potential investor may want to use GAAP-covered financial reporting as only a portion of his overall picture of a company and also consult non-GAAP financial measures such as pro forma earnings and free cash flow. These items can be viewed as both a non-GAAP and a comparable GAAP financial measure. U.S. Securities and Exchange Commission Regulation G requires public companies disclosing non-GAAP financial measures to simultaneously present and reconcile the GAAP measure most comparable.

Generally Accepted Accounting Principles

GAAP, or Generally Accepted Accounting Principles, is a commonly recognized set of rules and procedures designed to govern corporate accounting and financial reporting in the United States (US). The US GAAP is a comprehensive set of accounting practices that were developed jointly by the Financial Accounting Standards Board (FASB) and the Governmental Accounting Standards Board (GASB), so they are applied to governmental and non-profit accounting as well.

US securities law requires all publicly-traded companies, as well as any company that publicly releases financial statements, to follow the GAAP principles and procedures.

In addition, or as an alternative, are the International Financial Reporting Standards (IFRS) established by the International Accounting Standards Board (IASB). The IFRS rules govern accounting standards in the European Union, as well as in a number of countries in South America and Asia.

The Core GAAP Principles

GAAP is set forth in 10 primary principles, as follows:

- Principle of consistency: This principle ensures that consistent standards are followed in financial reporting from period to period.
- Principle of permanent methods: Closely related to the previous principle is that of consistent procedures and practices being applied in accounting and financial reporting to allow comparison.
- Principle of non-compensation: This principle states that all aspects of an organization's performance, whether positive or negative, are to be reported. In other words, it should not compensate (offset) a debt with an asset.
- Principle of prudence: All reporting of financial data is to be factual, reasonable, and not speculative.
- Principle of regularity: This principle means that all accountants are to consistently abide by the GAAP.
- Principle of sincerity: Accountants should perform and report with basic honesty and accuracy.
- Principle of good faith: Similar to the previous principle, this principle asserts that anyone involved in financial reporting is expected to be acting honestly and in good faith.
- Principle of materiality: All financial reporting should clearly disclose the organization's genuine financial position.
- Principle of continuity: This principle states that all asset valuations in financial reporting are based on the assumption that the business or other entity will continue to operate going forward.
- Principle of periodicity: This principle refers to entities abiding by commonly accepted financial reporting periods, such as quarterly or annually.

The Generally Accepted Accounting Principles further set out specific rules and principles governing such things as standardized currency units, cost and revenue recognition, financial statement format and presentation, and required disclosures. For example, it requires precise matching of expenses with revenues for the same accounting period (the matching principle).

Importance of GAAP

Generally Accepted Accounting Principles make financial reporting standardized and transparent, using commonly accepted terms, practices, and procedures. The consistency of presentation of financial reports that results from GAAP makes it easy for investors and other interested parties (such as a board of directors) to more easily comprehend financial statements and compare the financial statements of one company with those of another company.

GAAP also seeks to make non-profit and governmental entities more accountable by requiring them to clearly and honestly report their finances.

In short, GAAP is designed to ensure a consistent presentation of financial statements, making it easier for people to read and comprehend the information contained in the statements.

Applications in Financial Analysis

For financial analysts performing valuation work and financial modeling, it's important to have a solid understanding of accounting principles. While this is important, financial models focus more on cash flow and economic value, which is not significantly impacted by accounting principles (other than for the calculation of cash taxes).

Alternatives to GAAP

GAAP is the set of standards and practices that are followed in the United States, but what about other countries? Outside the US, the alternative in most countries is the International Financial Reporting Standards (IFRS), which is regulated by the International Accounting Standards Board (IASB). While the two systems have different principles, rules, and guidelines, IFRS and GAAP have been working towards merging the two systems.

Accounting Concepts

The term concept also known as postulates refer to such ideas which are accompanied with different accounting procedures. These are the fundamental ideas or the general assumptions underlying the theory and practice of financial accounting and are broad working rules for all accounting activities and developed by the accounting profession.

Business Entity Concept

The concept implies that a business unit is separate and distinct from the persons who supply capital to it (owners). It means that business has a separate legal entity from its owners. For the purpose of accounting the business and its owners are to be treated as two separate entities. Irrespective of the form of organisation, a business unit has got its own separate identity as distinguished from the persons who own or control it (owners). Business is kept separate from the proprietor so that transactions of the business may not be recorded with him. In case this concept is not followed, affairs of the business will be mixed up with the private affairs of the proprietor and the true picture of the business will not be revealed. Thus, in the books of the sole trader, a firm or a limited company, only business transactions are recorded and no note is taken of the personal transactions of the sole proprietor, the partners of the firm and the shareholders respectively.

For Example: If the proprietor of the business invests $60000 into the business, it will be deemed that he has given that much of money to the business as a loan which will be shown as a liability in the books of the firm. On receipt of the amount, cash account will be debited and the proprietor's capital account will be credited. Similarly, on withdrawal of the amount from the business for personal use of the proprietor, the proprietor's capital account will be debited and Cash account will be credited.

Money Measurement Concept

The concept of money measurement states that only those transactions, events and happenings in the organisation which can be expressed in terms of money (such as sale of goods, receipt of income etc.) are to be recorded in the book of accounts. All those transactions that cannot be expressed in monetary terms (such as appointment of the manager, creativity of its production department) should not be recorded. The advantage of maintaining business transactions in terms of money is that money serves a common denominator by means of which homogenous factors about a business can be expressed in terms of numbers (money), which are capable of additions and subtractions in future.

Going Concern Concept

The concept of going concern assumes that a business firm would continue to carry out its operations indefinitely, i.e., for a fairly long period of time and would not be liquidated or terminated in the foreseeable future. This is an important assumption of accounting as it provides the very basis for showing the value of assets in the balance sheet. A business unit is deemed to be a going concern and not a gone concern. This assumption provides much of the justification of recording fixed assets at original cost and depreciating them in a systematic manner year after year without reference to their current realizable value.

Cost Concept

The cost concept states that, an asset is recorded in the books at the price paid to acquire it and that this cost is the basis for all subsequent accounting for that asset. This does not mean that the asset will always be shown at cost, but it means that the acquiring cost becomes basis for all future accounting for the asset. Asset is recorded at cost at the time of its purchase but is reduced systematically in its value by charging depreciation by following any of the method.

In simple terms, the market value of an asset may change with the passage of time but for accounting purposes it continues to be shown in the books at its book value, i.e., the cost at which it was purchased minus Depreciation provided up to date. In the absence of cost concept, assets will be shown at their market values which will depend on the subjective views of persons who furnish financial statements, hence consistency will be hampered.

Dual aspect Concept

Dual aspect is the foundation or basic principle of accounting. It provides the very basis of recording business transactions in the books of accounts. This concept assumes that every transaction has a dual effect, i.e. it affects two accounts in their respective opposite sides. Therefore, the transaction should be recorded at two places. It means, both the aspects of the transaction must be recorded in the books of accounts. For example, goods purchased for cash has two aspects which are:

- Giving of cash.
- Receiving of goods.

These two aspects are to be recorded. Thus, the duality concept is commonly expressed in terms of fundamental accounting equation:

Assets = Liabilities + Capital

The above accounting equation states that the assets of a business are always equal to the claims of owner/owners and the outsiders. This claim is also termed as capital or owners' equity and that of outsiders, as liabilities or creditors' equity.

The knowledge of dual aspect helps in identifying the two aspects of a transaction which helps in applying the rules of recording the transactions in books of accounts. The implication of dual aspect concept is that every transaction has an equal impact on assets and liabilities in such a way that total assets are always equal to total liabilities.

Some more business transactions in terms of their dual aspect:

1. Capital brought in by the owner of the business the two aspects in this transaction are:

- Receipt of cash.
- Increase in Capital (owners' equity).

2. Purchase of machinery by Cheque

The two aspects in the transaction are:

- Reduction in Bank Balance.
- Owning of Machinery.

3. Goods sold for cash

The two aspects are:

- Receipt of cash.
- Delivery of goods to the customer.

4. Rent paid in cash to the landlord

The two aspects are:

- Payment of cash.
- Rent (Expenses incurred).

Once the two aspects of a transaction are known, it becomes easy to apply the rules of accounting and maintain the records in the books of accounts properly. The interpretation of the Dual aspect concept is that every transaction has an equal effect on assets and liabilities in such a way that total assets are always equal to total liabilities of the business.

Accrual Concept

The meaning of accrual is something that becomes due especially an amount of money that is yet to be paid or received at the end of the accounting period. It means that revenues are recognised when they become receivable. Though cash is received or not received and the expenses are recognised when they become payable though cash is paid or not paid. Both transactions will be recorded in the accounting period to which they relate. Therefore, the accrual concept makes a distinction between the accrual receipt of cash and the right to receive cash as regards revenue and actual payment of cash and obligation to pay cash as regards expenses.

The accrual concept under accounting assumes that revenue is realized at the time of sale of goods or services irrespective of the fact when the cash is received.

In brief, accrual concept requires that revenue is recognised when realized and expenses are recognised when they become due and payable without regard to the time of cash receipt or cash payment.

Significance

- It helps in knowing actual expenses and actual income during a particular time period.
- It helps in calculating the net profit of the business.

Matching Concept

The matching concept states that the revenue and the expenses incurred to earn the revenues must belong to the same accounting period. So once the revenue is realized, the next step is to allocate it to the relevant accounting period. This can be done with the help of accrual concept.

If the revenue is more than the expenses, it is called profit. If the expenses are more than revenue it is called loss. This is what exactly has been done by applying the matching concept. Therefore, the matching concept implies that all revenues earned during an accounting year, whether received/not received during that year and all cost incurred, whether paid/not paid during the year should be taken into account while ascertaining profit or loss for that year.

Significance

- It guides how the expenses should be matched with revenue for determining exact profit or loss for a particular period.
- It is very helpful for the investors/shareholders to know the exact amount of profit or loss of the business.

Accounting Conventions

Accounting conventions are guidelines used to help companies determine how to record certain business transactions that have not yet been fully addressed by accounting standards. These procedures and principles are not legally binding but are generally accepted by accounting bodies. Basically, they are designed to promote consistency and help accountants overcome practical problems that can arise when preparing financial statements.

Sometimes, there is not a definitive guideline in the accounting standards that govern a specific situation. In such cases, accounting conventions can be referred to.

Accounting is full of assumptions, concepts, standards, and conventions. Concepts such as relevance, reliability, materiality, and comparability are often supported by accounting conventions that help to standardize the financial reporting process.

In short, accounting conventions serve to fill in the gaps not yet addressed by accounting standards. If an oversight organization, such as the Securities and Exchange Commission (SEC) or the Financial Accounting Standards Board (FASB) sets forth a guideline that addresses the same topic as the accounting convention, the accounting convention is no longer applicable.

The scope and detail of accounting standards continue to widen, meaning that there are now fewer accounting conventions that can be used. Accounting conventions are not set in stone, either. Instead, they can evolve over time to reflect new ideas and opinions on the best way to record transactions.

Accounting conventions are important because they ensure that multiple different companies record transactions in the same way. Providing a standardized methodology makes it easier for investors to compare the financial results of different firms, such as competing ones operating in the same sector.

That said, accounting conventions are by no means flawless. They are sometimes loosely explained, presenting companies and their accountants with the opportunity to potentially bend or manipulate them to their advantage.

Areas where Accounting Conventions Apply

Accounting conservatism may be applied to inventory valuation. When determining the reporting value of inventory, conservatism dictates that the lower of historical cost or replacement cost should be the monetary value.

Accounting conventions also dictate that adjustments to line items should not be made for inflation or market value. This means book value can sometimes be less than market value. For example, if a building costs $50,000 when it is purchased, it should remain on the books at $50,000, regardless of whether it is worth more now.

Estimations such as uncollectible accounts receivables and casualty losses also use the conservatism convention. If a company expects to win a litigation claim, it cannot report the gain until it meets all revenue recognition principles. However, if a litigation claim is expected to be lost, an estimated economic impact is required in the notes to the financial statements. Contingent liabilities such as royalty payments or unearned revenue are to be disclosed, too.

Classification of Accounting Conventions

There are four widely recognized accounting conventions that guide the accountants throughout:

- Be Conservative – Conservatism.
- Disclose in Full – Full Disclosure.

- Be Consistent – Consistency.
- Report only that thing which is important – Materiality.

Generally Accepted Accounting Principles (GAAP) is updated regularly and reflects the latest accounting conventions.

Convention of Consistency

Accounting rules, methods, practices and conventions should be continuously and consistently observed and applied i.e. they should not change from one year to another. The accounting information provided by the financial statements would be useful in drawing conclusion regarding the working of an enterprise only when it allows comparisons over a period of time as well as with the working of other enterprises and this comparison is possible only when consistency is maintained throughout.

"The objective of the consistency standard is to ensure that if comparability of financial statements between periods has been materially affected by changes in accounting principles there will be appropriate reporting by the independent auditor regarding such changes."

The rationale behind this concept is that frequent changes in accounting treatment, would make the financial statements unstable, incomparable and unreliable and may seem difficult to be compared by the persons who use them. For Example: the principle of "valuing stock at cost or market price whichever is less" should be followed year after year without any change to get comparable results. Similarly, if depreciation on fixed assets is provided on straight line method in one accounting year, it should be followed year after year to maintain uniformity. Consistency serves to eliminate personal bias because the accountant will have to follow consistent rules, practices and conventions year after year and cannot apply his own judgment or views while maintaining records.

Consistency also means external consistency, i.e. the financial statements of one enterprise should be comparable with another. It means that every enterprise should follow same accounting methods, and procedures of recording and reporting business transactions. This will help in inter-firm as well as inter-period comparison. It should be pointed that the development of international and national accounting standards is due to the convention of consistency; they are framed so as to maintain global uniformity in accounts.

This convention does not completely prohibit changes. It does not debar from introducing improved accounting techniques. However, if a change becomes desirable, the change and its effects on profits and financial position of the company as compared to the previous year should be clearly stated in the financial statements. "Consistency serves to eliminate personal bias and to even out personal judgment but it must not become a fetish so as to ignore changed conditions or need for improvements in technique."

Importance of consistency: Being consistent in preparation of final accounts simply means that the organisation is following the set rules and standards and maintaining its financial image on the higher side in the eyes of the outsiders/investors. Consistent approach improves the comparability of the accounts with those of others or with themselves over years and removes the chance of biasness as well as reduces confusion in the minds of investors.

Convention of Full Disclosure

Information provided by the financial statements is used by the different group of people such as owners, investors, lenders, suppliers etc. in taking various financial decisions. So, in order to make sure that correct financial decisions are taken, the accounts should be prepared in such a manner that all the information whether good or bad should be disclosed in the report and no information be concealed from the interested parties. According to this convention, all accounting statements should be honestly prepared and to that end full disclosure of all significant information should be made. All information that carries some interest to proprietors, creditors and investors should be disclosed in accounting statements, in full. Since, financial statements are the only mode of communicating the financial information to all interested parties, it becomes essential that the accounts makes a full, fair and adequate disclosure of the information which is relevant for taking financial decisions. An obligation is put on the shoulders of those preparing the accounts to see that the books of accounts are as correct, reliable and informative as the circumstances allow and the important facts concerning the financial performance of the enterprise are fairly disclosed in:

- The financial statements.
- The accompanying footnotes of such statements.
- Special communications.
- The president's letter or other management reports in the annual report.

If there is no detailed disclosure in the profit and loss account, undisclosed reserves accumulated in the past periods may be used to increase the profits in years to come when the company is working badly and the shareholders may be misled into thinking that company is making profits. In such a case, the shareholders, investors and their advisers will not have the correct information to enable them to estimate the real value of the shares.

For Example: in case of sundry debtors not only the total amount of sundry debtors should be disclosed, but also the amount of good and secured debtors and amount of doubtful debtors should be stated. This does not mean disclosure of each and every item of information. It only means disclosure of such information which is of importance to owners, investors and creditors.

Importance of Full Disclosure Principle

For an accountant, the full disclosure principle is important because the notes to the financial statements and other financial accounts are subject to audit. To obtain an unqualified (or clean) opinion, one must have an intrinsic understanding of the full disclosure principle to ensure sufficient information for an unqualified opinion on the financial audit by the auditor. An opinion is said to be unqualified when the auditor concludes that the financial statements give a true, fair and transparent view in accordance with the financial reporting framework.

Convention of Conservatism

The concept of conservatism (also called prudence) provides guidance for recording transactions in the book of accounts and is based on the policy of caution or playing safe and has its origin as a protection against possible losses in the business world of uncertainty. This concept states that a conscious approach should be adopted in ascertaining income, so that profits of the enterprise are not overstated.

It compels a businessman to wear a "risk proof jacket" for the working rule is: anticipate no profits, but provide for all possible losses. This means over optimism in reporting results is considered more undesirable than over passionism results, because it shows position better than what actual financial position is. Some of the examples of the application of convention of conservatism are Valuing closing stock at cost or market value whichever is lower, creating provisions for doubtful debts, writing off intangible assets like goodwill and discount on debtors.

For Example: closing stock is valued at cost or market price whichever is lower. If market price is higher than the cost, the higher amount is ignored in the accounts and closing stock will be valued at cost which is lower than the market price. But if the market price is lower than the cost, the higher amount of cost will be ignored and stock will be valued at market price which is lower than the cost. Thus, as per the above example the principle of conservatism is inherent in the valuation of stock.

Importance of Conservatism

The benefit in being conservative while preparing the accounts is that at the end of the accounting year it is always better that the net assets and net income are understated rather than being overstated and misleading the investors by depicting their false image outside, which might ruin after the investors come to face the reality. And also, more of a rosy image of the organisation may also attract more tax liabilities as well. Following the conservatism approach, will keep the organisation on a safer side as this approach makes the management wear a risk proof jacket.

Conservatism of Materiality

The concept of materiality requires that accounting should focus on material facts. It means whether something should be disclosed or not in the financial statements will depend on whether it is material or not. Efforts and time should not be wasted in recording and presenting facts which are immaterial in the determination of income. The term "materiality" is a subjective term. The accountant should record an item as material even though it is of small amount and its knowledge seems to influence the decision of the proprietors or auditors or investors. For Example: commission paid to sole selling agents should be disclosed separately in the profit and loss account. Similarly, amount due to the directors or other officers should be disclosed separately in the balance sheet of Bank to know the exact amount of advances due from the directors or officers who are managing the affairs of bank.

Any fact would be considered as material if it is strongly believed that its knowledge would influence the decision of informed users of financial statements. For Example: money spend on creation of additional capacity of a customer interaction hall would be a material fact as it is going to increase the future earning capacity of the enterprise. Similarly, information about change in the method of depreciation adopted or any liability which is likely to arise in the near future would be considered important information.

Importance of Materiality Approach

If an organisation follows the materiality approach, it means that its financial statements are full of relevant data and the immaterial things are not shown in the accounts. This will maintain the accuracy of the accounts and only that information which is important to different users is disclosed. As a result only accurate accounts are communicated to the outside/inside world.

Difference between Accounting Concepts and Conventions

At the end of the financial year, financial statements are prepared by firms for a number of purposes, which include summarizing all activities and transactions, review the firm's financial position, evaluate performance and to make comparisons between previous years. The financial statements prepared must be consistent, complete and comparable and must also offer a true and a fair view of the firm's workings. In order to make sure that these standards of accuracy, fairness and consistency are met, a number of accounting concepts and conventions have been developed.

Accounting concepts and conventions are significant to the development of accounting theory in two ways. First, they are themselves part of an important process for developing the accounting principles. Second, they reflect the influence of the social, economic, historical and legal forces which shape the psychology of accounting in a given environment. Also both concepts and conventions aim to offer a more realistic and true view of the firm's financial statements. Despite of some similarities there are a number of differences between them: The main point of difference between accounting concepts and conventions is that accounting concepts are officially recorded, whereas accounting conventions are not recorded officially and are followed as generally accepted guidelines.

Accounting concepts have been established by professional Organisations/committees and are standard principles that must be followed while preparing financial accounts. Whereas, conventions are the generally accepted practices that can change and are updated over time, depending on the changes in the financial reporting arena.

In case of the accounting concepts, one has to follow all the concepts, there is no choice to leave any, and it is a legal binding to follow all. Whereas, in case of accounting conventions, there is a choice to select a particular convention and leave one.

BASIS OF DIFFERENCE	ACCOUNTING CONCEPTS	ACCOUNTING CONVENTIONS
MEANING	Accounting concepts are the assumptions that guide how the transactions should be recorded and reported.	Accounting convention may be defined as a custom or generally accepted practice which is adopted either by general agreement or common consent among accountants.
LEGAL POSITION	Accounting concepts have legal acceptance.	Accounting conventions are guidelines based upon custom or usage or general agreement.
RECORDING VS. FINANCIAL STATEMENTS	Accounting concepts are the basic assumptions on the basis of which transactions are recorded and accounts are maintained.	Accounting conventions are followed in preparing the Profit and loss account or Income Statement and Balance sheet or Position Statement.
SIGNIFICANCE	Accounting concepts are uniform set of rules followed in the recording of transactions.	Accounting concepts are not so important as accounting conventions.

ROLE OF PERSONAL JUDGMENT	There is no role of personal judgment or individual bias in the following of accounting concepts.	Personal judgments play an important role in the adoption of accounting conventions.
UNIFORM ADOPTION	There is uniform adoption of accounting concepts in different business enterprises.	There is no adoption of accounting conventions in various business enterprises.

Double Entry System

Every incorporated business is involved in the continuous business of sale and purchase of goods and services, and works for the purpose of earning the profits, attracting the customers and thereby satisfying them. They deal with the monetary transactions (those which are capable of being measured in terms of money) throughout the accounting year. This dealing with the transactions, affects the business in two ways: something is increased and something is deducted from the business. Items Description of Module Subject Name Management Paper Name Accounting & Financial Analysis Module Title Double Entry System Module Id Module No- 7 Pre-Requisites Debit and Credit Rules Objectives To understand the meaning, features and history of double entry Keywords Double Entry, Dual Effect This two way effect needs to be recorded carefully in order to get a complete and a clear image of the financial position of the enterprise at the end of the year. The recording of the transactions is done in a systematic and chronological order in the books of accounts, be it the journal, ledger, or trial balance. The entire process of recording the transactions in the books of accounts is termed as Book Keeping. It is clear that this recorded data is of no use, unless and until it is communicated to the interested users within time. The process of analyzing the data and communicating/ presenting it in the form of organised information to the management, is termed as Accounting. The data is presented in the form of final accounts, which include the summary of the entire working of the enterprise in quantitative terms. The aim of final accounts is to give a complete image of the enterprise, and this complete picture is possible only if the two way effect of each transaction is highlighted in the accounts, i.e. the debit effect and the credit effect. By this way the final accounts will be considered correct as well as complete.

Methods of Accounting

Accounting deals with the recording, analyzing and interpreting the accounting information to the interested users (both insiders and outsiders). Business transactions can be recorded in the books, in two ways:

- Single Entry System: Business Organisations if follow this system, prepare only cash book and personal accounts of debtors/creditors. Therefore complete record maintenance is not possible and trial balance cannot be prepared.
- Double Entry System: It maintains a two-fold effect of benefit giving and receiving aspects. It means that the record of equal debit and equal credit is maintained. In India, business transactions are recorded by the way of double entry system, hence depicting the debit and credit of every transaction.

Meaning of Double Entry System

As the name suggests, double entry system means a double effect of a transaction on the business. It means that every debit have a corresponding credit, with an equal amount. This further means that two accounting entries need to be passed in the books of accounts, to record each financial transaction. It is a modern and a new revised scientific method of recording the transactions in the books of accounts. In simple terms it means that every transaction have equal and opposite effects in two separate accounts. This system is based on the accounting equation of "Assets= Liabilities+ Equity". The transactions are always recorded in terms of Debit and Credit. Since both the debits and credits are recorded with the same amount, therefore at the end of accounting year all debits should be equal to all credits, which will also help in detecting the errors and accurately preparing the final accounts.

Features of Double Entry System

- Dual Effect: This means that when following a double entry system, each and every transaction will have a two way effect on the business, and both the effects will be recorded on the opposite sides of the account.
- Affected by same amount: As per the golden rule of double entry system, every debit has an equal and corresponding credit. Equal means with the same amount. It means that if there is a debit with $3000, the Credit will also be by $3000.
- Accurate recording: By following the system of double entry, the chance of any fault in recording reduces. As the amount is recorded on both the debit as well as credit side, of two separate books, at the end the debit side total always equals the credit side total. It maintains accuracy in the accounts.
- Involvement of two parties: A transaction is said to take place when two parties are involved, one being the receiver of benefit and the other, the giver of benefit. Each party is affected by the equal amount, one being debit and the other being credit.

It is important in maintaining an accurate financial system. Companies benefit greatly from using double-entry bookkeeping because it aids in accurate financial reporting and reduces errors and fraudulent activity.

Accuracy

Double-entry booking provides a more accurate look at a company's financial position than single-entry bookkeeping. One reason for this is because double-entry bookkeeping implements the matching principle. The matching principle uses accrual accounting rules to record revenue and the expenses related to revenue. Recording both revenue and expenses provides an accurate calculation of profits and losses. Profits and losses are represented on the income statement, which includes accounts calculated directly from the entries made in double-entry bookkeeping.

Error Reduction

Human errors can cause a misrepresentation of a company's financial position. Double-entry bookkeeping reduces errors because it provides checks and balances. With the advancement of technology, many accounting software programs automatically provide double-entry bookkeeping when a transaction is entered. This reduces the chance that a transaction is posted to the wrong offsetting account. Errors are easily caught with double-entry bookkeeping by making sure debit and credit amounts equal. Although errors are greatly reduced with double-entry bookkeeping, it does not totally prevent errors.

Leaves an Audit Trail

Double-entry bookkeeping reduces fraud by leaving an adult trail. An audit trail allows you to trace transactions from the journal entries that were posted to the general ledger. For example, if your cash balance seems too high on your balance sheet, you can trace back the transactions made to the cash account and see if they are accurate. You are able to see the exact accounts affected by posting transactions. Double-entry bookkeeping also uses reference numbers and provides brief descriptions with each entry made.

Financial Statement Preparation

Financial statements are easily prepared in companies using double-entry bookkeeping because information is gathered directly from the double-entry bookkeeping transactions. It is important for companies to produce accurate financial statements quickly and efficiently. Internal users, such as management, depend on financial statements to assess where the company is financially and to create operational budgets. External users, such as investors and vendors, depend on financial statements to determine a company's creditworthiness.

Debit and Credit Rules

In order to maintain a record of the transactions in the books of accounts, an accountant uses various rules in order to show the two way effect of the transaction. The rules of debit and credit can be classified into two heads under the double entry system: Traditional Approach and Modern Approach. The double effect of the transaction on the books of accounts remains the same, irrespective of which type of approach is being used by the accountant.

Traditional Approach

As per the traditional approach, the accounts are divided into real, personal and nominal:

- Real Account: refers to the accounts relating to the assets and liabilities.
- Personal Account: refers to the accounts of persons or Organisations, with whom the business deals with. Example: accounts of debtors and creditors.
- Nominal Account: means the accounts dealing with revenue, expenses, losses and gains.

If an accountant uses the traditional approach to record the transactions in the books of accounts, then the following Golden Rules must be followed, in case of different accounts:

ACCOUNT	DEBIT	CREDIT
Real	What Comes In	What Goes Out

Personal	The Receiver	The Giver
Nominal	All Expenses & Losses	All Incomes & Gains

Modern/Accounting Equation Approach

In order to follow this approach, the transaction is recorded keeping in mind the accounting equation i.e. (Assets= Liabilities+ Capital). For this purpose, the accounts are divided into five heads: Asset, Liability, Capital, Expenses/Losses and Income/Gains.

An increase in assets, losses and decrease in capital, gains, liability means Debit. On the other hand, a decrease in assets, losses and an increase in capital, gains, liability leads to a Credit. The following rules are summarized below:

	ASSETS	LIABILITIES	CAPITAL	INCOME/GAIN	INCOME/GAIN
INCREASE	Debit	Credit	Credit	Credit	Debit
DECREASE	Credit	Debit	Debit	Debit	Credit

Maintaining Accounts under Double Entry System

It is clear that the every transaction carried out by the business, have a dual effect on the business, debit and credit, with the same amount. This debit and credit of the account are presented in the form of a "T Account". T Account is an individual account depicting the increase or decrease in that particular account only. It is prepared horizontally. With Debit on the left side, whereas Credit on the right side. The difference between the two sides is known as the Account Balance.

Account Title

Left Side (Debit)	Left Side (Debit)

The preparation of T Account is just a one single step, from a sequence of steps involved in preparing a full- fledged financial statement. However, it provides a simple way of record keeping to the accountant. There is a proper procedure to be followed in order to record the transactions and show the dual effect of the transaction. The steps involved in recording are:

- Analyzing the source documents: The first step is to analyse the documents with respect to each transaction. Before recording the transactions, it is the responsibility of the person recording the transactions, to check for the evidence/proof for that transaction, either in the form of invoice or bank statement. Thereby, fulfilling the objective evidence concept.
- Recording in Journal: The next step is the preparation of journal. Also known as book of original entry, maintains a chronological record of all the monetary transactions, which took place in an accounting year.
- Posting from Journal to Ledger: After preparing the journal, a ledger account is maintained where the information about all the accounts is kept. A ledger account shows the two

sided effect of each transaction. For example: all the information regarding the increase and decrease in cash is recorded under the ledger to update the cash accounts.

- Preparation of Trial Balance: A trial balance shows a list of all the accounts with their respective balances. All the ledger accounts are listed in the trial balance with their amounts, and are totaled up so that the sum total of debit equals the sum total of credit. Such information helps in the preparation of the final accounts.
- Preparation of Financial Statements: After the preparation of the trial balance, and cross checking that the debit and credit totals are equal, the final step includes the preparation of the final accounts, which helps in predicting the financial position, solvency and effective working of any enterprise.

Traditional and Modern Accounting System

Traditional Accounting

There was a sales book, purchases book, cash book and more. Transcribing the transaction details from these "Books of Prime Entry" into ledgers that contained the accounts for income, expenses, assets, liabilities etc. For example, a credit sale to customer X was "posted" to both the Sales account and X's account. Each account has a "debit" column and a "credit" column, in addition to date, description and reference columns. The transaction amounts were entered either in the debit or the credit column, depending on the nature of the transaction Periodically, the debit and credit columns were totaled and each account's "balance" was extracted. It was a debit balance if total debits exceeded total credits, and vice versa. The balances were then listed in a "Trial Balance". If all transactions have been correctly accounted under double entry accounting principles, the total of Debit Account Balances will be the same as the total of Credit Account Balances and the trial balance will "agree." The balances in the Trial Balance were categorized into Income, Expense, Asset, Liability and Equity categories and summarized in an Income and Expense Statement and a Balance Sheet, which are the main financial statements.

Modern Accounting

Modern accounting eliminated all the steps above, excepting the first step of recording the transactions into a book of prime entry, in this case a computer data entry screen. Modern accounting mainly uses the computer device. The accounting software then sorted the entries by type of transaction and date to generate a day book "report", sorted them by affected accounts to generate a ledger report and did all the balance computations and summarizations to come up with Income & Expense Statement/Balance Sheet reports.

Golden Rules of Accounting

Traditional Accounting

Traditional accounting is also known as manual accounting.One of the most famous and commonly used term in the field of accounting and finance is "Three golden rules of accounting". The phrase itself shows that these rules form the very basis of accounting and act as a cornerstone for all record keeping. They are also called the traditional rules of accounting or the rules of debit and credit.

Type of Account	Debit	Credit
Personal A/C	The receiver	The giver
Real A/C	What comes in	What goes out
Nominal A/C	Expenses and losses	Income and gains

Modern Accounting

If you are passing an entry in the journal, you may use the Modern Accounting Approach instead of the usual Traditional Approach.

Accounts Involved	Debit/Credit	Rule Applied
Furniture A/C	50,000	Furniture is real a/c so Dr. what comes in

You should try to use the modern approach at least once to find out which one is easier to understand and apply. It is true that some people find the modern approach easier to apply than the traditional golden rules of accounting.

Type of Account	Debit	Credit
Asset A/C	Increase	Decrease
Liability A/C	Decrease	Increase
Capital A/C	Decrease	Increase
Revenue A/C	Decrease	Increase
Expenses A/C	Increase	Increase
Drawings A/C	Increase	Increase

Aspects of Traditional Accounting

Traditional accounting systems, even in today's world where modern accounting systems seem to triumph over paper based systems, can still provide an effective and useful way of recording business transactions and can deliver an efficient accounting information system for the small business owner. A Traditional accounts system, if developed correctly can deliver timely and accurate information. In many ways, particularly for the smaller business, in a well-designed Traditional accounting system the advantages outweigh the disadvantages. The Traditional system, though requires a greater understanding of how to book keep, can be easier to manage, once the key concepts of double entry book keeping have been learnt.

Aspects of Modern Accounting

Modern accounting is also known as computerized accounting. Accounting is a crucial function for every business – large or small.The following role played by modern accounting:

- To put information close to accountants.

- To improve the capacity of accounting research and extension specialists to organize, store retrieve and accounting information exchange.
- To evolve mechanism of information sharing.
- To develop accounting database for easy access and data base decision making.
- Access to the storehouse of information is easy.
- Accounting data will available universally.

Comparative Analysis: Traditional and Modern Accounting

Speed

The most glaring difference between traditional and computerized accounting is the speed of operations. With an accounting program, data is entered once and it is saved. The program provides management with reports in a speed never dreamed possible in the traditional days. No more waiting days or weeks to know whether your business is making a profit. Using computerized accounting, information can be accessed in a matter of minutes. Once data is available in the system, it can be used in reports, queries and analysis.

Accuracy

Computerized systems have drastically increased accuracy of calculations when compared to the traditional, manual system, in which columns had to be added up, numbers moved from one page to the next, and trial balance and financial statements manually compiled. If errors occurred, many hours had to be spent trying to find and correct them. With accounting software, this problem is eliminated. In the case of accounting spreadsheets, adding simple formulas still may be needed, but it is an easier and more accurate process. Efficiency goes through the roof when a computerized system is used.

Costs

The traditional manual accounting system with paper and pencil is cheaper than the computerized version, in which a firm needs a computer, software, printer and other expenses associated with a system. The manual system may work for small businesses up to a certain point, but with the affordable costs of computers and software, many firms are opting for the computerized system. They are easy to use, and finding experienced employees to run the system is not a hurdle.

Backups

When using a manual system, the risk of losing data is real. If important papers are damaged or destroyed, that work may have to be re-created. Copies of the original work can be made, but that could be expensive and time-consuming. Accounting on a computerized system offers the choice of saving work on a CD, portable or external hard drive, flash drive, or even online. Many firms back up data every night as a precaution. If something happens the next day, the data can be restored from the backup.

References

- Comparative-study-of-traditional: madeprojectseasy.blogspot.com, Retrieved 23, Jan 2020
- Importance-doubleentry-bookkeeping-8691783: bizfluent.com, Retrieved 25, Feb 2020
- Difference-between-accounting-concepts-and-conventions: commerceiets.com, Retrieved 27, April 2020
- accounting-convention: investopedia.com, Retrieved 08, May 2020
- Sample-notes-of-accounting: cms.sinhgad.edu, Retrieved 06, June 2020
- Importance-accounting-principles-4985: pocketsense.com, Retrieved 17, July 2020
- Basic-accounting-principles: accountingtools.com, Retrieved 02, August 2020

3

Tools and Standards in Accounting

Journal entry is the most basic tool used to record a transaction. Journals and ledgers are the standard methods to record financial transactions. Mercantilism, the systems of accounting, share capital, debenture, etc. are a few aspects which come under financial transactions. This chapter has been carefully written to provide the reader with a clearer understanding of the subject matter.

General Journal

The journal is where double entry bookkeeping entries are recorded by debiting one or more accounts and crediting another one or more accounts with the same total amount. The total amount debited and the total amount credited should always be equal, thereby ensuring the accounting equation is maintained. In accounting and bookkeeping, a journal is a record of financial transactions in order by date.

A journal is also named the *book of original entry*, from when transactions were written in a journal prior to manually posting them to the accounts in the general ledger or subsidiary ledger. Manual systems usually had a variety of journals such as a sales journal, purchases journal, cash receipts journal, cash disbursements journal, and a general journal. Depending on the business's accounting information system, specialized journals may be used in conjunction with the general journal for record-keeping. In such case, use of the general journal may be limited to non-routine and adjusting entries.

A general journal entry includes the date of the transaction, the titles of the accounts debited and credited, the amount of each debit and credit, and an explanation of the transaction also known as a Narration.

Journal

The transactions are first recorded in the book to show which accounts are effected. This book is called as "Journal".

Recording of transaction in journal is termed as journalizing the entries:

- Entries are recorded chronologically to maintain the records in an orderly manner.
- Journal entries are very important and form basis for all further records.

Specimen of Journal

Date	Particulars	L.F.	Debit (Amt)	Credit (Amt)

An entry in journal may appear as follows for the following transaction:

1.11.2010 Goods sold for cash of **₹ 5,000**

5.11.2010 Cash deposited in Bank **₹ 3,000**

Journal Entries

Date	**Particulars**	**L.F.**	**Debit (Amt)**	**Credit (Amt)**
1.11. 2010	Cash A/c....Dr.		5,000	
	To Sales A/c (Being Goods sold on cash)			5,000
5.11.2010	Bank A/c...Dr.		3,000	
	To Cash A/c (Being cash deposited in bank)			3,000

Sales Journal

A sales journal is a specialized accounting journal used in an accounting system to keep track of the sales of items that customers have purchased on account by charging a receivable on the debit side of an accounts receivable account and crediting revenue on the credit side. It differs from the cash receipts journal in that the latter will serve to book sales when cash is received. The sales journal is used to record all of the company sales on credit. Most often these sales are made up of inventory sales or other merchandise sales. Notice that only credit sales of inventory and merchandise items are recorded in the sales journal. Cash sales of inventory are recorded in the cash receipts journal. Both cash and credit sales of non-inventory or merchandise are recorded in the general journal.

Special Journals

Special Journals are designed to facilitate the process of journalizing and posting transactions. They are used for the most frequent transactions in a business. For example, in merchandising businesses, companies acquire merchandise from vendors, and then in turn sell the merchandise to individuals or other businesses. Sales and purchases are the most common transactions for the merchandising businesses. A business such as a retail store will record the following transactions many times a day for sales on account and cash sales.

Description	**Debit**	**Credit**
Accounts Receivable	XXX	
Sales		XXX
Sales Tax Payable		XXX

Description	Debit	Credit
Cash	XXX	
Sales		XXX
Sales Tax Payable		XXX

In order to save time for journalizing the entries, and posting the entries to the general ledgers and subledgers, Special Journals are used instead. An accountant can be specialized in a type of journal entry and several accountants can work each on 1 or more different types of journal entries only thereby using a better division of labour.

Types of Special Journals

The types of Special Journals that a business uses are determined by the nature of the business. Special journals are designed as a simple way to record the most frequently occurring transactions. There are four types of Special Journals that are frequently used by merchandising businesses: Sales journals, Cash receipts journals, Purchases journals, and Cash payments journals.

Sales Journal

Sales journals record transactions that involve sales purely on credit. Source documents here would probably be invoices. Provides a chronological record of all credit sales made in the life of a business. Credit sales are transactions where the goods are sold and payment is received at a later date. The source documents for the Sales journal are copies of all invoices given to the debtors.

Double entry Accounting is achieved by:

- Debit – debtors account with value of sales (increasing a current asset).
- Credit – sales account with total amount (increasing income).

Choose credit sales journal if this stock is then on-sold to customers who will pay later. The people/organizations here are known as debtors. Collectively, all these accounts that are to be paid to us by our customers are known as assets.

date	details	folio #	invoice #	amount
date sale was made	who did you sell it to		sequential - #order	

Cash Receipts Journal

A cash receipts journal (CRJ) records transactions that involve payments received with cash. Source documents would probably be receipts and cheque butts. The CRJ records the cash inflow of a business. Discount allowed is an expense as the discount allowed is the cost to the seller of obtaining an inflow of cash from a debtor weeks earlier than would be the case.

date	details	receipt #	discount allowed	sales	debtors	Other	BANK
date sale was made	who you received payment from				people who are also in sales journal	other types of income description	amount into bank

Expense Journals

Purchases Journal

Purchases Journals record transactions that involve purchases purely on credit. Source documents are invoices. For instance, the purchase of inventory on credit is recorded in the purchases journal.

date	details	folio #33	invoice #	amount
date sale was made	name of supplier		not sequential	

Cash Payments Journal

Cash Payments Journals record transactions that involve expenditures paid with cash. Source documents are likely receipts and cheque butts. The CPJ records the cash outflow of a business. If the owner of a business withdraws cash from the business an entry is made in the CPJ. Discount received is the cash discount received by a purchaser, it is an income item for the purchaser.

date	details	cheque #	discount received	purchases	creditors	Other	BANK
date payment was made	who you paid				people who are also in purchases journal	other types of expenses description	amount out of bank

Source Documents

When a transaction occur between a business and an external party, a source document will usually be created. Source documents are business forms that provide evidence of each transaction and give the details that are entered later into one of the journals in a computer accounting system. Some computer systems, such as payroll systems, also generate transactions that are recorded in one or more journals, but without paper source documents:

- *Receipt* when a business receives money or cheques over the shop counter it will usually issue a receipt. A receipt is a document that acknowledges that money or cheques have been received.
- *Check book stub.*
- *Invoice* includes business name (sellers) and address, invoice number, ABN, buyer details, date, description of goods purchased, quantity, unit price, amount (per item x quantity), total price and GST. An invoice is a document that records the details of a credit sale of inventory. The origin of the invoice is either delivered with the goods or sent separately to the customer. A number of copies are kept by the seller.
- *Delivery note* is a document that sets out the type and quantity of the inventory delivered to the purchaser. When the inventory arrives at the premises of the purchaser, the delivery note is signed by the purchaser and is evidence that the goods ordered have been delivered. A copy is kept by the seller.
- *Purchase order.*
- *Purchase requisition.*

- *Credit note* is a document issued by a seller that acknowledges that a customer is entitled to receive a reduction in the amount owing on goods purchased on credit.

Folio Number: Every page of a journal is numbered. This number is known as a folio number. The folio number is used as a cross reference between the journal and the ledger accounts. The use of folio numbers makes it easy to refer back from the ledger account to the journal entry or forward from the journal entry to the ledger account. In addition, folio numbers are a check that all journal entries have been recorded in the ledger system.

Each ledger account has a folio number column. The name and page of the journal from which the ledger entry came is recorded in the folio number column.

Each journal has a folio number column. The number of the ledger account to which the journal entry was posted is recorded in the folio number column of the journal.

Cash money, eftpos, cheques, credit cards. Receipts and payments.

Credit sale of inventory on credit Purchases.

Cash Journals record items sold or purchased with cash and they also record income received (debtor payment, interest) and daily expenses. If the transaction is of a cash nature, you must be convinced that money/cheque/credit card was also exchanged at the time that the good or service was exchanged.

Credit Journals record purchases or sales on credit. If the transaction is of a credit nature, you will assume that the cash will be exchanged after the exchange of the good or service. At this stage, these will only be concerned with your firm acquiring stock and the selling of that stock to customers who will pay later.

Format of Special Journals

In the General Journal, transactions are recorded in several lines, and each transaction is posted to the general ledger separately. For example, if fifty sales on account were made during one day, fifty ledger postings would have to be made to three general ledger accounts: Accounts Receivable, Sales, and Sale Tax Payable. In special journal, transactions are recorded in a single line, and the format of the journal made it possible to post only the total amount for each account to the general ledger. For example, if fifty sales on account were made during one day, only the total amount for Accounts Receivable, Sales, and Sales Tax Payable were posted to the general ledger. Thus the posting process is more efficient. Figure shows the example formats of the Special Journals.

Sales Journal

Date	Sale No.	To Whom Sold	Post. Ref.	Accounts Receivable Debit	Sales Credit	Sales Tax Payable Credit
April 1	900	A. Smith		$1,000.00	$940.00	$60.00
April 1	901	B. Johnson		$2,000.00	$1,880.00	$120.00
April 1	902	C. Chang		$1,000.00	$940.00	$60.00
April 4	904	D. Garcia		$1,000.00	$940.00	$60.00

Cash Receipt Journal

Date	Account Credited	Post Ref.	General Credit	Accounts Receivable Credit	Sales Credit	Sales Tax Payable Credit	Cash Debit
May 1	B. Johnson			$1,000			$1,000
May 3	C. Chang			$1,000			$1,000
May 5	A. Smith			$1,000			$1,000
May 8	Interest Receivable			$400			$400

Purchases Journal

Date	Invoice No.	From Whom Purchased	Post Ref.	Purchased Debit / Accounts Payable Credit
June 2	6321	BCD Corp.		$12,000
June 5	12D	Telecom8 Inc		$800
June 21	412	Furniture-X		$2,000

Cash Payments Journal

Date	Check No.	Account Debited	Post Ref.	General Debit	Accounts Payable Debit	Purchases Credit	Cash Credit
July 1	1254	Rent Expense		$1,200			$1,200
July 2	1255	BCD Corp.			$1,200		$1,200
July 2	1256	Furniture-X			$1,200		$1,200

Ledger

A ledger is the principal book or computer file for recording and totaling economic transactions measured in terms of a monetary unit of account by account type, with debits and credits in separate columns and a beginning monetary balance and ending monetary balance for each account.

Overview

The ledger is a permanent summary of all amounts entered in supporting journals which list individual transactions by date. Every transaction flows from a journal to one or more ledgers. A company's financial statements are generated from summary totals in the ledgers.

Ledgers include:

- Sales ledger, records accounts receivable. This ledger consists of the financial transactions made by customers to the company.
- Purchase ledger records money spent for purchasing by the company.
- General ledger representing the five main account types: assets, liabilities, income, expenses, and Capital.

- Distributed ledger, sometimes called a shared ledger, is a consensus of replicated, shared, and synchronized digital data geographically spread across multiple sites, countries, and/ or institutions.

For every debit recorded in a ledger, there must be a corresponding credit so that the debits equal the credits in the grand totals.

Etymology

Ledger from 1828.

The term *ledger* stems from the English dialect forms *liggen* or *leggen*, meaning "to lie or lay" (Dutch: *liggen* or *leggen*, German: *liegen* or *legen*); in sense it is adapted from the Dutch substantive *legger*, properly "a book laying or remaining regularly in one place". Originally, a ledger was a large volume of scripture or service book kept in one place in church and openly accessible. According to Charles Wriothesley's *Chronicle* (1538), "The curates should provide a booke of the bible in Englishe, of the largest volume, to be a ledger in the same church for the parishioners to read on."

In application of this original meaning the commercial usage of the term is for the "principal book of account" in a business house.

After recording transaction in journal, recorded entries are classified and grouped by preparation of accounts, is known as "ledger". It is also known as principal books of accounts.

Specimen of Ledger

Dr. ABC Account Cr.

Date	Particulars	J.F.	Amt	Date	Particulars	J.F.	Amt

- A ledger account has two sides debit and credit.
- Separate account is opened in ledger book for different set of transaction.
- It is practice to use word 'To' and 'By' while posting transaction on debit and credit side of account.
- To ascertain the balance in any account, what is done is to total the sides and ascertain the difference; the difference is balance.

Case 1: Ram & Co.

Prepare ledger accounts for Ram & Co from the following details:

Opening balances:

Cash A/c	Rs. 1,500
Creditors A/c	Rs. 800
Debtors A/c	Rs. 1,200
Capital A/c	Rs. 1,900

Transactions:

- 2 Apr. Purchased goods of Rs. 3,000 on credit.
- 4 Apr. Cash sales of Rs. 2,400.
- 7 Apr. Goods sold on credit Rs. 1,250.
- 15 Apr. Paid cash of Rs. 250 for expenses.
- 18 Apr. cash received from debtors Rs. 1,200.
- 22 Apr. paid cash to creditors Rs. 800.

In the books of Ram & Company

Dr. Cash A/c Cr.

Date	Particulars	J.F.	Amt	Date	Particulars	J.F.	Amt
01-Apr	To balance b/d		1,500	15-Apr	By Expenses A/c		250
04-Apr	To Sales A/c		2,400	22-Apr	By Creditors A/c		800
18-Apr	To Debtors A/c		1,200	30-Apr	By Balance C/d		4,050
	Total		**5,100**		**Total**		**5,100**
01-May	To balance b/d		4,050				

Dr. Purchase A/c Cr.

Date	Particulars	J.F.	Amt	Date	Particulars	J.F.	Amt
02-Apr	To Creditors A/c		3,000	30-Apr	By Balance C/d		3,000
	Total		**3,000**		**Total**		**3,000**
01-May	To balance b/d		3,000				

Dr. Sales A/c Cr.

Date	Particulars	J.F.	Amt	Date	Particulars	J.F.	Amt
30-Apr	To Balance C/d		3,650	04-Apr	By Cash A/c		2,400
				07-Apr	By Debtors A/c		1,250
	Total		**3,650**		**Total**		**3,650**
				01-May	By Balance b/d		3,650

Dr.			Debtors A/c				Cr.
Date	Particulars	J.F.	Amt	Date	Particulars	J.F.	Amt
01-Apr	To Balance b/d		1,200	18-Apr	By Cash A/c		1,200
07-Apr	To Sales A/c		1,250	30-Apr	By Balance c/d		1,250
	Total		**2,450**		**Total**		**2,450**
01-May	To Balance b/d		1,250				

Dr.			Creditors A/c				Cr.
Date	Particulars	J.F.	Amt	Date	Particulars	J.F.	Amt
22-Apr	To Cash A/c		800	01-Apr	By Balance b/d		800
30-Apr	To Balance c/d		3,000	02-Apr	By Purchase A/c		3,000
	Total		**3,800**		**Total**		**3,800**
				01-May	By Balance b/d		3,000

Dr.			Expenses A/c				Cr.
Date	Particulars	J.F.	Amt	Date	Particulars	J.F.	Amt
15-Apr	To Cash A/c		250	30-Apr	By Balance C/d		250
	Total		**250**		**Total**		**250**
01-May	To Balance b/d		250				

Dr.			Capital A/c				Cr.
Date	Particulars	J.F.	Amt	Date	Particulars	J.F.	Amt
30-Apr	To Balance c/d		1,900	01-Apr	By Balance b/d		1,900
	Total		**1,900**		**Total**		**1,900**
				01-May	To Balance b/d		1,900

Subsidiary Books

- In case of large business organisation numerous transactions takes place with respect to purchase, sales, cash etc. Journalization of each of these transactions separately is laborious and time-consuming.

To solve this problem subsidiary books are prepared.

- Subsidiary book is a book of original entry generally maintained by large organisation wherein cash and cash transactions are directly recorded avoiding cumbersome process of Journalization without sacrificing the fundamental principle of double entry book keeping system.

Normally, the following subsidiary books are used in business:

- Cash book: To record cash, bank and discount transactions.
- Purchase book: To record transaction relating to credit purchases of goods in trade.

- Sales book: To record transaction relating to credit sales.
- Purchase return book: To record transaction relating to purchase return.
- Sales return book: To record transaction relating to sales return.
- Bills receivable book: To record the receipts of the promissory notes or hundies.
- Bills payable book: To record the issue of the promissory notes or hundies.
- Journal proper: To record other transactions for which no specific book is maintained, and for recording entries to rectify mistakes in books of accounts.

Mercantilism

An imaginary seaport painted by Claude Lorrain around 1639, at the height of mercantilism.

Mercantilism was an economic theory and practice that was dominant in Western Europe during the 15th to the mid-18th centuries. Mercantilism is a form of economic nationalism. Its goal is to enrich and empower the nation and state to the maximum degree, by acquiring and retaining as much economic activity as possible within the nation's borders. Manufacturing and industry, particularly of goods with military applications, was prioritized. Mercantilism sought to ensure the nation produced as much volume and variety of output as possible, so as to limit its dependence upon foreign suppliers. Economic autarky was a critical element of mercantilism. These aims were primarily accomplished by:

1. Imposing high tariffs on the importation of finished goods; and imposing low, or no, taxes on the importation of raw materials or exotic products.
2. Imposing low, or no taxes on the export of finished goods; and imposing high taxes on the exportation of raw materials.
3. Seeking new markets for domestic manufactured products, so as to artificially increase the demand for domestic production.

These policies generally resulted in a positive balance of trade, which led to the accumulation of precious metals, which is how accounts used to be balanced.

Historically, such policies sometimes led to war and may have motivated colonial expansion. Indeed, with the establishment of overseas colonies by northern Europe powers early in the 17th century, mercantile theory gained a new and wider significance, in which its aim and ideal became both national and imperialistic. While it has been noted that both the United States under the American System, and Imperial China under the Canton System, pursued de facto mercantile policies, they did not engage in significant colonial activities. High tariffs, especially on manufactured goods, are an almost universal feature of mercantilist policy. Other policies have included:

- Forbidding colonies to trade with other nations.
- Monopolizing markets with staple ports.
- Banning the export of gold and silver, even for payments.
- Forbidding trade to be carried in foreign ships, for example, the Navigation Acts.
- Subsidies on exports.
- Promoting manufacturing and industry through research or direct subsidies.
- Maximizing the use of domestic resources.
- Restricting domestic consumption through non-tariff barriers to trade.

Mercantilism has been linked to bullionism ever since Adam Smith made the accusation. However, due to the fact that no author self-consciously used the label to refer to their own thoughts mercantilist authors can only be identified retrospectively. There are exceptions, for example, Antoine de Montchrestien, the "godfather" of French mercantilism, wrote:

it is not the abundance of gold and silver, the quantity of pearls and diamonds, which makes states opulent... it is the supply of things necessary for life and suitable for clothing.

John Maynard Keynes observed that the accumulation of gold may have served an important purpose in states before the advent of fiat money, since it increased liquidity in currency-starved early modern markets. The core of mercantile policy was a coherent national industrial policy, which was aimed at generating as much material wealth within the nation as possible. Doing so, it was thought, was the best way to increase the state's military and political power.

The term "mercantile system" was used by its foremost critic, Adam Smith, but "mercantilism" had been used earlier by Mirabeau.

Many nations applied the theory, one prime example being France which was the most important state economically in Europe at the time. King Louis XIV followed the guidance of Jean Baptiste Colbert, his controller general of finances (1665–83). It was determined that the state should rule in the economic realm as it did in the diplomatic, and that the interests of the state as identified by the king were superior to those of merchants and everyone else. The goal of mercantilist economic policies was to build up the state, especially in an age of incessant warfare, and the state should look for ways to strengthen the economy and weaken foreign adversaries.

Influence

Mercantilism was the dominant school of economic thought in Europe throughout the late Renaissance and early modern period (from the 15th to the 18th century). Mercantilism encouraged the many intra-European wars of the period and arguably fueled European expansion and imperialism—both in Europe and throughout the rest of the world—until the 19th century or early 20th century.

Evidence of mercantilistic practices appeared in early modern Venice, Genoa, and Pisa regarding control of the Mediterranean trade of bullion. However, as a codified school of economic theories, mercantilism's real birth was marked by the empiricism of the Renaissance, which first began to quantify large-scale trade accurately.

England began the first large-scale and integrative approach to mercantilism during the Elizabethan Era (1558–1603). An early statement on national balance of trade appeared in *Discourse of the Common Weal of this Realm of England*, 1549: "We must always take heed that we buy no more from strangers than we sell them, for so should we impoverish ourselves and enrich them." The period featured various but often disjointed efforts by the court of Queen Elizabeth to develop a naval and merchant fleet capable of challenging the Spanish stranglehold on trade and of expanding the growth of bullion at home. Queen Elizabeth promoted the Trade and Navigation Acts in Parliament and issued orders to her navy for the protection and promotion of English shipping. A systematic and coherent explanation of balance of trade was made public through Thomas Mun's argument *England's Treasure by Forraign Trade, or the Balance of our Forraign Trade is The Rule of Our Treasure.* It was written in the 1620s and published in 1664.

These efforts organized national resources sufficiently in the defense of England against the far larger and more powerful Spanish Empire, and in turn paved the foundation for establishing a global empire in the 19th century. The authors noted most for establishing the English mercantilist system include Gerard de Malynes and Thomas Mun, who first articulated the Elizabethan system, which in turn was then developed further by Josiah Child. Numerous French authors helped cement French policy around mercantilism in the 17th century. This French mercantilism was best articulated by Jean-Baptiste Colbert (in office, 1665–1683), though policy liberalised greatly under Napoleon.

In Europe, academic belief in mercantilism began to fade in the late 18th century, especially in Britain, in light of the arguments of Adam Smith and the classical economists. The repeal of the Corn Laws by Robert Peel symbolised the emergence of free trade as an alternative system.

Neomercantilism is a 20th-century economic policy that uses the ideas and methods of neoclassical economics. The new mercantilism has different goals and focuses on more rapid economic growth based on advanced technology. It promotes such policies as substitution state taxation, subsidies, expenditures, and general regulatory powers for tariffs and quotas, and protection through the formation of supranational trading blocs.

Theory

Most of the European economists who wrote between 1500 and 1750 are today generally considered mercantilists; this term was initially used solely by critics, such as Mirabeau and Smith, but was quickly adopted by historians. Originally the standard English term was "mercantile system". The word "mercantilism" was introduced into English from German in the early 19th century.

The bulk of what is commonly called "mercantilist literature" appeared in the 1620s in Great Britain. Smith saw the English merchant Thomas Mun (1571–1641) as a major creator of the mercantile system, especially in his posthumously published *Treasure by Foreign Trade* (1664), which Smith considered the archetype or manifesto of the movement. Perhaps the last major mercantilist work was James Steuart's *Principles of Political Economy*, published in 1767.

Mercantilist literature also extended beyond England. Italy and France produced noted writers of mercantilist themes, including Italy's Giovanni Botero (1544–1617) and Antonio Serra (1580–?) and, in France, Jean Bodin, Colbert. Themes also existed in writers from the German historical school from List, as well as followers of the American system and British free-trade imperialism, thus stretching the system into the 19th century. However, many British writers, including Mun and Misselden, were merchants, while many of the writers from other countries were public officials. Beyond mercantilism as a way of understanding the wealth and power of nations, Mun and Misselden are noted for their viewpoints on a wide range of economic matters.

Merchants in Venice

The Austrian lawyer and scholar Philipp Wilhelm von Hornick, one of the pioneers of Cameralism, detailed a nine-point program of what he deemed effective national economy in his *Austria Over All, If She Only Will* of 1684, which comprehensively sums up the tenets of mercantilism:

- That every little bit of a country's soil be utilized for agriculture, mining or manufacturing.
- That all raw materials found in a country be used in domestic manufacture, since finished goods have a higher value than raw materials.
- That a large, working population be encouraged.
- That all export of gold and silver be prohibited and all domestic money be kept in circulation.
- That all imports of foreign goods be discouraged as much as possible.
- That where certain imports are indispensable they be obtained at first hand, in exchange for other domestic goods instead of gold and silver.
- That as much as possible, imports be confined to raw materials that can be finished [in the home country].
- That opportunities be constantly sought for selling a country's surplus manufactures to foreigners, so far as necessary, for gold and silver.
- That no importation be allowed if such goods are sufficiently and suitably supplied at home.

Other than Von Hornick, there were no mercantilist writers presenting an overarching scheme for the ideal economy, as Adam Smith would later do for classical economics. Rather, each mercantilist writer tended to focus on a single area of the economy. Only later did non-mercantilist scholars integrate these "diverse" ideas into what they called mercantilism. Some scholars thus reject the idea of mercantilism completely, arguing that it gives "a false unity to disparate events". Smith saw the mercantile system as an enormous conspiracy by manufacturers and merchants against consumers, a view that has led some authors, especially Robert E. Ekelund and Robert D. Tollison, to call mercantilism "a rent-seeking society". To a certain extent, mercantilist doctrine itself made a general theory of economics impossible. Mercantilists viewed the economic system as a zero-sum game, in which any gain by one party required a loss by another. Thus, any system of policies that benefited one group would by definition harm the other, and there was no possibility of economics being used to maximize the commonwealth, or common good. Mercantilists' writings were also generally created to rationalize particular practices rather than as investigations into the best policies.

Mercantilist domestic policy was more fragmented than its trade policy. While Adam Smith portrayed mercantilism as supportive of strict controls over the economy, many mercantilists disagreed. The early modern era was one of letters patent and government-imposed monopolies; some mercantilists supported these, but others acknowledged the corruption and inefficiency of such systems. Many mercantilists also realized that the inevitable results of quotas and price ceilings were black markets. One notion that mercantilists widely agreed upon was the need for economic oppression of the working population; laborers and farmers were to live at the "margins of subsistence". The goal was to maximize production, with no concern for consumption. Extra money, free time, and education for the lower classes were seen to inevitably lead to vice and laziness, and would result in harm to the economy.

Infinite Growth

The mercantilists saw a large population as a form of wealth which made possible the development of bigger markets and armies. The opposing doctrine of physiocracy predicted that mankind would outgrow its resources. The idea of mercantilism was to protect the markets, but it also helped to maintain the agriculture and those who were dependent upon it.

Scholars debate over why mercantilism dominated economic ideology for 250 years. One group, represented by Jacob Viner, sees mercantilism as simply a straightforward, common-sense system whose logical fallacies remained opaque to people at the time, as they simply lacked the required analytical tools.

The second school, supported by scholars such as Robert B. Ekelund, portrays mercantilism not as a mistake, but rather as the best possible system for those who developed it. This school argues that rent-seeking merchants and governments developed and enforced mercantilist policies. Merchants benefited greatly from the enforced monopolies, bans on foreign competition, and poverty of the workers. Governments benefited from the high tariffs and payments from the merchants. Whereas later economic ideas were often developed by academics and philosophers, almost all mercantilist writers were merchants or government officials.

Monetarism offers a third explanation for mercantilism. European trade exported bullion to pay for goods from Asia, thus reducing the money supply and putting downward pressure on prices and economic activity. The evidence for this hypothesis is the lack of inflation in the British economy until the Revolutionary and Napoleonic Wars, when paper money came into vogue.

A fourth explanation lies in the increasing professionalisation and technification of the wars of the era, which turned the maintenance of adequate reserve funds (in the prospect of war) into a more and more expensive and eventually competitive business.

Mercantilism developed at a time of transition for the European economy. Isolated feudal estates were being replaced by centralized nation-states as the focus of power. Technological changes in shipping and the growth of urban centres led to a rapid increase in international trade. Mercantilism focused on how this trade could best aid the states. Another important change was the introduction of double-entry bookkeeping and modern accounting. This accounting made extremely clear the inflow and outflow of trade, contributing to the close scrutiny given to the balance of trade. Of course, the impact of the discovery of America cannot be ignored. New markets and new mines propelled foreign trade to previously inconceivable volumes, resulting in "the great upward movement in prices" and an increase in "the volume of merchant activity itself".

Prior to mercantilism, the most important economic work done in Europe was by the medieval scholastic theorists. The goal of these thinkers was to find an economic system compatible with Christian doctrines of piety and justice. They focused mainly on microeconomics and on local exchanges between individuals. Mercantilism was closely aligned with the other theories and ideas that began to replace the medieval worldview. This period saw the adoption of the very Machiavellian realpolitik and the primacy of the *raison d'état* in international relations. The mercantilist idea of all trade as a zero-sum game, in which each side was trying to best the other in a ruthless competition, was integrated into the works of Thomas Hobbes. This dark view of human nature also fit well with the Puritan view of the world, and some of the most stridently mercantilist legislation, such as the Navigation Ordinance of 1651, was enacted by the government of Oliver Cromwell.

Jean-Baptiste Colbert's work in 17th-century France came to exemplify classical mercantilism. In the English-speaking world its ideas were criticized by Adam Smith with the publication of *The Wealth of Nations* and later by David Ricardo with his explanation of comparative advantage. Mercantilism was rejected by Britain and France by the mid-19th century. The British Empire embraced free trade and used its power as the financial centre of the world to promote the same. The Guyanese historian Walter Rodney describes mercantilism as the period of the worldwide development of European commerce, which began in the 15th century with the voyages of Portuguese and Spanish explorers to Africa, Asia, and the New World.

Policies

French finance minister and mercantilist Jean-Baptiste Colbert served for over 20 years.

Mercantilist ideas were the dominant economic ideology of all of Europe in the early modern period, and most states embraced it to a certain degree. Mercantilism was centred on England and France, and it was in these states that mercantilist polices were most often enacted.

France

Mercantilism arose in France in the early 16th century soon after the monarchy had become the dominant force in French politics. In 1539, an important decree banned the import of woolen goods from Spain and some parts of Flanders. The next year, a number of restrictions were imposed on the export of bullion.

Over the rest of the 16th century, further protectionist measures were introduced. The height of French mercantilism is closely associated with Jean-Baptiste Colbert, finance minister for 22 years in the 17th century, to the extent that French mercantilism is sometimes called Colbertism. Under Colbert, the French government became deeply involved in the economy in order to increase exports. Protectionist policies were enacted that limited imports and favored exports. Industries were organized into guilds and monopolies, and production was regulated by the state through a series of more than one thousand directives outlining how different products should be produced.

To encourage industry, foreign artisans and craftsmen were imported. Colbert also worked to decrease internal barriers to trade, reducing internal tariffs and building an extensive network of roads and canals. Colbert's policies were quite successful, and France's industrial output and economy grew considerably during this period, as France became the dominant European power. He was less successful in turning France into a major trading power, and Britain and the Netherlands remained supreme in this field.

New France

France imposed its mercantilist philosophy on its colonies in North America, especially New France. It sought to derive the maximum material benefit from the colony, for the homeland, with a minimum of imperial investment in the colony itself. The ideology was embodied in New France through the establishment under Royal Charter of a number of corporate trading monopolies including La Compagnie des Marchands, which operated from 1613 to 1621 and the Compagnie de Montmorency, from that date until 1627. It was in turn replaced by La Compagnie des Cent-Associés created in 1627, by King Louis XIII and the Communauté des habitants in 1643. These were the first corporations to operate in what is now Canada.

Great Britain

In England, mercantilism reached its peak during the Long Parliament government (1640–60). Mercantilist policies were also embraced throughout much of the Tudor and Stuart periods, with Robert Walpole being another major proponent. In Britain, government control over the domestic economy was far less extensive than on the Continent, limited by common law and the steadily increasing power of Parliament. Government-controlled monopolies were common, especially before the English Civil War, but were often controversial.

The Anglo-Dutch Wars were fought between the English and the Dutch for control over the seas and trade routes.

With respect to its colonies, British mercantilism meant that the government and the merchants became partners with the goal of increasing political power and private wealth, to the exclusion of other empires. The government protected its merchants—and kept others out—through trade barriers, regulations, and subsidies to domestic industries in order to maximize exports from and minimize imports to the realm. The government had to fight smuggling, which became a favorite American technique in the 18th century to circumvent the restrictions on trading with the French, Spanish, or Dutch. The goal of mercantilism was to run trade surpluses, so that gold and silver would pour into London. The government took its share through duties and taxes, with the remainder going to merchants in Britain. The government spent much of its revenue on a superb Royal Navy, which not only protected the British colonies but threatened the colonies of the other empires, and sometimes seized them. Thus the British Navy captured New Amsterdam (New York) in 1664. The colonies were captive markets for British industry, and the goal was to enrich the mother country.

British mercantilist writers were themselves divided on whether domestic controls were necessary. British mercantilism thus mainly took the form of efforts to control trade. A wide array of regulations were put in place to encourage exports and discourage imports. Tariffs were placed on imports and bounties given for exports, and the export of some raw materials was banned completely. The Navigation Acts expelled foreign merchants from England's domestic trade. The nation aggressively sought colonies and once under British control, regulations were imposed that allowed the colony to only produce raw materials and to only trade with Britain. This led to friction with the inhabitants of these colonies, and mercantilist policies (such as forbidding trade with other empires and controls over smuggling) were a major irritant leading to the American Revolution.

Mercantalism taught that trade was a zero-sum game, with one country's gain equivalent to a loss sustained by the trading partner. Overall, however, mercantilist policies had a positive impact on Britain helping turn it into the world's dominant trader and the global hegemon. De facto mercantile policies continued until the 1850s, when Britain began to embrace freer trade. For example, during the Industrial Revolution, Britain's average tariff on manufactured goods rose from 30% to 50%, peaking at 57% in the 1820s. This worked in concert with Britain's imperialistic expansion, which was motivated, in part, to acquire new markets for British manufactured goods—the quintessential mercantile paradigm. One domestic policy that had a lasting impact was the conversion of "waste lands" to agricultural use. Mercantilists believed that to maximize a nation's power, all land and resources had to be used to their utmost, and this era thus saw projects like the draining of The Fens.

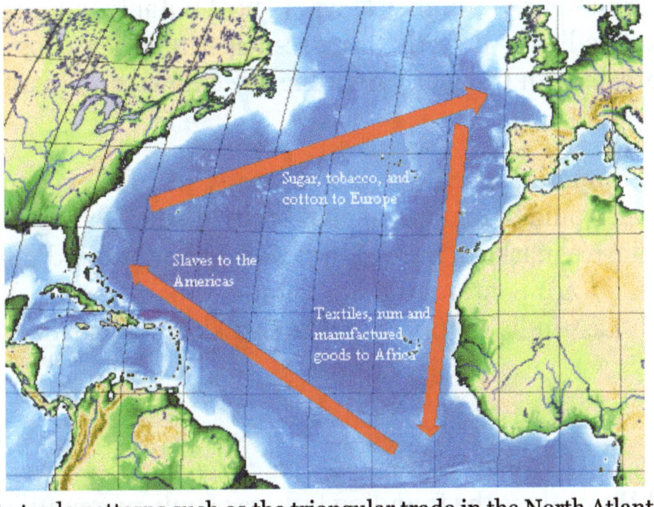

Mercantilism helped create trade patterns such as the triangular trade in the North Atlantic, in which raw materials were imported to the metropolis and then processed and redistributed to other colonies.

Other Countries

The other nations of Europe also embraced mercantilism to varying degrees. Perhaps the earliest coherent mercantile policy developed in the Italian city-state of Venice, which monopolized the Mediterranean pilgrim and spice trades. Venice prohibited the importation of finished products, and forced all Venetian naval traffic to make a stop in Venice, regardless of the cargoes final destination. This ensured that additional economic activity occurred within Venice. This enriched Venice at its consumers expense. The policy was summed up by a prominent Venetian merchant:

Nothing is better to increase and enrich the condition of our city than to give all liberty and occasion that commodities of our city be brought here and procured here rather than elsewhere, because this results in advantage both to the state and to private persons.

The Netherlands, which had become the financial centre of Europe by being its most efficient trader, had little interest in seeing trade restricted and adopted few mercantilist policies. Mercantilism became prominent in Central Europe and Scandinavia after the Thirty Years' War (1618–48), with Christina of Sweden, Jacob Kettler of Courland, and Christian IV of Denmark being notable proponents. The Habsburg Holy Roman Emperors had long been interested in mercantilist policies, but the vast and decentralized nature of their empire made implementing such notions difficult.

Some constituent states of the empire did embrace Mercantilism, most notably Prussia, which under Frederick the Great had perhaps the most rigidly controlled economy in Europe. During the economic collapse of the 17th century, Spain had little coherent economic policy, but French mercantilist policies were imported by Philip V with some success. Russia under Peter I (Peter the Great) attempted to pursue mercantilism, but had little success because of Russia's lack of a large merchant class or an industrial base.

Wars and Imperialism

Mercantilism was the economic version of warfare using economics as a tool for warfare by other means backed up by the state apparatus, and was well suited to an era of military warfare. Since the level of world trade was viewed as fixed, it followed that the only way to increase a nation's trade was to take it from another. A number of wars, most notably the Anglo-Dutch Wars and the Franco-Dutch Wars, can be linked directly to mercantilist theories. Most wars had other causes but they reinforced mercantilism by clearly defining the enemy, and justified damage to the enemy's economy.

Mercantilism fueled the imperialism of this era, as many nations expended significant effort to conquer new colonies that would be sources of gold (as in Mexico) or sugar (as in the West Indies), as well as becoming exclusive markets. European power spread around the globe, often under the aegis of companies with government-guaranteed monopolies in certain defined geographical regions, such as the Dutch East India Company or the British Hudson's Bay Company (operating in present-day Canada).

Criticisms

Adam Smith and David Hume were the founding fathers of anti-mercantilist thought. A number of scholars found important flaws with mercantilism long before Adam Smith developed an ideology that could fully replace it. Critics like Hume, Dudley North, and John Locke undermined much of mercantilism, and it steadily lost favor during the 18th century.

Much of Adam Smith's *The Wealth of Nations* is an attack on mercantilism.

In 1690, John Locke argued that prices vary in proportion to the quantity of money. Locke's *Second Treatise* also points towards the heart of the anti-mercantilist critique: that the wealth of the world is not fixed, but is created by human labor (represented embryonically by Locke's labor theory of value). Mercantilists failed to understand the notions of absolute advantage and comparative advantage (although this idea was only fully fleshed out in 1817 by David Ricardo) and the benefits of trade.

For instance, imagine that Portugal was a more efficient producer of wine than England, yet in England cloth could be produced more efficiently than it could in Portugal. Thus if Portugal specialized in wine and England in cloth, *both* states would end up *better off* if they traded. This is an example of the reciprocal benefits of trade (whether due to comparative or absolute advantage). In modern economic theory, trade is *not* a zero-sum game of cutthroat competition, because both sides can benefit.

Hume famously noted the impossibility of the mercantilists' goal of a constant positive balance of trade. As bullion flowed into one country, the supply would increase, and the value of bullion in that state would steadily decline relative to other goods. Conversely, in the state exporting bullion, its value would slowly rise. Eventually it would no longer be cost-effective to export goods from the high-price country to the low-price country, and the balance of trade would reverse. Mercantilists fundamentally misunderstood this, long arguing that an increase in the money supply simply meant that everyone gets richer.

The importance placed on bullion was also a central target, even if many mercantilists had themselves begun to de-emphasize the importance of gold and silver. Adam Smith noted that at the core of the mercantile system was the "popular folly of confusing wealth with money", that bullion was just the same as any other commodity, and that there was no reason to give it special treatment. More recently, scholars have discounted the accuracy of this critique. They believe Mun and Misselden were not making this mistake in the 1620s, and point to their followers Josiah Child and Charles Davenant, who in 1699 wrote, "Gold and Silver are indeed the Measure of Trade, but that the Spring and Original of it, in all nations is the Natural or Artificial Product of the Country; that is to say, what this Land or what this Labour and Industry Produces." The critique that mercantilism was a form of rent seeking has also seen criticism, as scholars such Jacob Viner in the 1930s pointed out that merchant mercantilists such as Mun understood that they would not gain by higher prices for English wares abroad.

The first school to completely reject mercantilism was the physiocrats, who developed their theories in France. Their theories also had several important problems, and the replacement of mercantilism did not come until Adam Smith published *The Wealth of Nations* in 1776. This book outlines the basics of what is today known as classical economics. Smith spent a considerable portion of the book rebutting the arguments of the mercantilists, though often these are simplified or exaggerated versions of mercantilist thought.

Scholars are also divided over the cause of mercantilism's end. Those who believe the theory was simply an error hold that its replacement was inevitable as soon as Smith's more accurate ideas were unveiled. Those who feel that mercantilism amounted to rent seeking hold that it ended only when major power shifts occurred. In Britain, mercantilism faded as the Parliament gained the monarch's power to grant monopolies. While the wealthy capitalists who controlled the House of Commons benefited from these monopolies, Parliament found it difficult to implement them because of the high cost of group decision making.

Mercantilist regulations were steadily removed over the course of the 18th century in Britain, and during the 19th century the British government fully embraced free trade and Smith's laissez-faire economics. On the continent, the process was somewhat different. In France, economic control remained in the hands of the royal family, and mercantilism continued until the French Revolution. In Germany mercantilism remained an important ideology in the 19th and early 20th centuries, when the historical school of economics was paramount.

Legacy

Adam Smith.

Adam Smith rejected the mercantilist focus on production, arguing that consumption was paramount to production. He added that mercantilism was popular among merchants because it was what is now called rent seeking. However, John Maynard Keynes argued that encouraging production was just as important as encouraging consumption, and he favoured the "new mercantilism". Keynes also noted that in the early modern period the focus on the bullion supplies was reasonable. In an era before paper money, an increase in bullion was one of the few ways to increase the money supply. Keynes said mercantilist policies generally improved both domestic and foreign investment—domestic because the policies lowered the domestic rate of interest, and investment by foreigners by tending to create a favorable balance of trade.

Keynes and other economists of the 20th century also realized that the balance of payments is an important concern. Keynes also supported government intervention in the economy as necessity, as did mercantilism.

As of 2010, the word "mercantilism" remains a pejorative term, often used to attack various forms of protectionism. The similarities between Keynesianism (and its successor ideas) and mercantilism have sometimes led critics to call them neo-mercantilism. Paul Samuelson, writing within a Keynesian framework, wrote of mercantilism, "With employment less than full and Net National Product suboptimal, all the debunked mercantilist arguments turn out to be valid."

Some other systems that copy several mercantilist policies, such as Japan's economic system, are also sometimes called neo-mercantilist. In an essay appearing in the 14 May 2007 issue of *Newsweek*, business columnist Robert J. Samuelson wrote that China was pursuing an essentially neo-mercantilist trade policy that threatened to undermine the post–World War II international economic structure.

Murray Rothbard, representing the Austrian School of economics, describes it this way:

Mercantilism, which reached its height in the Europe of the seventeenth and eighteenth centuries, was a system of statism which employed economic fallacy to build up a structure of imperial state power, as well as special subsidy and monopolistic privilege to individuals or groups favored by the state. Thus, mercantilism held exports should be encouraged by the government and imports discouraged.

John Maynard Keynes.

In specific instances, protectionist mercantilist policies also had an important and positive impact on the state that enacted them. Adam Smith, for instance, praised the Navigation Acts, as they greatly expanded the British merchant fleet and played a central role in turning Britain into the world's naval and economic superpower from the 18th century onward. Some economists thus feel that protecting infant industries, while causing short-term harm, can be beneficial in the long term.

System of Accounting

Accounting system is followed majorly in two ways:

- Cash.
- Mercantile.

Cash System

Definition and Explanation:

- It is a system in which accounting entries are made only when cash is received or paid. No entry is made when a payment or receipt is merely due.
- Government system of accounting is mostly on the cash system.

For example:

- The salary for December 2010 has not been paid till 5th Jan. 2011. Under cash basis, Salary expense for the month of December will not be recorded as payment has not been made.

Mercantile System

Definition and Explanation

- It is a system in which accounting entries are made on the basis of amount having become due for payment or receipt.
- This system recognizes the fact that if a transaction or an event occurred, its consequences cannot be avoided and therefore, should be brought into book in order to present a meaningful picture of profit earned or loss suffered.
- The mercantile system is also known as the accrual system.

Difference Between Cash and Mercantile System of Accounting

- Under cash basis accounting, Revenues are recognized and earned only when cash is received irrespective of when and how the services were performed or goods delivered.

To put it in different terms, the cash basis of accounting takes into consideration all those incomes/gains that have been received and expenses/losses that have been paid during the accounting period in consideration.

Under accrual or mercantile basis accounting, Revenues are recognized and earned when they are realized or realizable irrespective of when the cash is received.

To put it in different terms, the accrual basis of accounting, records all incomes/gains and expenses/ losses pertaining to the accounting period under consideration, irrespective of receipt or payment.

Preparation of Financial Statement

Particulars	Amount (₹)
Cash	5,600
Trade debtors	8,400
Rent	5,500
Salaries	12,000
Trade Creditors	18,700
Insurance	4,000
Petty Expenses	3,000
Opening Stock	20,000
Sales	2,65,000
Purchases	1,80,000
Capital	1,05,900
Motor Vehicle	65,000
Machinery	54,000
Office Expenses	2,950
Repairs & Maintenance	5,000
Electricity exps.	2,550

Prepare Profit & Loss A/c and Balance Sheet from the above trial balance.

Solution

Trading & Profit & Loss A/c for the Year Ended 31st March ....

Particulars	₹	Particulars	₹
Opening Stock	20,000	Sales	2,65,000
Purchases	1,80,000		
Gross Profit	65,000		
Total	**2,65,000**	**Total**	**2,65,000**

Particulars	₹	Particulars	₹
Rent	5,500	Gross Profit b/d	65,000
Salaries	12,000		
Insurance	4,000		
Petty Exps.	3,000		
Office Exps.	2,950		
Repairs & Maintenance	5,000		
Electricity Exp.	2,250		
Net Profit	30,300		

Balance Sheet as on 31st March ....

Liabilities	₹	Assets	₹
Capital	1,05,900	Motor Vehicle	65,000
Net Profit	30,300	Machinery	54,000
Trade Creditors	8,400	Trade debtors	20,000
		Cash	5,600
	1,44,600		**1,44,600**

Share Capital

A corporation's share capital (or capital stock in US English) is the portion of a corporation's equity that has been obtained by the issue of shares in the corporation to a shareholder, usually for cash.

In a strict accounting sense, share capital is the nominal value of issued shares (that is, the sum of their par values, as indicated on share certificates). If the allocation price of shares is greater than their par value, e.g. as in a rights issue, the shares are said to be sold at a premium (variously called *share premium, additional paid-in capital* or *paid-in capital in excess of par*). Commonly, the share capital is the total of the aforementioned nominal share capital and the premium share capital. Conversely, when shares are issued below par, they are said to be issued at a discount or part-paid.

Sometimes shares are allocated in exchange for non-cash consideration, most commonly when company A acquires company B for shares. Here the share capital is increased to the par value of the new shares, and the merger reserve is increased to the balance of the price of company B.

Besides its meaning in accounting, described above, "share capital" may also describe the number and types of shares that compose a company's share structure. For an example of the different meanings: a company might have an "outstanding share capital" of 500,000 shares (the "structure" usage); it has received for them a total of 2 million dollars, which in the balance sheet is the "share capital" (the accounting usage).

The legal aspects of share capital are mostly dealt with in a jurisdiction's corporate law system. An example of such an issue is that when a company allocates new shares, it must do so in a way that does not inequitably dilute existing shareholders without their agreement.

- Total capital of the company is divided into a number of small indivisible units of a fixed amount and each such unit is called a share.
- As the total capital of the company is divided into shares, the capital of the company is called 'share capital'.
- The fixed value of a share, printed on the share certificate is called nominal/ par/ face value of a share.
- A company can issue shares at a price different from the face value of a share; this is issue price of share.
- Types of shares Shares issued by a company are divided into two categories:
    - Preference Shares:

      The shares which are assured of preferential dividend at a fixed rate during the life of company and carry a preferential right over other shareholders to be paid first in case of winding up of company.
    - Equity Shares.

      Equity shares are those shares, which are not preference shares. It means that they do not enjoy any preferential rights in the matter of payment of dividend or repayment of capital.

Issue of Share Capital

- The shares can be issued by company either for cash or for the consideration other than cash.
- A public company issues a prospectus inviting general public to subscribe for its shares. On the basis of prospectus, application are deposited in a scheduled bank by the interested parties along with the amount payable at the time of application in cash which is called as application money.
- Company reserves the right to reject or accept an application fully or partially. Successful applicants become shareholders of the company and are required to pay the second installment which is known as allotment money.
- Subsequent installments, if any, to be called by the company are known as calls.
- Journal Entries for issues of shares for cash.
    - On the receipt of the application money
      Bank A/c...... Dr.
      To Shares Application money

- On the allotment of share
  Share Allotment A/c.....Dr.
  Share Application A/c...Dr.
  To Share Capital A/c
  To Securities Premium A/c
  (if shares are issued at premium)
- On the receipt of allotment money
  Bank A/c.....Dr.
  To Share Allotment A/c
- On the call being made
  Share call A/c.....Dr.
  To Share Capital A/c
- On receipt of call money
  Bank A/c......Dr.
  To Share Call A/c
- If call money is received from shareholders even before making call
  Bank A/c....Dr.
  To Calls in Advance A/c
- If money is not received from shareholders on any call
  Calls in Arrears A/c....Dr.
  To Share Allotment A/c
  To Share Call A/c

The Articles of Association of a company usually empower the director to charge interest at a stipulated rate on calls in arrears. According to Table A of Companies Act 1956 interest at the rate of 5% p.a. is to be charged on unpaid calls from the due date of the call up to the actual payment.

JE for interest receivable on call in arrears
Shareholders A/c....Dr.
To Interest on Calls in Arrears A/c

For receipt of interest
Interest on Calls in Arrears A/c...Dr.
Shareholders A/c

According to Table A of Companies Act 1956 interest at the rate of 6% p.a. is to be paid on calls in advance from the actual payment up to due date of the call.

JE for Interest due
Interest on Calls in Arrears A/c...Dr.
To Shareholders A/c

Payment of interest
Shareholders A/c ...Dr.
Interest on Calls in Advance A/c

Issued Shares

Issued shares is a term of law and finance for the number of shares of a corporation which have been allocated (allotted) and are subsequently held by shareholders. The act of creating new issued shares is called *issuance, allocation* or *allotment.* Allotment is simply the creation of shares and their transfer to a subscriber. After allotment, a subscriber becomes a shareholder, though usually that also requires formal entry in the members register.

The number of shares that can be issued is limited to the total authorized shares. Issued shares are those shares which the board of directors and/or shareholders have agreed to allocate. Issued shares are the sum of outstanding shares held by shareholders; and treasury shares are shares which had been issued but have been repurchased by the corporation, and which generally have no voting rights or rights to dividends.

The issued shares of a corporation form the equity capital of the corporation, and some corporations are required by law to have a minimum value of equity capital, while others may not need any or just a nominal number. The value of the issued shares are determined at the time they are issued and the value does not change, in relation to the issuing corporation after that time.

Shares are most commonly issued fully paid, in which case the liability of the shareholders is limited to the amount paid on the shares; but they may also be issued partly paid, with unlimited liability, subject to guarantee, or some other form.

Basic Formulae

- Shares authorized = Shares issued + Shares unissued
- Shares issued = Shares outstanding + Treasury shares

Capital Surplus

Capital surplus, also called share premium, is an account which may appear on a corporation's balance sheet, as a component of shareholders' equity, which represents the amount the corporation raises on the issue of shares in excess of their par value (nominal value) of the shares (common stock).

This is called Additional paid in capital in US GAAP terminology but, additional paid in capital is not limited to share premium. It is a very broad concept and includes tax related and conversion related adjustments.

Taken together, common stock (and sometimes preferred stock) issued and paid plus capital surplus represent the total amount actually paid by investors for shares when issued (assuming no subsequent adjustments or changes).

Shares for which there is no par value will generally not have any form of capital surplus on the balance sheet; all funds from issuing shares will be credited to common stock issued.

Some other scenarios for triggering a capital surplus include when the Government donates a piece of land to the company.

The capital surplus/share premium account (SPA) is generally not distributable, but may be used to:

- Write off the expenses/commission relating to the issue of those shares, or
- Make a bonus share issue of fully paid-up shares.

It may also be used to account for any gains the firm may derive from selling treasury stock, although this is less commonly seen.

Capital surplus is also a term used by economists to denote capital inflows in excess of capital outflows on a country's balance of payments.

Background

Many firms authorize shares with some nominal par value, often the smallest unit of currency commonly in use (such as one penny or $0.01), in many jurisdictions due to legal requirements. The firm may then sell these shares for a much higher price (as the par value is a largely archaic and fictional concept).

Any premium received over the par value is credited to capital surplus.

Share Premium Reserve Account

According to Companies Act 2006 s.610 in the United Kingdom the share premium account may be put only to certain specified uses. However UK company law in this connection was significantly relaxed in 2008 by permitting the share premium account to be converted into share capital and then the share capital to be reduced (effectively allowing the elimination of the share premium account by a two-stage process).

Under companies ordinance 1984 (Nepal) s.84:

(1) If a company issues shares at a premium, whether for cash or otherwise, a sum equal to the aggregate amount or value of the premiums on those shares shall be transferred to an account called "the share premium account".

(2) The share premium account may be applied by the company in paying up unissued shares to be allotted to members as fully paid bonus shares, or in writing off- (a) the company's preliminary expenses; or (b) the expenses of, or the commission paid or discount allowed on, any issue of shares or debentures of the company, or (c) in providing for the premium payable on redemption of debentures of the company.

(3) Subject to this, the provisions of this Act relating to the reduction of a company's share capital apply as if the share premium account were part of its paid up share capital.

A company's SPA is a part of creditors' buffer.

Assets:

Cash: $450

Liabilities:

Nil

Shareholders' equity:

Common stock: $100

Preference stock: $25

Share premium: $325

SPA = Number of new shares issued x (issue price - par value).

Preferred Stock

Preferred stock (also called preferred shares, preference shares or simply preferreds) is a type of stock which may have any combination of features not possessed by common stock including properties of both an equity and a debt instrument, and is generally considered a hybrid instrument. Preferred stocks are senior (i.e., higher ranking) to common stock, but subordinate to bonds in terms of claim (or rights to their share of the assets of the company) and may have priority over common stock (ordinary shares) in the payment of dividends and upon liquidation. Terms of the preferred stock are described in the articles of association.

Like bonds, preferred stocks are rated by the major credit-rating companies. The rating for preferreds is generally lower than for bonds because preferred dividends do not carry the same guarantees as interest payments from bonds and because preferred-stock holders' claims are junior to those of all creditors.

Features

Preferred stock is a special class of shares which may have any combination of features not possessed by common stock. The following features are usually associated with preferred stock:

- Preference in dividends.
- Preference in assets, in the event of liquidation.
- Convertibility to common stock.
- Callability (ability to be redeemed before it matures), at the option of the corporation.
- Nonvoting.

Preference in Dividends

In general, preferred stock has *preference* in dividend payments. The preference does not assure the payment of dividends, but the company must pay the stated dividends on preferred stock before paying any dividends on common stock.

Preferred stock can be *cumulative* or *noncumulative*. A cumulative preferred requires that if a company fails to pay a dividend (or pays less than the stated rate), it must make up for it at a later time. Dividends accumulate with each passed dividend period (which may be quarterly, semi-annually or annually). When a dividend is not paid in time, it has "passed"; all passed dividends on a cumulative stock make up a dividend in arrears. A stock without this feature is known as a noncumulative, or *straight*, preferred stock; any dividends passed are lost if not declared.

Other Features or Rights

- Preferred stock may or may not have a fixed liquidation value (or par value) associated with it. This represents the amount of capital which was contributed to the corporation when the shares were first issued.
- Preferred stock has a claim on liquidation proceeds of a stock corporation equal to its par (or liquidation) value, unless otherwise negotiated. This claim is senior to that of common stock, which has only a residual claim.
- Almost all preferred shares have a negotiated, fixed-dividend amount. The dividend is usually specified as a percentage of the par value or as a fixed amount (for example, Pacific Gas & Electric 6% Series A Preferred). Sometimes, dividends on preferred shares may be negotiated as *floating*; they may change according to a benchmark interest-rate index (such as LIBOR).
- Some preferred shares have special voting rights to approve extraordinary events (such as the issuance of new shares or approval of the acquisition of a company) or to elect directors, but most preferred shares have no voting rights associated with them; some preferred shares gain voting rights when the preferred dividends are in arrears for a substantial time. This is all variable on the rights assigned to the preferred shares at the time of incorporation.

The above list (which includes several customary rights) is not comprehensive; preferred shares (like other legal arrangements) may specify nearly any right conceivable. Preferred shares in the U.S. normally carry a call provision, enabling the issuing corporation to repurchase the share at its (usually limited) discretion.

Types

In addition to straight preferred stock, there is diversity in the preferred stock market. Additional types of preferred stock include:

- *Prior preferred stock*—Many companies have different issues of preferred stock outstanding at one time; one issue is usually designated highest-priority. If the company has only enough money to meet the dividend schedule on one of the preferred issues, it makes the payments on the prior preferred. Therefore, prior preferreds have less credit risk than other preferred stocks (but usually offers a lower yield).
- *Preference preferred stock*—Ranked behind a company's prior preferred stock (on a seniority basis) are its preference preferred issues. These issues receive preference over all other classes of the company's preferred (except for prior preferred). If the company issues more than one issue of preference preferred, the issues are ranked by seniority. One issue is designated first preference, the next-senior issue is the second and so on.
- *Convertible preferred stock*—These are preferred issues which holders can exchange for a predetermined number of the company's common-stock shares. This exchange may occur at any time the investor chooses, regardless of the market price of the common stock. It is a one-way deal; one cannot convert the common stock back to preferred stock. A variant of

this is the *anti-dilutive convertible preferred* recently made popular by investment banker Stan Medley who structured several variants of these preferred for some forty plus public companies. In the variants used by Stan Medley the preferred share converts to either a percentage of the company's common shares or a fixed dollar amount of common shares rather than a set number of shares of common. The intention is to ameliorate the bad effects investors suffer from rampant shorting and dilutive efforts on the OTC markets.

- *Cumulative preferred stock*—If the dividend is not paid, it will accumulate for future payment.
- *Exchangeable preferred stock*—This type of preferred stock carries an embedded option to be exchanged for some other security.
- *Participating preferred stock*—These preferred issues offer holders the opportunity to receive extra dividends if the company achieves predetermined financial goals. Investors who purchased these stocks receive their regular dividend regardless of company performance (assuming the company does well enough to make its annual dividend payments). If the company achieves predetermined sales, earnings or profitability goals, the investors receive an additional dividend.
- *Perpetual preferred stock*—This type of preferred stock has no fixed date on which invested capital will be returned to the shareholder (although there are redemption privileges held by the corporation); most preferred stock is issued without a redemption date.
- *Putable preferred stock*—These issues have a "put" privilege, whereby the holder may (under certain conditions) force the issuer to redeem shares.
- *Monthly income preferred stock*—A combination of preferred stock and subordinated debt.
- *Non-cumulative preferred stock*—Dividends for this type of preferred stock will not accumulate if they are unpaid; very common in TRuPS and bank preferred stock, since under BIS rules preferred stock must be non-cumulative if it is to be included in Tier 1 capital.
- *Supervoting stock*—a "class of stock that provides its holders with larger than proportionate voting rights compared with another class of stock issued by the same company." It enables a limited number of stockholders to control a company. Usually, the purpose of the super voting shares is to give key company insiders greater control over the company's voting rights, and thus its board and corporate actions. The existence of super voting shares can also be an effective defense against hostile takeovers, since key insiders can maintain majority voting control of their company without actually owning more than half of the outstanding shares.

Usage

Preferred stocks offer a company an alternative form of financing—for example through pension-led funding; in some cases, a company can defer dividends by going into arrears with little penalty or risk to its credit rating, however, such action could have a negative impact on the company meeting the terms of its financing contract. With traditional debt, payments are required; a missed payment would put the company in default.

Occasionally companies use preferred shares as means of preventing hostile takeovers, creating preferred shares with a poison pill (or forced-exchange or conversion features) which are exercised upon a change in control. Some corporations contain provisions in their charters authorizing the issuance of preferred stock whose terms and conditions may be determined by the board of directors when issued. These "blank checks" are often used as a takeover defense; they may be assigned very high liquidation value (which must be redeemed in the event of a change of control), or may have great super-voting powers.

When a corporation goes bankrupt, there may be enough money to repay holders of preferred issues known as "senior" but not enough money for "junior" issues. Therefore, when preferred shares are first issued their governing document may contain protective provisions preventing the issuance of new preferred shares with a senior claim. Individual series of preferred shares may have a senior, pari-passu (equal), or junior relationship with other series issued by the same corporation.

Users

Preferred shares are more common in private or pre-public companies, where it is useful to distinguish between the control of and the economic interest in the company. Government regulations and the rules of stock exchanges may either encourage or discourage the issuance of publicly traded preferred shares. In many countries, banks are encouraged to issue preferred stock as a source of Tier 1 capital. On the other hand, the Tel Aviv Stock Exchange prohibits listed companies from having more than one class of capital stock.

A company may issue several classes of preferred stock. It may undergo several rounds of financing, with each round receiving separate rights and having a separate class of preferred stock. Such a company might have "Series A Preferred," "Series B Preferred," "Series C Preferred" and common stock.

In the United States there are two types of preferred stocks: *straight* preferreds and *convertible* preferreds. Straight preferreds are issued in perpetuity (although some are subject to call by the issuer, under certain conditions) and pay a stipulated rate of interest to the holder. Convertible preferreds—in addition to the foregoing features of a straight preferred—contain a provision by which the holder may convert the preferred into the common stock of the company (or, sometimes, into the common stock of an affiliated company) under certain conditions (among which may be the specification of a future date when conversion may begin, a certain number of common shares per preferred share or a certain price per share for the common stock).

There are income-tax advantages generally available to *corporations* investing in preferred stocks in the United States.

But for *individuals*, a *straight* preferred stock, a hybrid between a bond and a stock, bears some disadvantages of each type of securities without enjoying the advantages of either. Like a bond, a straight preferred does not participate in future earnings and dividend growth of the company, or growth in the price of the common stock. However, a bond has greater security than the preferred and has a maturity date at which the principal is to be repaid. Like the common, the preferred has less security protection than the bond. However, the potential increase in the market price of the common (and its dividends, paid from future growth of the company) is lacking for the preferred. One advantage of the preferred to its issuer is that the preferred receives better equity credit at rating agencies than straight debt (since it is usually perpetual). Also, certain types of preferred stock qualify as Tier 1 capital; this allows financial institutions to satisfy regulatory requirements without diluting common shareholders. Through preferred stock, financial institutions are able to gain leverage while receiving Tier 1 equity credit.

If an investor paid par ($100) today for a typical straight preferred, such an investment would give a current yield of just over six percent. If, in a few years, 10-year Treasuries were to yield more than 13 percent to maturity (as they did in 1981) these preferreds would yield at least 13 percent; since the rate of dividend is fixed, this would reduce their market price to $46, a 54-percent loss. The difference between straight preferreds and Treasuries (or any investment-grade Federal-agency or corporate bond) is that the bonds would move up to par as their maturity date approaches; however, the straight preferred (having no maturity date) might remain at these $40 levels (or lower) for a long time.

Advantages of straight preferreds may include higher yields and—in the U.S. at least—tax advantages; they yield about 2 percent more than 10-year Treasuries, rank ahead of common stock in case of bankruptcy and dividends are taxable at a maximum rate of 15% rather than at ordinary-income rates (as with bond interest).

Advantages of Preference Shares

1. No obligation for dividends: A company is not bound to pay a dividend on preference shares if its profits in a particular year are insufficient. It can postpone the dividend in case of cumulative preference shares also. No fixed burden is created on its finances.
2. No interference: Generally, preference shares do not carry voting rights.Therefore, a company can raise capital without dilution of control. Equity shareholders retain exclusive control over the company.
3. Trading on equity: The rate of dividend on preference shares is fixed. Therefore, with the rise in its earnings, the company can provide the benefits of trading on equity to the equity shareholders.
4. No charge on assets: Preference shares do not create any mortgage or charge on the assets of the company. The company can keep its fixed assets free for raising loans in future.
5. Variety: Different types of preference shares can be issued depending on the needs of investors. Participating preference shares or convertible preference shares may be issued to attract bold and enterprising investors.

Country-by-country Perspectives

Canada

Preferred shares represent a significant portion of Canadian capital markets, with over C$11.2 billion in new preferred shares issued in 2016. Many Canadian issuers are financial organizations which may count capital raised in the preferred-share market as Tier 1 capital (provided that the shares issued are perpetual). Another class of issuer includes split share corporations. Investors in Canadian preferred shares are generally those who wish to hold fixed-income investments in a taxable portfolio. Preferential tax treatment of dividend income (as opposed to interest income) may, in many cases, result in a greater after-tax return than might be achieved with bonds.

Preferred shares are often used by private corporations to achieve Canadian tax objectives. For instance, the use of preferred shares can allow a business to accomplish an estate freeze. By transferring common shares in exchange for fixed-value preferred shares, business owners can allow future gains in the value of the business to accrue to others (such as a discretionary trust).

Germany

The rights of holders of preference shares in Germany are usually rather similar to those of ordinary shares, except for some dividend preference and no voting right in many topics of shareholders' meetings. Preference shares in German stock exchanges are usually indicated with *V*, *VA* or *Vz* (short for *Vorzugsaktie*)—for example, "BMW Vz"—in contrast to *St*, *StA* (short for *Stammaktie*) or *NA* (short for *Namensaktie*) for standard shares. Preference shares with multiple voting rights, e.g. at RWE or Siemens, have been abolished.

Preferred stock may comprise up to half of total equity. It is convertible into common stock, but its conversion requires approval by a majority vote at the stockholders' meeting. If the vote passes, German law requires consensus with preferred stockholders to convert their stock (which is usually encouraged by offering a one-time premium to preferred stockholders). The firm's intention to do so may arise from its financial policy (i.e. its ranking in a specific index). Industry stock indices usually do not consider preferred stock in determining the daily trading volume of a company's stock; for example, they do not qualify the company for a listing due to a low trading volume in common stocks.

United Kingdom

Perpetual non-cumulative preference shares may be included as Tier 1 capital. Perpetual cumulative preferred shares are Upper Tier 2 capital. Dated preferred shares (normally having an original maturity of at least five years) may be included in Lower Tier 2 capital.

United States

In the United States, the issuance of publicly listed preferred stock is generally limited to financial institutions, REITs and public utilities. Because in the U.S. dividends on preferred stock are not tax-deductible at the corporate level (in contrast to interest expense), the effective cost of capital raised by preferred stock is 35 percent greater than issuing the equivalent amount of debt at the same interest rate. This has led to the development of TRuPS: debt instruments with the same properties as preferred stock. With the passage of the Dodd-Frank Wall Street Reform and Consumer Protection Act in 2010, TRuPS will be phased out as a vehicle for raising Tier 1 capital by bank holding companies. Outstanding TRuPS issues will be phased out completely by 2015.

However, with a qualified dividend tax of 15 percent (compared to a top ordinary marginal tax rate of 35 percent), $1 of dividend income taxed at this rate provides the same after-tax income as approximately $1.30 in interest. The size of the preferred stock market in the United States has been estimated as $100 billion (as of early 2008), compared to $9.5 trillion for equities and US$4.0 trillion for bonds. The amount of new issuance in the United States was $34.1 billion in 2016.

Other Countries

- In Nigeria preferred shares make up a small percentage of a company's stock with no voting rights except in cases were they are not paid dividends; owners of preferred shares are entitled to a greater percentage of company profits.
- *Czech Republic*—Preferred stock cannot be more than 50 percent of total equity.
- *France*—By a law enacted in June 2004 France allows the creation of preferred shares.
- *South Africa*—Dividends from preference shares are not taxable as income when held by individuals.
- *Brazil*—In Brazil, up to 50 percent of the capital stock of a company may be composed of preferred stock. The preferred stock will have at least one less right than the common stock (normally voting power), but will have a preference in receiving dividends.
- *Russia*—No more than 25% of capital may be preferred stock. Voting rights are limited, but if dividends are not fully paid, shareholders obtain full voting rights.

Common Stock

Common stock is a form of corporate equity ownership, a type of security. The terms voting share and ordinary share are also used frequently in other parts of the world; "common stock" being primarily used in the United States. They are known as Equity shares or Ordinary shares in the UK and other Commonwealth realms. This type of share gives the stockholder the right to share in the profits of the company, and to vote on matters of corporate policy and the composition of the members of the board of directors.

It is called "common" to distinguish it from preferred stock. If both types of stock exist, common/equity stockholders usually cannot be paid dividends until all preferred/preference stock dividends are paid in full; it is possible to have common stock that has dividends that are paid alongside the preferred stock.

In the event of bankruptcy, common stock investors receive any remaining funds after bondholders, creditors (including employees), and preferred stockholders are paid.

Common stockholders can also earn money through capital appreciation. Common shares may perform better than preferred shares or bonds over time, in part to accommodate the increased risk.

Shareholder Rights

Shareholder rights are more conceptual than technical or factual. Their most common source is in the statutory and case law of the jurisdiction in which the company was formed. Information about what people think of as shareholder rights can also be found in the corporate charter and governance documents, but companies do not actually have documentation outlining specific "Shareholder Rights." Some shareholders elect to enter into shareholder agreements that create new rights among the shareholders, and it is common for the company to be a party to that agreement.

Some common stock shares have voting rights on certain matters, such as electing the board of directors. However in the United States, a company can have both a "voting" and "non-voting" series of common stock, as with preferred stock, but not in countries which have laws against multiple voting and non-voting shares.

Hypothetically speaking, holders of voting common stock can influence the corporation through votes on establishing corporate objectives and policy, stock splits, and electing the company's board of directors. In practice, it's questionable whether or not such actions can be organized or ruled in their favor. Some shareholders, including holders of common stock, also receive preemptive rights, which enable them to retain their proportional ownership in a company if it issues additional stock or other securities. There is no fixed dividend paid out to common/equity stockholders and so their returns are uncertain, contingent on earnings, company reinvestment, and efficiency of the market to value and sell stock.

Classification

Common/Equity stock is classified to differentiate it from preferred stock. Each is considered a "class" of stock, with different series of each issued from time to time such as Series B Preferred Stock. Nevertheless, using "Class B Common Stock" is a common label for a super-voting series of common stock.

Debenture

In corporate finance, a debenture is a medium to long-term debt instrument used by large companies to borrow money, at a fixed rate of interest. The legal term "debenture" originally referred to a document that either creates a debt or acknowledges it, but in some countries the term is now used interchangeably with bond, loan stock or note. A debenture is thus like a certificate of loan or a loan bond evidencing the fact that the company is liable to pay a specified amount with interest and although the money raised by the debentures becomes a part of the company's capital structure, it does not become share capital. Senior debentures get paid before subordinate debentures, and there are varying rates of risk and payoff for these categories.

Debentures are generally freely transferable by the debenture holder. Debenture holders have no rights to vote in the company's general meetings of shareholders, but they may have separate meetings or votes e.g. on changes to the rights attached to the debentures. The interest paid to them is a charge against profit in the company's financial statements.

Attributes

- A movable property.
- Issued by the company in the form of a certificate of indebtedness.
- Generally specifying the dates of redemption, repayment of principal and payment of interest.

- May or may not create a charge on the assets of the company.
- Corporations in the US often issue bonds of around $1,000, while government bonds are more likely to be $5,000.

Debentures gave rise to the idea of the rich "clipping their coupons," which means that a bond-holder will present their "coupon" to the bank and receive a payment each quarter (or in whatever period is specified in the agreement).

There are also other features that minimize risk, such as a "sinking fund," which means that the debtor must pay some of the value of the bond after a specified period of time. This decreases risk for the creditors, as a hedge against inflation, bankruptcy, or other risk factors. A sinking fund makes the bond less risky, and therefore gives it a smaller "coupon" (or interest payment). There are also options for "convertibility," which means a creditor may turn their bonds into equity in the company if it does well. Companies also reserve the right to call their bonds, which mean they can call it sooner than the maturity date. Often there is a clause in the contract that allows this; for example, if a bond issuer wishes to rebuy a 30-year bond at the 25th year, they must pay a premium. If a bond is called, it means that less interest is paid out.

Failure to pay a bond effectively means bankruptcy. Bondholders who have not received their interest can throw an offending company into bankruptcy, or seize its assets if that is stipulated in the contract.

Security in Different Jurisdictions

In the United States, debenture refers specifically to an unsecured corporate bond, i.e. a bond that does not have a certain line of income or piece of property or equipment to guarantee repayment of principal upon the bond's maturity. Where security is provided for loan stocks or bonds in the US, they are termed 'mortgage bonds'.

However, in the United Kingdom a debenture is usually secured.

In Canada, a debenture refers to a secured loan instrument where security is generally over the debtor's credit, but security is not pledged to specific assets. Like other secured debts, the debenture gives the debtor priority status over unsecured creditors in a bankruptcy; however debt instruments where security is pledged to specific assets (such as a bond) receive a higher priority status in a bankruptcy than do debentures.

In Asia, if repayment is secured by a charge over land, the loan document is called a mortgage; where repayment is secured by a charge against other assets of the company, the document is called a debenture; and where no security is involved, the document is called a note or 'unsecured deposit note'.

Convertibility

There are two types of debentures:

1. Convertible debentures, which are convertible bonds or bonds that can be converted into equity shares of the issuing company after a predetermined period of time. "Convertibility" is

a feature that corporations may add to the bonds they issue to make them more attractive to buyers. In other words, it is a special feature that a corporate bond may carry. As a result of the advantage a buyer gets from the ability to convert, convertible bonds typically have lower interest rates than non-convertible corporate bonds.

2. Non-convertible debentures, which are simply regular debentures, cannot be converted into equity shares of the liable company. They are debentures without the convertibility feature attached to them. As a result, they usually carry higher interest rates than their convertible counterparts.

Issue of Debentures

Issue of debentures can be categorized into the following:

1. Debenture issued at par and redeemable at par or at a discount.
2. Debenture issued at discount and redeemable at par or at a discount.
3. Debenture issued at premium and redeemable at par or at a discount.
4. Debenture issued at par and redeemable at premium.
5. Debenture issued at a discount and redeemable at premium.

Journal Entries in each of the above cases are discussed below:

1. Debenture issued at par and redeemable at par or at a discount
   For receipt of application money:
   Bank A/c......Dr.
   To Debenture Application Money A/c
   For transfer of application money to debenture account:
   Debenture Application A/c
   To Debenture A/c

2. Debenture issued at discount and redeemable at par or at a discount
   For receipt of application money:
   Bank A/c......Dr.
   To Debenture Application Money A/c
   For transfer of application money to debenture account:
   Debenture Application A/c
   To Debenture A/c

3. Debenture issued at discount and redeemable at par or at a discount
   For receipt of application money:
   Bank A/c......Dr.
   To Debenture Application Money A/c
   For transfer of application money to debenture account:
   Debenture Application A/c
   Discount on issue of debenture A/c
   To Debenture A/c

4. Debenture issued at premium and redeemable at par or at a discount
For receipt of application money:
Bank A/c......Dr.
To Debenture Application
Money A/c
For transfer of application money to debenture account:
Debenture Application A/c
To Debenture A/c
To Securities premium A/c

5. Debenture issued at par and redeemable at premium
For receipt of application money:
Bank A/c......Dr.
To Debenture Application
Money A/c
For transfer of application money to debenture account:
Debenture Application A/c
To Debenture A/c
Call made consequent upon allotment:
Debenture Allotment A/c
Loss on issue of Debenture A/c
To Debenture A/c
To Debenture redemption
Premium A/c

6. Debenture issued at a discount and redeemable at premium
For receipt of application money:
Bank A/c......Dr.
To Debenture Application Money A/c
For transfer of application money to debenture account:
Debenture Application A/c
To Debenture A/c
Call made consequent upon allotment:
Debenture Allotment A/c
Discount /Loss on issue of Debenture A/c (Discount + premium on redemption)
To Debenture A/c
To Debenture redemption
Premium A/c

7. Debenture issued at a premium and redeemable at premium
For receipt of application money:
Bank A/c......Dr.
To Debenture Application
Money A/c
For transfer of application money to debenture account:
Debenture Application A/c
To Debenture A/c

Call made consequent upon allotment:
Debenture Allotment A/c
Loss on issue of Debenture A/c (amount equal to premium on redemption)
To Debenture A/c
To Debenture redemption
Premium A/c

Redemption of Debentures

Redemption of debentures can be categorized into the following:

1. Debenture issued at par and redeemable at par.
2. Debenture issued at discount and redeemable at par.
3. Debenture issued at premium and redeemable at par.
4. Debenture issued at par and redeemable at premium.
5. Debenture issued at a discount and redeemable at premium.
6. Debenture issued at a premium and redeemable at premium.

Journal Entries in Each of the Above Cases are Discussed Below

1. Debenture issued at par and redeemable at par
   -Closing debenture account
   Debenture A/c......Dr.
   To Debenture holders A/c
   -For payment of money to debenture holders:
   Debenture holders A/c
   To Bank A/c

2. Debenture issued at discount and redeemable at par
   -For transfer of loss of discount to profit & loss account:
   Profit & Loss A/c......Dr.
   To Discount on issue of debenture A/c
   the above entry may be repeated during the tenure of the debenture for writing off proportionate discount every year.
   -Closing debenture account
   Debenture A/c......Dr.
   To Debenture holders A/c
   -For payment of money to debenture holders:
   Debenture holders A/c
   To Bank A/c

3. Debenture issued at premium and redeemable at par
   -Closing debenture account
   Debenture A/c......Dr.
   To Debenture holders A/c
   -For payment of money to debenture holders:

Debenture holders A/c
To Bank A/c

4. Debenture issued at par and redeemable at premium
-For transfer of loss of premium to profit & loss account:
Profit & Loss A/c......Dr.
To Loss on issue of debenture A/c

the above entry may be repeated during the tenure of the debenture for writing off pro-portionate premium to be paid on redemption every year.
-Closing debenture and premium account
Debenture A/c......Dr.
Debenture redemption Premium A/c......Dr.
To Debenture holders A/c
-For payment of money to debenture holders:
Debenture holders A/c
To Bank A/c

5. Debenture issued at a discount and redeemable at premium
-For transfer of loss of discount and premium to profit & loss account:
Profit & Loss A/c......Dr.
To Discount / Loss on issue of debenture A/c (Discount + Premium)
-Closing debenture and premium account
Debenture A/c......Dr.
Debenture redemption Premium A/c......Dr.
To Debenture holders A/c
-For payment of money to debenture holders:
Debenture holders A/c
To Bank A/c

6. Debenture issued at a premium and redeemable at premium
-For transfer of loss of discount to profit & loss account:
Profit & Loss A/c......Dr.
To Loss on issue of debenture A/c (Premium on redemption)
-Closing debenture and premium account
Debenture A/c......Dr.
Debenture redemption Premium A/c......Dr.
To Debenture holders A/c
-For payment of money to debenture holders:
Debenture holders A/c
To Bank A/c

Purchase of Debenture

Debentures sometime are purchased in an open market and then cancelled on due date.

Example,

Company has issued 1000 9 % debentures for Rs. 100000. interest being payable half yearly The company purchases 100 debentures at Rs. 98 per debenture cum interest (interest for 6 months).

Journal Entries:

Own Debenture A/c....Dr. 9350

Interest A/c....Dr. 450

To Bank 9800

Suppose out of these debentures 40 debentures sold at Rs. 102 ex interest and remaining are cancelled at the end of 6 months from date of purchase.

Journal Entries:

Bank A/c...DR. 4080

To Own Debentures 4080

To Interest A/c 60

Own Debentures A/c...DR. 340

To Profit & Loss 340

(Profit on sale transferred to P & L A/c)

At the end of 6 months

9% debentures A/c....Dr. 6000

To Own Debenture 5610

To Capital Reserve 390

(Profit on cancellation transferred).

Accounting Principles

For communicating the results of business to outside world, it should be based on certain uniform and scientifically laid down principles or postulates.

Accounting principles mean those rules of conduct or procedures which are adopted by accountants universally while recording the accounting transactions to ensure uniformity, clarity and understanding while recording transactions.

Accounting Concepts

Accounting Concepts are those basic assumptions or conditions upon which accounting is based. Important accounting concepts are:

Business Entity Concept: – Entity is different from it's owner for accounting purposes.

Dual Aspect Concept: – Recording simultaneously debits credits.

Equity+ Liabilities = Assets

Cost Concept: – Assets are normally recorded basis of historical cost i.e. acquisition cost. Market value immaterial, except on concepts of revaluation.

Going Concern Concept: – Always on anticipation that a business will continue for long and will not be liquidated.

Accounting Period Concept: – Though business continues indefinitely, life of business sub-divided into accounting periods (generally of 1 year).

Money Measurement Concept: – Those transactions which are expressed in money terms are only recorded.

Realisation Concept: - Revenue is recognised only when, an agreement is reached or sale is made. Exceptions may be on certain businesses such on HP/sale on contract etc.

Constant Value Concept: - Assumption of constant value of currency e.g. rupee.

Accrual Concept: - Under this concept, the effects of transactions and other events are recognised on mercantile basis i.e. when they occur (and not as cash received or paid).

Consistency: – In order to achieve comparability of the financial statements of a enterprise through time, the accounting policies are followed consistently from the one period to another. A change in accounting policy is made only in certain exceptional circumstances.

Fundamental Accounting Assumptions are:

Going Concern, Consistency, and Accrual.

If nothing has been mentioned about fundamental accounting assumptions in the financial statements then it is assumed that they have already been followed in the preparation of financial statements.

However, if any of the above mentioned fundamental accounting assumption is not followed then this fact should be disclosed.

Exercise

Consider the following data pertaining to L Ltd.

Cost of the land purchased on 1st April 2010 Rs. 2,50,000.

Registration Charges Rs. 5,000.

Market Value as on 31st 2012 Rs.5,00,000.

While finalising the annual accounts, if the company values land at Rs. 5,00,000.

Which of the following concept is violated by L Ltd?

Cost, Accrual, Matching, Conservatism.

Accounting Standards

- Accounting Standards are written policy document issued by expert accounting body or by government or regulatory body covering the aspects of recognition, treatment, measurement, presentation and disclosure of accounting transaction and events in the financial statements.
- Accounting Standards (ASs) provide framework and standard accounting policies so that financial statements of different enterprises become comparable.
- The Accounting Standards seek to ensure that the financial statements of an enterprise should give a true and fair view of its financial position and working results.
- The Accounting Standards not only prescribe appropriate accounting treatment of complex business transactions but also foster greater transparency and market discipline.

Accounting Standards promote:

- Uniformity.
- Rationalization.
- Comparability.
- Transparency.

Generally Accepted Accounting Principles

Financial statements prepared and presented by a company typically follow an external standard that specifically guides their preparation. These standards vary across the globe and are typically overseen by some combination of the private accounting profession in that specific nation and the various government regulators. Variations across countries may be considerable making cross country evaluation of financial data challenging.

Publicly traded companies typically are subject to the most rigorous standards. Small and midsize businesses often follow more simplified standards, plus any specific disclosures required by their specific lenders and shareholders. Some firms operate on the cash method of accounting which can often be simple and straight forward. Larger firms most often operate on an accrual basis. Accounting standards prescribe in considerable detail what accruals must be made, how the financial statements are to be presented, and what additional disclosures are required.

Some important elements that accounting standards cover include: identifying the exact entity which is reporting, discussing any "going concern" questions, specifying monetary units, and reporting time frames.

Limitations

Accounting standards were largely written in the early 21st century. Massive *accounting irregularities* at large firms such as Worldcom and Enron illustrate that despite all the efforts widespread fraud can still occur, and even be missed by the outside auditors.

Benefits of Accounting Standards

The lack of transparent accounting standards in some nations has been cited as increasing the difficulty of doing business in them. In particular, the Asian financial meltdown in the late 1990s has been partially attributed due to the lack of detailed accounting standards. Giant firms in some Asian countries were able to take advantage of their poorly devised accounting standards to cover up immense debts and losses, which yielded a collective effect that eventually led the whole region into financial crisis.

Common Accounting Standards Around the Globe

- International Financial Reporting Standards.

This standard is adopted in whole, or in large part, by many countries. Its acceptable in the U.S. (for a firm located outside of the U.S.) to report in this widely accepted format.

Accounting Standards by Nation

- China - Chinese Accounting Standards.
- Canada - Generally Accepted Accounting Principles.
- France - Generally Accepted Accounting Practice (*Plan Comptable Général*).
- Germany - Generally Accepted Accounting Practice (*Grundsätze ordnungsmäßiger Buchführung*).
- India - Indian Accounting Standards.
- Nepal - Nepal Financial Reporting Standards.
- Russia - Russian GAAP.
- United Kingdom - Generally Accepted Accounting Practice (UK).
- United States - Generally Accepted Accounting Principles (United States) Domestic firms typically report in this format. Foreign firms that trade in the U.S. typically report in IFRS format.

Global Standardization and IFRS

Many countries use or are converging on the International Financial Reporting Standards (IFRS) that were established and are maintained by the International Accounting Standards Board. In some countries, local accounting principles are applied for regular companies but listed or large companies must conform to IFRS, so statutory reporting is comparable internationally.

All listed and grouped EU companies have been required to use IFRS since 2005, Canada moved in 2009, Taiwan in 2013, and other countries are adopting local versions.

In the United States, while *"...the SEC published a statement of continued support for a single set of high-quality, globally accepted accounting standards, and acknowledged that IFRS is best positioned to serve this role..."* progress is less evident.

Accounting Standards in India

The Institute of Chartered Accountants of India (ICAI) being apex accounting body in India, constituted the Accounting Standards Board (ASB) on 21st April, 1977, with a view to harmonies the diverse accounting policies and practices in use in India.

- While formulating accounting standards, the ASB takes into consideration the applicable laws, customs, usages and business environment prevailing in the country.
- The ASB also gives due consideration to International Financial Reporting Standards (IFRSs)/ International Accounting Standards (IASs) issued by IASB and tries to integrate them, to the extent possible, in the light of conditions and practices prevailing in India.

Ind AS

In accordance with India's assurance to converge with IFRS, the Ministry of Corporate Affairs (MCA) issued a press release on 25 February 2011, notifying the Ind AS (Indian Accounting Standards).

Several of the requirements of Ind AS are considerably dissimilar from policies and practices presently followed by Indian companies. Further, while finalising the Ind AS, the Indian standard setters have examined individual IFRS and modified the requirements, wherever necessary, to suit Indian requirements. This has resulted in differences between Ind AS and equivalent requirements under IFRS (referred to as 'carve outs').

- Ind AS 101: First-time Adoption of Indian Accounting Standards.
- Ind AS 102: Share based Payment.
- Ind AS 103: Business Combinations.
- Ind AS 104: Insurance Contracts.
- Ind AS 105: Non current Assets Held for Sale and Discontinued Operations.
- Ind AS 106: Exploration for and Evaluation of Mineral Resources.
- Ind AS 107: Financial Instruments: Disclosures.
- Ind AS 108: Operating Segments.
- Ind AS 1: Presentation of Financial Statements.

- Ind AS 2: Inventories.
- Ind AS 7: Statement of Cash Flows.
- Ind AS 8: Accounting Policies, Changes in Accounting Estimates and Errors.
- Ind AS 10: Events after the Reporting Period.
- Ind AS 11: Construction Contracts.
- Ind AS 12: Income Taxes.
- Ind AS 16: Property, Plant and Equipment.
- Ind AS 17: Leases.
- Ind AS 18: Revenue.
- Ind AS 19: Employee Benefits.
- Ind AS 20: Accounting for Government Grants and Disclosure of Government Assistance.
- Ind AS 21: The Effects of Changes in Foreign Exchange Rate.
- Ind AS 23: Borrowing Costs.
- Ind AS 24: Related Party Disclosures.
- Ind AS 27: Consolidated and Separate Financial Statements.
- Ind AS 28: Investments in Associates.
- Ind AS 29: Financial Reporting in Hyperinflationary Economies.
- Ind AS 31: Interests in Joint Ventures.
- Ind AS 32: Financial Instruments: Presentation.
- Ind AS 33: Earnings per Share.
- Ind AS 34: Interim Financial Reporting.
- Ind AS 36: Impairment of Assets.
- Ind AS 37: Provisions, Contingent Liabilities and Contingent Assets.
- Ind AS 38: Intangible Assets.
- Ind AS 39: Financial Instruments: Recognition and Measurement.
- Ind AS 40: Investment Property.

International Financial Reporting Standards

International Financial Reporting Standards (IFRS) are designed as a common global language for business affairs so that company accounts are understandable and comparable across international boundaries. They are a consequence of growing international shareholding and trade and are particularly important for companies that have dealings in several countries. They are progressively replacing the many different national accounting standards. They are the rules to be followed by accountants to maintain books of accounts which are comparable, understandable, reliable and relevant as per the users internal or external.

IFRS, with the exception of *IAS 29 Financial Reporting in Hyperinflationary Economies* and *IFRIC 7 Applying the Restatement Approach under IAS 29*, are authorized in terms of the historical cost paradigm. IAS 29 and IFRIC 7 are authorized in terms of the units of constant purchasing power paradigm.

IFRS began as an attempt to harmonize accounting across the European Union but the value of harmonization quickly made the concept attractive around the world. However, it has been debated whether or not de facto harmonization has occurred. Standards that were issued by IASC (the predecessor of IASB) are still within use today and go by the name International Accounting Standards (IAS), while standards issued by IASB are called IFRS. IAS were issued between 1973 and 2001 by the Board of the International Accounting Standards Committee (IASC). On 1 April 2001, the new International Accounting Standards Board (IASB) took over from the IASC the responsibility for setting International Accounting Standards. During its first meeting the new Board adopted existing IAS and Standing Interpretations Committee standards (SICs). The IASB has continued to develop standards calling the new standards "International Financial Reporting Standards".

In the absence of a Standard or an Interpretation that specifically applies to a transaction, management must use its judgement in developing and applying an accounting policy that results in information that is relevant and reliable. In making that judgement, IAS 8.11 requires management to consider the definitions, recognition criteria, and measurement concepts for assets, liabilities, income, and expenses in the Framework.

Criticisms of IFRS are (1) that they are not being adopted in the US, (2) a number of criticisms from France and (3) that *IAS 29 Financial Reporting in Hyperinflationary Economies* had no positive effect at all during 6 years in Zimbabwe's hyperinflationary economy. The IASB offered responses to the first two criticisms, but has offered no response to the last criticism while IAS 29 was as of March 2014 being implemented in its original ineffective form in Venezuela and Belarus.

Objective of Financial Statements

Financial statements are a structured representation of the financial positions and financial performance of an entity. The objective of financial statements is to provide information about the financial position, financial performance and cash flows of an entity that is useful to a wide range of users in making economic decisions. Financial statements also show the results of the management's stewardship of the resources entrusted to it.

To meet this objective, financial statements provide information about an entity's:

a. assets.

b. liabilities.

c. equity.

d. income and expenses, including gains and losses.

e. contributions by and distributions to owners in their capacity as owners.

f. cash flows.

This information, along with other information in the notes, assists users of financial statements in predicting the entity's future cash flows and, in particular, their timing and certainty.

The following are the general features in IFRS:

- Fair presentation and compliance with IFRS: Fair presentation requires the faithful representation of the effects of the transactions, other events and conditions in accordance with the definitions and recognition criteria for assets, liabilities, income and expenses set out in the Framework of IFRS.
- Going concern: Financial statements are present on a going concern basis unless management either intends to liquidate the entity or to cease trading, or has no realistic alternative but to do so.
- Accrual basis of accounting: An entity shall recognise items as assets, liabilities, equity, income and expenses when they satisfy the definition and recognition criteria for those elements in the Framework of IFRS.
- Materiality and aggregation: Every material class of similar items has to be presented separately. Items that are of a dissimilar nature or function shall be presented separately unless they are immaterial.
- Offsetting: Offsetting is generally forbidden in IFRS. However certain standards require offsetting when specific conditions are satisfied (such as in case of the accounting for defined benefit liabilities in IAS 19 and the net presentation of deferred tax liabilities and deferred tax assets in IAS 12).
- Frequency of reporting: IFRS requires that at least annually a complete set of financial statements is presented. However listed companies generally also publish interim financial statements (for which the accounting is fully IFRS compliant)for which the presentation is in accordance with IAS 34 *Interim Financing Reporting*.
- Comparative information: IFRS requires entities to present comparative information in respect of the preceding period for all amounts reported in the current period's financial statements. In addition comparative information shall also be provided for narrative and descriptive information if it is relevant to understanding the current period's financial statements. The standard IAS 1 also requires an additional statement of financial position (also called a third balance sheet) when an entity applies an accounting policy retrospectively or makes a retrospective restatement of items in its financial statements, or when it reclassifies items in its financial statements. This for example occurred with the adoption of the revised standard IAS 19 (as of 1 January 2013) or when the new consolidation standards IFRS 10-11-12 were adopted (as of 1 January 2013 or 2014 for companies in the European Union).
- Consistency of presentation: IFRS requires that the presentation and classification of items in the financial statements is retained from one period to the next unless:

a. It is apparent, following a significant change in the nature of the entity's operations or a review of its financial statements, that another presentation or classification would be more appropriate having regard to the criteria for the selection and application of accounting policies in IAS 8.

b. An IFRS standard requires a change in presentation.

Qualitative Characteristics of Financial Information

Fundamental qualitative characteristics of financial information include:

- Relevance.
- Faithful representation.

Enhancing qualitative characteristics include:

- Comparability.
- Verifiability.
- Timeliness.
- Understandability.

Elements of Financial Statements

The elements directly related to the measurement of the statement of financial position include:

- Asset: An asset is a resource controlled by the entity as a result of past events and from which future economic benefits are expected to flow to the entity.
- Liability: A liability is a present obligation of the entity arising from the past events, the settlement of which is expected to result in an outflow from the entity of resources embodying economic benefits, i.e. assets.
- Equity: Nominal equity is the nominal residual interest in the nominal assets of the entity after deducting all its liabilities in nominal value.

The financial performance of an entity is presented in the statement of comprehensive income, which consists of the income statement (Statement of Profit/Loss) and the statement of other comprehensive income (usually presented in two separate statements). Financial performance includes the following elements (which are recognised in the income statement or other comprehensive income as required by the applicable IFRS standard):

- Revenues: increases in economic benefit during an accounting period in the form of inflows or enhancements of assets, or decrease of liabilities that result in increases in equity. However, it does not include the contributions made by the equity participants (for example owners, partners or shareholders).

- Expenses: decreases in economic benefits during an accounting period in the form of outflows, or depletions of assets or incurrences of liabilities that result in decreases in equity. However, these don't include the distributions made to the equity participants.

Results recognised in other comprehensive income are limited to the following specific circumstances:

- Remeasurements of defined benefit assets or liabilities (as defined in the standard IAS 19).
- Increases or decreases in the fair value of financial assets classified as available for sale (with the exception of impairment losses)(as defined in the standard IAS 39).
- Increases or decreases resulting from the application of a revaluation of property, plant and equipment or intangible assets.
- Exchange differences resulting from the translation of foreign operations (subsidiary, associate, joint arrangement or branch of a reporting entity, the activities of which are conducted in a country or currency other than those of the reporting entity) according to the standard IAS 21.
- The portion of the gain or loss on the hedging instrument in a cash flow hedge (or a hedge of a net investment in a foreign operation, as this is accounted similarly) that is determined to be an effective hedge.

The statement of changes in equity consists of a reconciliation of the changes in equity in which the following information is provided:

- Total comprehensive income for the period, showing separately the total amounts attributable to owners of the parent and to non-controlling interests.
- For each component of equity, the effects of retrospective application or retrospective restatement recognised in accordance with IAS 8.
- For each component of equity, a reconciliation between the carrying amount at the beginning and the end of the period, separately disclosing changes resulting from:
  - Profit or loss.
  - Other comprehensive income.
  - Transactions with owners in their capacity as owners, showing separately contributions by and distributions to owners and changes in ownership interests in subsidiaries that do not result in a loss of control.

Statement of Cash Flows

- Operating cash flows: the principal revenue-producing activities of the entity and are generally calculated by applying the indirect method, whereby profit or loss is adjusted for the effects of transaction of a non-cash nature, any deferrals or accruals of past or future cash receipts or payments, and items of income or expense associated with investing or financing cash flows.

- Investing cash flows: the acquisition and disposal of long-term assets and other investments not included in cash equivalents. These represent the extent to which expenditures have been made for resources intended to generate future income and cash flows. Only expenditures that result in a recognised asset in the statement of financial position are eligible for classification as investing activities.
- Financing cash flows: activities that result in changes in the size and composition of the contributed equity and borrowings of the entity. These are important because they are useful in predicting claims on future cash flows by providers of capital to the entity.

Notes to the Financial Statements: These shall (a) present information about the basis of preparation of the financial statements and the specific accounting policies used; (b) disclose the information required by IFRSs that is not presented elsewhere in the financial statements; and (c) provide information that is not presented elsewhere in the financial statements, but is relevant to an understanding of any of them.

Recognition of Elements of Financial Statements

An item is recognized in the financial statements when:

- It is probable future economic benefit will flow to or from an entity.
- The resource can be reliably measured.

In some cases specific standards add additional conditions before recognition is possible or prohibit recognition altogether.

An example is the recognition of internally generated brands, mastheads, publishing titles, customer lists and items similar in substance, for which recognition is prohibited by IAS 38. In addition research and development expenses can only be recognised as an intangible asset if they cross the threshold of being classified as 'development cost'.

Whilst the standard on provisions, IAS 37, prohibits the recognition of a provision for contingent liabilities, this prohibition is not applicable to the accounting for contingent liabilities in a business combination. In that case the acquirer shall recognise a contingent liability even if it is not probable that an outflow of resources embodying economic benefits will be required.

International Financial Reporting Standards (IFRS) are designed as a common global language for business affairs so that company accounts are understandable and comparable across international boundaries. They are a consequence of growing international.

Concepts of Capital and Capital Maintenance

Concepts of Capital

Par. 102. A financial concept of capital is adopted by most entities in preparing their financial statements. Under a financial concept of capital, such as invested money or invested purchasing power, capital is synonymous with the net assets or equity of the entity. Under a physical concept of capital, such as operating capability, capital is regarded as the productive capacity of the entity based on, for example, units of output per day.

Par. 103. The selection of the appropriate concept of capital by an entity should be based on the needs of the users of its financial statements. Thus, a financial concept of capital should be adopted if the users of financial statements are primarily concerned with the maintenance of nominal invested capital or the purchasing power of invested capital. If, however, the main concern of users is with the operating capability of the entity, a physical concept of capital should be used. The concept chosen indicates the goal to be attained in determining profit, even though there may be some measurement difficulties in making the concept operational.

Concepts of Capital Maintenance and the Determination of Profit

Par. 104. The concepts of capital in paragraph 102 give rise to the following two concepts of capital maintenance:

(a) Financial capital maintenance. Under this concept a profit is earned only if the financial (or money) amount of the net assets at the end of the period exceeds the financial (or money) amount of net assets at the beginning of the period, after excluding any distributions to, and contributions from, owners during the period. Financial capital maintenance can be measured in either nominal monetary units or units of constant purchasing power.

(b) Physical capital maintenance. Under this concept a profit is earned only if the physical productive capacity (or operating capability) of the entity (or the resources or funds needed to achieve that capacity) at the end of the period exceeds the physical productive capacity at the beginning of the period, after excluding any distributions to, and contributions from, owners during the period.

The concepts of capital in paragraph 102 give rise to the following three concepts of capital during low inflation and deflation:

- (A) Physical capital.
- (B) Nominal financial capital.
- (C) Constant item purchasing power financial capital.

The concepts of capital in paragraph 102 give rise to the following three concepts of capital maintenance during low inflation and deflation:

(1) Physical capital maintenance: optional during low inflation and deflation. Current Cost Accounting model prescribed by IFRS.

(2) Financial capital maintenance in nominal monetary units (Historical cost accounting): authorized by IFRS but not prescribed—optional during low inflation and deflation. (a) Historical cost accounting. Financial capital maintenance in nominal monetary units per se during inflation and deflation is a fallacy: it is impossible to maintain the real value of financial capital constant with measurement in nominal monetary units per se during inflation and deflation.

(3) Financial capital maintenance in units of constant purchasing power (Capital Maintenance in Units of Constant Purchasing Power): authorized by IFRS but not prescribed—optional during low inflation and deflation. Capital Maintenance in Units of Constant Purchasing

Power is prescribed during hyperinflation in IAS 29: i.e. the restatement of Historical Cost or Current Cost period-end financial statements in terms of the period-end monthly published Consumer Price Index. Only financial capital maintenance in units of constant purchasing power (Capital Maintenance in Units of Constant Purchasing Power) in terms of a daily index per se can automatically maintain the real value of financial capital constant at all levels of inflation and deflation in all entities that at least break even in real value—ceteris paribus—for an indefinite period of time. This would happen whether these entities own revaluable fixed assets or not and without the requirement of more capital or additional retained profits to simply maintain the existing constant real value of existing shareholders' equity constant. Financial capital maintenance in units of constant purchasing power requires the calculation and accounting of net monetary losses and gains from holding monetary items during low inflation and deflation. The calculation and accounting of net monetary losses and gains during low inflation and deflation have thus been authorized in IFRS since 1989.

Par. 105. The concept of capital maintenance is concerned with how an entity defines the capital that it seeks to maintain. It provides the linkage between the concepts of capital and the concepts of profit because it provides the point of reference by which profit is measured; it is a prerequisite for distinguishing between an entity's return on capital and its return of capital; only inflows of assets in excess of amounts needed to maintain capital may be regarded as profit and therefore as a return on capital. Hence, profit is the residual amount that remains after expenses (including capital maintenance adjustments, where appropriate) have been deducted from income. If expenses exceed income the residual amount is a loss.

Par. 106. The physical capital maintenance concept requires the adoption of the current cost basis of measurement. The financial capital maintenance concept, however, does not require the use of a particular basis of measurement. Selection of the basis under this concept is dependent on the type of financial capital that the entity is seeking to maintain.

Par. 107. The principal difference between the two concepts of capital maintenance is the treatment of the effects of changes in the prices of assets and liabilities of the entity. In general terms, an entity has maintained its capital if it has as much capital at the end of the period as it had at the beginning of the period. Any amount over and above that required to maintain the capital at the beginning of the period is profit.

Par. 108. Under the concept of financial capital maintenance where capital is defined in terms of nominal monetary units, profit represents the increase in nominal money capital over the period. Thus, increases in the prices of assets held over the period, conventionally referred to as holding gains, are, conceptually, profits. They may not be recognised as such, however, until the assets are disposed of in an exchange transaction. When the concept of financial capital maintenance is defined in terms of constant purchasing power units, profit represents the increase in invested purchasing power over the period. Thus, only that part of the increase in the prices of assets that exceeds the increase in the general level of prices is regarded as profit. The rest of the increase is treated as a capital maintenance adjustment and, hence, as part of equity.

Par. 109. Under the concept of physical capital maintenance when capital is defined in terms of the physical productive capacity, profit represents the increase in that capital over the period. All price changes affecting the assets and liabilities of the entity are viewed as changes in the measurement of the physical productive capacity of the entity; hence, they are treated as capital maintenance adjustments that are part of equity and not as profit.

Par. 110. The selection of the measurement bases and concept of capital maintenance will determine the accounting model used in the preparation of the financial statements. Different accounting models exhibit different degrees of relevance and reliability and, as in other areas, management must seek a balance between relevance and reliability. This Framework is applicable to a range of accounting models and provides guidance on preparing and presenting the financial statements constructed under the chosen model. At the present time, it is not the intention of the Board of IASC to prescribe a particular model other than in exceptional circumstances, such as for those entities reporting in the currency of a hyperinflationary economy. This intention will, however, be reviewed in the light of world developments.

Requirements

- A Statement of Financial Position.
- A Statement of Comprehensive Income separate statements comprising an Income Statement and separately a Statement of Comprehensive Income, which reconciles Profit or Loss on the Income statement to total comprehensive income.
- A Statement of Changes in Equity (SOCE).
- A Cash Flow Statement or Statement of Cash Flows.
- Notes, including a summary of the significant accounting policies.

Comparative information is required for the prior reporting period (IAS 1.36). An entity preparing IFRS accounts for the first time must apply IFRS in full for the current and comparative period although there are transitional exemptions (IFRS1.7).

On 6 September 2007, the IASB issued a revised IAS 1 Presentation of Financial Statements. The main changes from the previous version are to require that an entity must:

- Present all non-owner changes in equity (that is, 'comprehensive income') *either* in one Statement of comprehensive income or in two statements (a separate income statement and a statement of comprehensive income). Components of comprehensive income may *not* be presented in the Statement of changes in equity.
- Present a statement of financial position (balance sheet) as at the beginning of the earliest comparative period in a complete set of financial statements when the entity applies the new standard.
- Present a statement of cash flow.
- Make necessary disclosure by the way of a note.

The revised IAS 1 is effective for annual periods beginning on or after 1 January 2009. Early adoption is permitted.

Criticisms of IFRS

In 2012 the US Securities and Exchange Commission Staff issued a 127-page report of potential issues with IFRS that would need to be addressed before adoption by the United States. The staff of the IFRS Foundation provided a detailed answer on the main criticisms in the SEC staff report.

A number of criticisms were voiced in the beginning of 2013 in the French media to which the IASB Board member Philippe Danjou responded in his document 'An Update on International Financial Reporting Standards (IFRSs).'

It is widely acknowledged that *IAS 29 Financial Reporting in Hyperinflationary Economies* had no positive effect during the six years it was implemented during hyperinflation in Zimbabwe. This led people to ask the purpose of IAS 29. As of March 2014, IAS 29 was being implemented in its original ineffective form in Venezuela and Belarus. It was suggested to the IASB in 2012 that IAS 29 should be corrected to require daily indexation which would result in effective constant purchasing power accounting and would stabilize the non-monetary economy during hyperinflation. The IASB has offered no response to date (March 2014) to this criticism and has not yet altered IAS 29 to require daily indexation.

Adoption

IFRS are used in many parts of the world, including the South Korea, European Union, India, Hong Kong, Australia, Malaysia, Pakistan, GCC countries, Russia, Chile, Philippines, South Africa, Singapore and Turkey, but not in the United States. Please refer to PricewaterhouseCoopers' "IFRS by country" publication for a detailed explanation of the level of IFRS adoption per country. 140 Jurisdiction profiles are available online.

It is generally expected that IFRS adoption worldwide will be beneficial to investors and other users of financial statements, by reducing the costs of comparing alternative investments and increasing the quality of information. Companies are also expected to benefit, as investors will be more willing to provide financing. Companies that have high levels of international activities are among the group that would benefit from a switch to IFRS. Companies that are involved in foreign activities and investing benefit from the switch due to the increased comparability of a set accounting standard. However, Ray J. Ball has expressed some skepticism of the overall cost of the international standard; he argues that the enforcement of the standards could be lax, and the regional differences in accounting could become obscured behind a label. He also expressed concerns about the fair value emphasis of IFRS and the influence of accountants from non-common-law regions, where losses have been recognized in a less timely manner.

To assess progress towards the goal of a single set global accounting standards, the IFRS Foundation has developed and posted profiles about the use of IFRSs in individual jurisdictions. These were based on information from various sources. The starting point was the responses provided by standard-setting and other relevant bodies to a survey that the IFRS Foundation conducted. Currently, profiles are completed for 124 jurisdictions, including all of the G20 jurisdictions plus 104 others. Eventually, the plan is to have a profile for every jurisdiction that has adopted IFRSs, or is on a programme toward adoption of IFRSs.

Australia

The Australian Accounting Standards Board (AASB) has issued 'Australian equivalents to IFRS' (A-IFRS), numbering IFRS standards as AASB 1–8 and IAS standards as AASB 101–141. Australian equivalents to SIC and IFRIC Interpretations have also been issued, along with a number of 'domestic' standards and interpretations. These pronouncements replaced previous Australian generally accepted accounting principles with effect from annual reporting periods beginning on or after 1 January 2005 (i.e. 30 June 2006 was the first report prepared under IFRS-equivalent standards for June year ends). To this end, Australia, along with Europe and a few other countries, was one of the initial adopters of IFRS for domestic purposes (in the developed world). It must be acknowledged, however, that IFRS and primarily IAS have been part and parcel of accounting standard package in the developing world for many years since the relevant accounting bodies were more open to adoption of international standards for many reasons including that of capability.

The AASB has made certain amendments to the IASB pronouncements in making A-IFRS, however these generally have the effect of eliminating an option under IFRS, introducing additional disclosures or implementing requirements for not-for-profit entities, rather than departing from IFRS for Australian entities. Accordingly, for-profit entities that prepare financial statements in accordance with A-IFRS are able to make an unreserved statement of compliance with IFRS.

The AASB continues to mirror changes made by the IASB as local pronouncements. In addition, over recent years, the AASB has issued so-called 'Amending Standards' to reverse some of the initial changes made to the IFRS text for local terminology differences, to reinstate options and eliminate some Australian-specific disclosure. There are some calls for Australia to simply adopt IFRS without 'Australianising' them and this has resulted in the AASB itself looking at alternative ways of adopting IFRS in Australia.

Brazil

Brazil has already adopted IFRS for all companies whose securities are publicly traded and for most financial institutions whose securities are not publicly traded, for both consolidated and separate (individual) company financial statements.

Canada

The use of IFRS became a requirement for Canadian publicly accountable profit-oriented enterprises for financial periods beginning on or after 1 January 2011. This includes public companies and other "profit-oriented enterprises that are responsible to large or diverse groups of shareholders."

European Union

In 2002 the European Union agreed that from 1 January 2005 International Accounting Standards / International Financial Reporting Standards would apply for the consolidated accounts of the EU listed companies.

In order to be approved for use in the EU, standards must be endorsed by the Accounting Regulatory Committee (ARC), which includes representatives of member state governments and is advised by a group of accounting experts known as the European Financial Reporting Advisory Group. As a result, IFRS as applied in the EU may differ from that used elsewhere.

Parts of the standard IAS 39: Financial Instruments: Recognition and Measurement were not originally approved by the ARC. IAS 39 was subsequently amended, removing the option to record financial liabilities at fair value, and the ARC approved the amended version. The IASB is working with the EU to find an acceptable way to remove a remaining anomaly in respect of hedge accounting. The World Bank Centre for Financial Reporting Reform is working with countries in the ECA region to facilitate the adoption of IFRS and IFRS for SMEs.

Whilst the IASB set the effective dates for the new consolidation standards IFRS 10 *Consolidated Financial Statements*, IFRS 11 *Joint Arrangements* and IFRS 12 *Disclosure of Interests in Other Entities* at 1 January 2013, the ARC decided to delay the mandatory effective date for the companies listed in the European Union by one year. The standards therefore only became effective on 1 January 2014.

The European Commission has launched a general analysis of the impacts of 8 years of use of international financial reporting standards (IFRSs) in the EU for preparers and users of financial statements from the private sector. The study will include an overall assessment of whether the Regulation 1606/2002 of the European Parliament and the Council ('IAS Regulation') has met the two-fold initial objectives of ensuring a high degree of transparency and comparability of the financial statements of European companies and an efficient functioning of the market, in comparison with the situation before IFRS implementation in 2005. It will also include a cost-benefit analysis and an assessment and analysis of the benefits and drawbacks brought by the IAS Regulation for different stakeholder groups.

Ghana

Ghana transitioned from the Ghana Accounting Standards (GAS) to adopt the IFRS on January 1, 2007. As of 2008 and beyond, a legislative injunction has been imposed on the Bank of Ghana to prepare financial statements in accordance with IFRS; thereby making it mandatory for all public entities in the country.

India

The Institute of Chartered Accountants of India (ICAI) has announced that IFRS will be mandatory in India for financial statements for the periods beginning on or after 1 April 2016 in a phased manner. There is a roadmap issued by MCA for adoption of IFRS.

Reserve Bank of India has stated that financial statements of banks need to be IFRS-compliant for periods beginning on or after 1 April 2011.

The ICAI has also stated that IFRS will be applied to companies above INR 1000 crore (INR 10 billion) from April 2011. Phase wise applicability details for different companies in India:

Phase 1: Opening balance sheet as at 1 April 2011*

i. Companies which are part of NSE Index – Nifty 50.

ii. Companies which are part of BSE Index – Sensex 30.

   a. Companies whose shares or other securities are listed on a stock exchange outside India.

   b. Companies, whether listed or not, having net worth of more than INR 1000 crore (INR 10 billion).

Phase 2: Opening balance sheet as at 1 April 2012*

Companies not covered in phase 1 and having net worth exceeding INR 500 crore (INR 5 billion).

Phase 3: Opening balance sheet as at 1 April 2014*

Listed companies not covered in the earlier phases * If the financial year of a company commences at a date other than 1 April, then it shall prepare its opening balance sheet at the commencement of immediately following financial year.

On 22 January 2010, the Ministry of Corporate Affairs issued the road map for transition to IFRS. It is clear that India has deferred transition to IFRS by a year. In the first phase, companies included in Nifty 50 or BSE Sensex, and companies whose securities are listed on stock exchanges outside India and all other companies having net worth of INR 10 billion will prepare and present financial statements using Indian Accounting Standards converged with IFRS. According to the press note issued by the government, those companies will convert their first balance sheet as at 1 April 2011, applying accounting standards convergent with IFRS if the accounting year ends on 31 March. This implies that the transition date will be 1 April 2011. According to the earlier plan, the transition date was fixed at 1 April 2010.

The press note does not clarify whether the full set of financial statements for the year 2011–12 will be prepared by applying accounting standards convergent with IFRS. The deferment of the transition may make companies happy, but it will undermine India's position. Presumably, lack of preparedness of Indian companies has led to the decision to defer the adoption of IFRS for a year. This is unfortunate that India, which boasts for its IT and accounting skills, could not prepare itself for the transition to IFRS over last four years. But that might be the ground reality.

Transition in Phases

Companies, whether listed or not, having net worth of more than INR 5 billion will convert their opening balance sheet as at 1 April 2013. Listed companies having net worth of INR 5 billion or less will convert their opening balance sheet as at 1 April 2014. Un-listed companies having net worth of Rs5 billion or less will continue to apply existing accounting standards, which might be modified from time to time. Transition to IFRS in phases is a smart move.

The transition cost for smaller companies will be much lower because large companies will bear the initial cost of learning and smaller companies will not be required to reinvent the wheel. However, this will happen only if a significant number of large companies engage Indian accounting firms to provide them support in their transition to IFRS. If, most large companies, which will comply with Indian accounting standards convergent with IFRS in the first phase, choose one of the international firms, Indian accounting firms and smaller companies will not benefit from the learning in the first phase of the transition to IFRS.

It is likely that international firms will protect their learning to retain their competitive advantage. Therefore, it is for the benefit of the country that each company makes judicious choice of the accounting firm as its partner without limiting its choice to international accounting firms. Public sector companies should take the lead and the Institute of Chartered Accountants of India (ICAI) should develop a clear strategy to diffuse the learning.

Size of Companies

The government has decided to measure the size of companies in terms of net worth. This is not the ideal unit to measure the size of a company. Net worth in the balance sheet is determined by accounting principles and methods. Therefore, it does not include the value of intangible assets. Moreover, as most assets and liabilities are measured at historical cost, the net worth does not reflect the current value of those assets and liabilities. Market capitalisation is a better measure of the size of a company. But it is difficult to estimate market capitalisation or fundamental value of unlisted companies. This might be the reason that the government has decided to use 'net worth' to measure size of companies. Some companies, which are large in terms of fundamental value or which intend to attract foreign capital, might prefer to use Indian accounting standards convergent with IFRS earlier than required under the road map presented by the government. The government should provide that choice.

Japan

The minister for Financial Services in Japan announced in late June 2011 that mandatory application of the IFRS should not take place from fiscal year-ending March 2015; five to seven years should be required for preparation if mandatory application is decided; and to permit the use of U.S. GAAP beyond the fiscal year ending 31 March 2016.

Montenegro

Montenegro gained independence from Serbia in 2006. Its accounting standard setter is the Institute of Accountants and Auditors of Montenegro (IAAM). In 2005, IAAM adopted a revised version of the 2002 "Law on Accounting and Auditing" which authorized the use of IFRS for all entities. IFRS is currently required for all consolidated and standalone financial statements, however, enforcement is not effective except in the banking sector. Financial statements for banks in Montenegro are, generally, of high quality and can be compared to those of the European Union. Foreign companies listed on Montenegro's two stock exchanges (Montenegro Stock Exchange and NEX Stock Exchange) are also required to apply IFRS in their financial statements. Montenegro does not have a national GAAP. Currently, no Montenegrin translation of IFRS exists, and because of this Montenegro applies the Serbian translation from 2010. IFRS for SMEs is not currently applied in Montenegro.

Nepal

In Nepal the Accounting Standards Board (ASB) is in charge of standard setting. Nepal closely models its Financial Reporting Standards (FRS) according to the IFRS, with appropriate changes made to suit the Nepalese context. It has issued Nepal Financial Reporting Standards in 2013. The 2013 version of standards almost resembles IFRS with slight modification.

Pakistan

All listed companies must follow all issued IAS/IFRS except the following:

IAS 39 and IAS 41: Implementation of these standards has been held in abeyance by State Bank of Pakistan for Banks and DFIs.

IFRS-1: Effective for the annual periods beginning on or after 1 January 2004. This IFRS is being considered for adoption for all companies other than banks and DFIs.

IFRS-9: Under consideration of the relevant Committee of the Institutes (ICAP & ICMAP). This IFRS will be effective for the annual periods beginning on or after 1 January 2013.

Russia

The government of Russia has been implementing a program to harmonize its national accounting standards with IFRS since 1998. Since then twenty new accounting standards were issued by the Ministry of Finance of the Russian Federation aiming to align accounting practices with IFRS. Despite these efforts essential differences between Russian accounting standards and IFRS remain. Since 2004 all commercial banks have been obliged to prepare financial statements in accordance with both Russian accounting standards and IFRS. Full transition to IFRS is delayed but starting 2012 new modifications making Russian GAAP converging to IFRS have been made. They notably include the booking of reserves for bad debts and contingent liabilities and the devaluation of inventory and financial assets.

Still, several differences between the two sets of account still remain. Major reasons for deviation between Russian GAAP and IFRS / US-GAAP (e.g. when the Russian affiliate of a larger group need to be consolidated to the mother company) are the following:

1. Booking of payables in the General Ledger according to national accounting standards can only be made upon receipt of the actual acceptance protocol (good's receipt). Indeed, in Russia, in contrast to IFRS and US-GAAP, the invoice (outgoing or incoming) is not an official tax or accounting document and does not trigger any booking. There is also no provision to book in the General Ledger any expense for goods and services that according to a contract are effectively received but for whom documents are still not exchanged.
2. There is no possibility under Russian GAAP to recognise the good-will as an intangible asset in the balance sheet of a company. This has a major consequence when a company is sold. Indeed, if a company (or part of it) is sold at a higher value than its book value (i.e. to account for the good-will value), the selling party need to pay tax at the relevant profit tax rate (20% in 2013) on the difference in value between selling and accounting value and the buyer has no possibility to amortize the cost and deduct it from present and future revenues.
3. There is no equivalent of IAS 37 in the Russian GAAP. Loans and monetary securities are not discounted, so the present value of such financial assets is not discounted for the relevant interest rates at the different maturities of the loans.

Singapore

In Singapore the Accounting Standards Committee (ASC) is in charge of standard setting. Singapore closely models its Financial Reporting Standards (FRS) according to the IFRS, with appropriate changes made to suit the Singapore context. Before a standard is enacted, consultations with the IASB are made to ensure consistency of core principles.

South Africa

All companies listed on the Johannesburg Stock Exchange have been required to comply with the requirements of International Financial Reporting Standards since 1 January 2005.

The IFRS for SMEs may be applied by 'limited interest companies', as defined in the South African Corporate Laws Amendment Act of 2006 (that is, they are not 'widely held'), if they do not have public accountability (that is, not listed and not a financial institution). Alternatively, the company may choose to apply full South African Statements of GAAP or IFRS.

South African Statements of GAAP are entirely consistent with IFRS, although there may be a delay between issuance of an IFRS and the equivalent SA Statement of GAAP (can affect voluntary early adoption).

Taiwan

Adoption scope and timetable:

(1) Phase I companies: listed companies and financial institutions supervised by the Financial Supervisory Commission (FSC), except for credit cooperatives, credit card companies and insurance intermediaries:

A. They will be required to prepare financial statements in accordance with Taiwan-IFRS starting from 1 January 2013.

B. Early optional adoption: Firms that have already issued securities overseas, or have registered an overseas securities issuance with the FSC, or have a market capitalization of greater than NT$10 billion, will be permitted to prepare additional consolidated financial statements in accordance with Taiwan-IFRS starting from 1 January 2012. If a company without subsidiaries is not required to prepare consolidated financial statements, it will be permitted to prepare additional individual financial statements on the above conditions.

(2) Phase II companies: unlisted public companies, credit cooperatives and credit card companies:

A. They will be required to prepare financial statements in accordance with Taiwan-IFRS starting from 1 January 2019.

B. They will be permitted to apply Taiwan-IFRS starting from 1 January 2013.

(3) Pre-disclosure about the IFRS adoption plan, and the impact of adoption.

To prepare properly for IFRS adoption, domestic companies should propose an IFRS adoption plan and establish a specific taskforce. They should also disclose the related information from 2 years prior to adoption, as follows:

A. Phase I companies:

(A) They will be required to disclose the adoption plan, and the impact of adoption, in 2011 annual financial statements, and in 2012 interim and annual financial statements.

(B) Early optional adoption:

a. Companies adopting IFRS early will be required to disclose the adoption plan, and the impact of adoption, in 2010 annual financial statements, and in 2011 interim and annual financial statements.

b. If a company opts for early adoption of Taiwan-IFRS after 1 January 2011, it will be required to disclose the adoption plan, and the impact of adoption, in 2011 interim and annual financial statements commencing on the decision date.

B. Phase II companies will be required to disclose the related information from 2 years prior to adoption, as stated above.

Year Work Plan

2008:

- Establishment of IFRS Taskforce.

2009~2011:

- Acquisition of authorization to translate IFRS.
- Translation, review, and issuance of IFRS.
- Analysis of possible IFRS implementation problems, and resolution thereof.
- Proposal for modification of the related regulations and supervisory mechanisms.
- Enhancement of related publicity and training activities.

2012:

- IFRS application permitted for Phase I companies.
- Study on possible IFRS implementation problems, and resolution thereof.
- Completion of amendments to the related regulations and supervisory mechanisms.
- Enhancement of the related publicity and training activities.

2013:

- Application of IFRS required for Phase I companies, and permitted for Phase II companies.

- Follow-up analysis of the status of IFRS adoption, and of the impact.

2014:

- Follow-up analysis of the status of IFRS adoption, and of the impact.

2015:

- Applications of IFRS required for Phase II companies.

Expected Benefits

(1) More efficient formulation of domestic accounting standards, improvement of their international image, and enhancement of the global rankings and international competitiveness of our local capital markets.

(2) Better comparability between the financial statements of local and foreign companies.

(3) No need for restatement of financial statements when local companies wish to issue overseas securities, resulting in reduction in the cost of raising capital overseas.

(4) For local companies with investments overseas, use of a single set of accounting standards will reduce the cost of account conversions and improve corporate efficiency.

Above is quoted from Accounting Research and Development Foundation.

Turkey

The Banking Regulation and Supervision Agency and Capital Markets Board of Turkey translated IFRS into Turkish in 2002. Banks and Turkish companies listed on the Istanbul Stock Exchange are required to prepare IFRS reports since then. The Turkish Accounting Standards Board (called the Public Oversight Authority after 2011) also translated IFRS in 2005. The new Commercial Code came into force in 2012. The Public Oversight Authority is the only authorized board regarding auditing and financial reporting standards. Most businesses authorized by the Council of Ministers in addition to banks and Turkish companies listed on the Istanbul Stock Exchange are required to prepare IFRS reports since 2012.

Zimbabwe

Zimbabwe also adopted IFRS.

IASs

- IAS 1 Presentation of Financial Statements.
- IAS 2 Inventories.
- IAS 7 Cash Flow Statements.
- IAS 8 Accounting Policies, Changes in Accounting Estimates and Errors.

- IAS 10 Events After the Balance Sheet Date.
- IAS 11 Construction Contracts.
- IAS 12 Income Taxes.
- IAS 16 Property, Plant and Equipment.
- IAS 17 Leases.
- IAS 18 Revenue.
- IAS 19 Employee Benefits.
- IAS 20 Accounting for Government Grants and Disclosure of Government Assistance.
- IAS 21 The Effects of Changes in Foreign Exchange Rates.
- IAS 23 Borrowing Costs.
- IAS 24 Related Party Disclosures.
- IAS 26 Accounting and Reporting by Retirement Benefit Plans.
- IAS 27 Consolidated and Separate Financial Statements.
- IAS 28 Investments in Associates.
- IAS 29 Financial Reporting in Hyperinflationary Economies.
- IAS 31 Interests in Joint Ventures.
- IAS 32 Financial Instruments: Presentation.
- IAS 33 Earnings per Share.
- IAS 34 Interim Financial Reporting.
- IAS 36 Impairment of Assets.
- IAS 37 Provisions, Contingent Liabilities and Contingent Assets.
- IAS 38 Intangible Assets.
- IAS 39 Financial Instruments: Recognition and Measurement.
- IAS 40 Investment Property.
- IAS 41 Agriculture.

GAAP

- To avoid confusion and to achieve uniformity, accounting process is applied within the conceptual framework of 'Generally Accepted Accounting Principles' (GAAP).

- The Financial Statements of entity cannot be said to be showing a true and fair view, unless these Financial Statements have been drawn up on GAAP.
- GAAP consist of four components:
  - The requirements of law.
  - The judgments by courts of law.
  - Pronouncement by the governing bodies (Like ICAI, FASB in US).
  - Requirements of regulatory authority (Like RBI, SEBI, SEC in US).
- GAAPs are the backbone of the accounting information system, without which whole system cannot even stand erectly.
- GAAPs and Accounting Standard are considered as the theory base of accounting.

References

- "AcSB Confirms Changeover Date to IFRSs". Canadian Institute of Chartered Accountants. 13 February 2008. Retrieved 13, March 2020
- Jerry J. Weygandt; Paul D. Kimmel; Donald E. Kieso (5 January 2010). Accounting Principles. John Wiley and Sons. p. 608. ISBN 978-0-470-57725-7. Retrieved 23, February 2020
- Claudia B. Gilbertson; Mark W. Lehman (12 March 2008). Fundamentals of Accounting: Course 1. Cengage Learning. p. 242. ISBN 978-0-538-44826-0. Retrieved 18, April 2020
- "Stammaktie, Vorzugsaktie, Inhaberaktie, Namensakti Die Arten von Aktien" (in German). 2004-03-24. Retrieved 04, June 2020
- Jan Bebbington; Rob Gray; Richard Laughlin (16 August 2001). Financial accounting: practice and principles. Cengage Learning EMEA. p. 6. ISBN 978-1-86152-771-4. Retrieved 13, July 2020

4

Financial Statement and its Types

Financial statement is a written report or record which conveys the business activities and financial performance of a company and includes a summary of the financial results, position and cash flow. Balance sheets, liabilities, income statements, equities, etc. are a few types of financial statements. This chapter covers the financial statements and its types in a clear and concise manner.

Financial Statement

STATEMENT
—OF—
WACHOVIA NATIONAL BANK,
WINSTON, N. C.
JANUARY 29TH, 1906.
(CONDENSED FROM REPORT TO THE COMPTROLLER OF THE CURRENCY.)

RESOURCES.		LIABILITIES.	
Loans, including Overdrafts	$ 511,789.61	Capital	$ 150,000.00
U. S. Bonds and Premiums	52,300.00	Surplus and Undivided Profits	171,167.89
Real Estate, Furniture and Fixtures	4,500.00	Circulation	50,000.00
Redemption fund with U. S. Treasurer	2,500.00	Deposits	468,153.02
Cash and Due from Banks	268,231 30		
	$839,320.91		$839,320.91

W. A. LEMLY, President. JAS. A. GRAY, Cashier.

Historical financial statements.

A financial statements (or financial report) is a formal record of the financial activities and position of a business, person, or other entity.

Relevant financial information is presented in a structured manner and in a form easy to understand. They typically include basic financial statements, accompanied by a management discussion and analysis:

1. A balance sheet, also referred to as a statement of financial position, reports on a company's assets, liabilities, and owners equity at a given point in time.
2. An income statement, also known as a statement of comprehensive income, statement of revenue & expense, P&L or profit and loss report, reports on a company's income, expenses, and profits over a period of time. A profit and loss statement provides information on the operation of the enterprise. These include sales and the various expenses incurred during the stated period.

3. A Statement of changes in equity, also known as equity statement or statement of retained earnings, reports on the changes in equity of the company during the stated period.
4. A cash flow statement reports on a company's cash flow activities, particularly its operating, investing and financing activities.

For large corporations, these statements may be complex and may include an extensive set of footnotes to the financial statements and management discussion and analysis. The notes typically describe each item on the balance sheet, income statement and cash flow statement in further detail. Notes to financial statements are considered an integral part of the financial statements.

Purpose for Business Entities

"The objective of financial statements is to provide information about the financial position, performance and changes in financial position of an enterprise that is useful to a wide range of users in making economic decisions." Financial statements should be understandable, relevant, reliable and comparable. Reported assets, liabilities, equity, income and expenses are directly related to an organization's financial position.

Financial statements are intended to be understandable by readers who have "a reasonable knowledge of business and economic activities and accounting and who are willing to study the information diligently." Financial statements may be used by users for different purposes:

- Owners and managers require financial statements to make important business decisions that affect its continued operations. Financial analysis is then performed on these statements to provide management with a more detailed understanding of the figures. These statements are also used as part of management's annual report to the stockholders.
- Employees also need these reports in making collective bargaining agreements (CBA) with the management, in the case of labor unions or for individuals in discussing their compensation, promotion and rankings.
- Prospective investors make use of financial statements to assess the viability of investing in a business. Financial analyses are often used by investors and are prepared by professionals (financial analysts), thus providing them with the basis for making investment decisions.
- Financial institutions (banks and other lending companies) use them to decide whether to grant a company with fresh working capital or extend debt securities (such as a long-term bank loan or debentures) to finance expansion and other significant expenditures.

Consolidated

Consolidated financial statements are defined as "Financial statements of a group in which the assets, liabilities, equity, income, expenses and cash flows of the parent (company) and its subsidiaries are presented as those of a single economic entity", according to International Accounting Standard 27 "Consolidated and separate financial statements", and International Financial Reporting Standard 10 "Consolidated financial statements".

Government

The rules for the recording, measurement and presentation of government financial statements may be different from those required for business and even for non-profit organizations. They may use either of two accounting methods: accrual accounting, or cost accounting, or a combination of the two (OCBOA). A complete set of chart of accounts is also used that is substantially different from the chart of a profit-oriented business.

Personal

Personal financial statements may be required from persons applying for a personal loan or financial aid. Typically, a personal financial statement consists of a single form for reporting personally held assets and liabilities (debts), or personal sources of income and expenses, or both. The form to be filled out is determined by the organization supplying the loan or aid.

Audit and Legal Implications

Although laws differ from country to country, an audit of the financial statements of a public company is usually required for investment, financing, and tax purposes. These are usually performed by independent accountants or auditing firms. Results of the audit are summarized in an audit report that either provide an unqualified opinion on the financial statements or qualifications as to its fairness and accuracy. The audit opinion on the financial statements is usually included in the annual report.

There has been much legal debate over who an auditor is liable to. Since audit reports tend to be addressed to the current shareholders, it is commonly thought that they owe a legal duty of care to them. But this may not be the case as determined by common law precedent. In Canada, auditors are liable only to investors using a prospectus to buy shares in the primary market. In the United Kingdom, they have been held liable to potential investors when the auditor was aware of the potential investor and how they would use the information in the financial statements. Nowadays auditors tend to include in their report liability restricting language, discouraging anyone other than the addressees of their report from relying on it. Liability is an important issue: in the UK, for example, auditors have unlimited liability.

In the United States, especially in the post-Enron era there has been substantial concern about the accuracy of financial statements. Corporate officers (the chief executive officer (CEO) and chief financial officer (CFO)) are personally responsible for fair financial reporting allowing those reading the report to have a good sense of the organization.

Standards and Regulations

Different countries have developed their own accounting principles over time, making international comparisons of companies difficult. To ensure uniformity and comparability between financial statements prepared by different companies, a set of guidelines and rules are used. Commonly referred to as Generally Accepted Accounting Principles (GAAP), these set of guidelines provide the basis in the preparation of financial statements, although many companies voluntarily disclose information beyond the scope of such requirements.

Recently there has been a push towards standardizing accounting rules made by the International Accounting Standards Board ("IASB"). IASB develops International Financial Reporting Standards that have been adopted by Australia, Canada and the European Union (for publicly quoted companies only), are under consideration in South Africa and other countries. The United States Financial Accounting Standards Board has made a commitment to converge the U.S. GAAP and IFRS over time.

Inclusion in Annual Reports

To entice new investors, public companies assemble their financial statements on fine paper with pleasing graphics and photos in an annual report to shareholders, attempting to capture the excitement and culture of the organization in a "marketing brochure" of sorts. Usually the company's chief executive will write a letter to shareholders, describing management's performance and the company's financial highlights.

In the United States, prior to the advent of the internet, the annual report was considered the most effective way for corporations to communicate with individual shareholders. Blue chip companies went to great expense to produce and mail out attractive annual reports to every shareholder. The annual report was often prepared in the style of a coffee table book.

Notes

Notes to financial statements (notes) are additional information added to the end of financial statements that help explain specific items in the statements as well as provide a more comprehensive assessment of a company's financial condition. Notes to financial statements can include information on debt, going concern criteria, accounts, contingent liabilities or contextual information explaining the financial numbers (e.g. to indicate a lawsuit).

The notes clarify individual statement line-items. For example, if a company lists a loss on a fixed asset impairment line in their income statement, notes could state the reason for the impairment by describing how the asset became impaired. Notes are also used to explain the accounting methods used to prepare the statements and they support valuations for how particular accounts have been computed.

In consolidated financial statements, all subsidiaries are listed as well as the amount of ownership (controlling interest) that the parent company has in the subsidiaries. Any items within the financial statements that are valuated by estimation are part of the notes if a substantial difference exists between the amount of the estimate previously reported and the actual result. Full disclosure of the effects of the differences between the estimate and actual results should be included.

Management Discussion and Analysis

Management discussion and analysis or MD&A is an integrated part of a company's annual financial statements. The purpose of the MD&A is to provide a narrative explanation, through the eyes of management, of how an entity has performed in the past, its financial condition, and its future prospects. In so doing, the MD&A attempt to provide investors with complete, fair, and balanced information to help them decide whether to invest or continue to invest in an entity.

The section contains a description of the year gone by and some of the key factors that influenced the business of the company in that year, as well as a fair and unbiased overview of the company's past, present, and future.

MD&A typically describes the corporation's liquidity position, capital resources, results of its operations, underlying causes of material changes in financial statement items (such as asset impairment and restructuring charges), events of unusual or infrequent nature (such as mergers and acquisitions or share buybacks), positive and negative trends, effects of inflation, domestic and international market risks, and significant uncertainties.

Moving to Electronic

Financial statements have been created on paper for hundreds of years. The growth of the Web has seen more and more financial statements created in an electronic form which is exchangeable over the Web. Common forms of electronic financial statements are PDF and HTML. These types of electronic financial statements have their drawbacks in that it still takes a human to read the information in order to reuse the information contained in a financial statement.

More recently a market driven global standard, XBRL (Extensible Business Reporting Language), which can be used for creating financial statements in a structured and computer readable format, has become more popular as a format for creating financial statements. Many regulators around the world such as the U.S. Securities and Exchange Commission have mandated XBRL for the submission of financial information.

The UN/CEFACT created, with respect to Generally Accepted Accounting Principles, (GAAP), internal or external financial reporting XML messages to be used between enterprises and their partners, such as private interested parties (e.g. bank) and public collecting bodies (e.g. taxation authorities). Many regulators use such messages to collect financial and economic information.

Financial statements are records that provide an information of an individual's, organization's, or business' financial status.

They are normally prepared general or specific purposes.

General purpose Financial Statement examples:

- Balance Sheet.
- Profit and Loss A/c.

- Cash Flow Statement.
- Fund Flow Statement.
- Segment Revenue Report

Specific purpose Financial Statement examples:

- Departmental Budget.
- Computation prepared for Income Tax Purpose.

Balance Sheet

In financial accounting, a balance sheet or statement of financial position is a summary of the financial balances of an individual or organisation, whether it be a sole proprietorship, a business partnership, a corporation, private limited company or other organization such as Government or not-for-profit entity. Assets, liabilities and ownership equity are listed as of a specific date, such as the end of its financial year. A balance sheet is often described as a "snapshot of a company's financial condition". Of the four basic financial statements, the balance sheet is the only statement which applies to a single point in time of a business' calendar year.

A standard company balance sheet has two sides: assets, on the left and financing, which itself has two parts, liabilities and ownership equity, on the right. The main categories of assets are usually listed first, and typically in order of liquidity. Assets are followed by the liabilities. The difference between the assets and the liabilities is known as equity or the net assets or the net worth or capital of the company and according to the accounting equation, net worth must equal assets minus liabilities.

Another way to look at the balance sheet equation is that total assets equals liabilities plus owner's equity. Looking at the equation in this way shows how assets were financed: either by borrowing money (liability) or by using the owner's money (owner's or shareholders' equity). Balance sheets are usually presented with assets in one section and liabilities and net worth in the other section with the two sections "balancing".

A business operating entirely in cash can measure its profits by withdrawing the entire bank balance at the end of the period, plus any cash in hand. However, many businesses are not paid immediately; they build up inventories of goods and they acquire buildings and equipment. In other words: businesses have assets and so they cannot, even if they want to, immediately turn these into cash at the end of each period. Often, these businesses owe money to suppliers and to tax authorities, and the proprietors do not withdraw all their original capital and profits at the end of each period. In other words, businesses also have liabilities.

Types

A balance sheet summarizes an organization or individual's assets, equity and liabilities at a specific point in time. Two forms of balance sheet exist. They are the report form and the account form. Individuals and small businesses tend to have simple balance sheets. Larger businesses tend to have more complex balance sheets, and these are presented in the organization's annual report. Large businesses also may prepare balance sheets for segments of their businesses. A balance sheet is often presented alongside one for a different point in time (typically the previous year) for comparison.

Personal

A personal balance sheet lists current assets such as cash in checking accounts and savings accounts, long-term assets such as common stock and real estate, current liabilities such as loan debt and mortgage debt due, or overdue, long-term liabilities such as mortgage and other loan debt. Securities and real estate values are listed at market value rather than at historical cost or cost basis. Personal net worth is the difference between an individual's total assets and total liabilities.

US Small Business

Sample Small Business Balance Sheet				
Assets (current)		**Liabilities and Owners' Equity**		
Cash	$6,600	**Liabilities**		
Accounts Receivable	$6,200	Notes Payable	$5,000	
Assets (non-current)		Accounts Payable	$25,000	
Tools and equipment	$25,000	*Total liabilities*		$30,000
		Owners' equity		
		Capital Stock	$7,000	
		Retained Earnings	$800	
		Total owners' equity		$7,800
Total	$37,800	*Total*		$37,800

A small business balance sheet lists current assets such as cash, accounts receivable, and inventory, fixed assets such as land, buildings, and equipment, intangible assets such as patents, and liabilities such as accounts payable, accrued expenses, and long-term debt. Contingent liabilities such as warranties are noted in the footnotes to the balance sheet. The small business's equity is the difference between total assets and total liabilities.

Public Business Entities Structure

Guidelines for balance sheets of public business entities are given by the International Accounting Standards Board and numerous country-specific organizations/companies. The standard used by companies in the USA adhere to U.S. Generally Accepted Accounting Principles (GAAP). The Federal Accounting Standards Advisory Board (FASAB) is a United States federal advisory committee whose mission is to develop generally accepted accounting principles (GAAP) for federal financial reporting entities.

Balance sheet account names and usage depend on the organization's country and the type of organization. Government organizations do not generally follow standards established for individuals or businesses.

If applicable to the business, summary values for the following items should be included in the balance sheet: Assets are all the things the business owns. This will include property, tools, vehicles, furniture, machinery, and so on.

Assets

Non-current assets (Fixed assets):

1. Property, plant and equipment.
2. Investment property, such as real estate held for investment purposes.
3. Intangible assets such as (patents, copyrights and goodwill).
4. Financial assets (excluding investments accounted for using the equity method, accounts receivables, and cash and cash equivalents), such as notes receivables.
5. Investments accounted for using the equity method.
6. Biological assets, which are living plants or animals. Bearer biological assets are plants or animals which bear agricultural produce for harvest, such as apple trees grown to produce apples and sheep raised to produce wool.
7. Loan To (More than one financial period).

Current Assets

1. Prepaid expenses for future services that will be used within a year.
2. Accounts receivable.
3. Cash and cash equivalents.
4. Cash at bank, Petty Cash, Cash On Hand.
5. Revenue Earned In Arrears (Accrued Revenue) for services done but not yet received for the year.
6. Loan To (Less than one financial period).

Liabilities

1. Accounts payable.
2. Provisions for warranties or court decisions (contingent liabilities that are both probable and measurable).
3. Financial liabilities (excluding provisions and accounts payables), such as promissory notes and corporate bonds.
4. Liabilities and assets for current tax.
5. Deferred tax liabilities and deferred tax assets.
6. Unearned revenue for services paid for by customers but not yet provided.
7. Interests on loan stock.

Equity / Capital

The net assets shown by the balance sheet equals the third part of the balance sheet, which is known as the shareholders' equity. It comprises:

1. Issued capital and reserves attributable to equity holders of the parent company (controlling interest).
2. Non-controlling interest in equity.

Formally, shareholders' equity is part of the company's liabilities: they are funds "owing" to shareholders (after payment of all other liabilities); usually, however, "liabilities" is used in the more restrictive sense of liabilities excluding shareholders' equity. The balance of assets and liabilities (including shareholders' equity) is not a coincidence. Records of the values of each account in the balance sheet are maintained using a system of accounting known as double-entry bookkeeping. In this sense, shareholders' equity by construction must equal assets minus liabilities, and thus the shareholders' equity is considered to be a residual.

Regarding the items in equity section, the following disclosures are required:

1. Numbers of shares authorized, issued and fully paid, and issued but not fully paid.
2. Par value of shares.
3. Reconciliation of shares outstanding at the beginning and the end of the period.
4. Description of rights, preferences, and restrictions of shares.
5. Treasury shares, including shares held by subsidiaries and associates.
6. Shares reserved for issuance under options and contracts.
7. A description of the nature and purpose of each reserve within owners' equity.

Substantiation

Balance sheet substantiation is the accounting process conducted by businesses on a regular basis to confirm that the balances held in the primary accounting system of record (e.g. SAP, Oracle, other ERP system's General Ledger) are reconciled (in balance with) with the balance and transaction records held in the same or supporting sub-systems.

Balance sheet substantiation includes multiple processes including reconciliation (at a transactional or at a balance level) of the account, a process of review of the reconciliation and any pertinent supporting documentation and a formal certification (sign-off) of the account in a predetermined form driven by corporate policy.

Balance sheet substantiation is an important process that is typically carried out on a monthly, quarterly and year-end basis. The results help to drive the regulatory balance sheet reporting obligations of the organization.

Historically, balance sheet substantiation has been a wholly manual process, driven by spreadsheets, email and manual monitoring and reporting. In recent years software solutions have been developed to bring a level of process automation, standardization and enhanced control to the balance sheet substantiation or account certification process. These solutions are suitable for organizations with a high volume of accounts and/or personnel involved in the Balance Sheet Substantiation process and can be used to drive efficiencies, improve transparency and help to reduce risk.

Balance sheet substantiation is a key control process in the SOX 404 top-down risk assessment.

Sample

The following balance sheet is a very brief example prepared in accordance with IFRS. It does not show all possible kinds of assets, liabilities and equity, but it shows the most usual ones. Because it shows goodwill, it could be a consolidated balance sheet. Monetary values are not shown, summary (subtotal) rows are missing as well.

Under IFRS items are always shown based on liquidity from the least liquid assets at the top, usually land and buildings to the most liquid, i.e. cash. Then liabilities and equity continue from the most immediate liability to be paid (usual account payable) to the least i.e. long term debt such a mortgages and owner's equity at the very bottom.

Consolidated Statement of Finance Position of XYZ, Ltd.

As of 31 December 2015

ASSETS

Non-Current Assets (Fixed Assets)

Property, Plant and Equipment **(PPE)**

Less : Accumulated Depreciation

Goodwill

Intangible Assets **(Patent, Copyright, Trademark, etc.)**

Less : Accumulated Amortization

Investments in Financial assets **due after one year**

Investments **in** Associates **and** Joint Ventures

Other Non-Current Assets, e.g. Deferred Tax **Assets,** Lease Receivable **and Receivables due after one year**

Current Assets

Inventories

Prepaid Expenses

Investments in Financial assets due within one year

Non-Current and Current Assets Held for sale

Accounts Receivable (Debtors) due within one year

Less : Allowances for Doubtful debts

Cash and Cash Equivalents

TOTAL ASSETS (this will match/balance the total for Liabilities and Equity below)

LIABILITIES and EQUITY

Current Liabilities (Creditors: amounts falling due within one year)

Accounts Payable

Current Income Tax Payable

Current portion of Loans Payable

Short-term Provisions

Other Current Liabilities, e.g. Deferred income, Security deposits

Non-Current Liabilities (Creditors: amounts falling due after more than one year)

Loans Payable

Issued Debt Securities, e.g. Notes/Bonds Payable

Deferred Tax Liabilities

Provisions, e.g. Pension Obligations

Other Non-Current Liabilities, e.g. Lease Obligations

EQUITY

Paid-in Capital

Share Capital (Ordinary Shares, Preference Shares)

Share Premium

Less: Treasury Shares

Retained Earnings

Revaluation Reserve

Other Accumulated Reserves

Accumulated Other Comprehensive Income

Non-Controlling Interest

TOTAL LIABILITIES and EQUITY (this will match/balance the total for Assets above)

Assets

Fixed Asset

Fixed assets, also known as tangible assets or property, plant, and equipment (PP&E), is a term used in accounting for assets and property that cannot easily be converted into cash. This can be compared with current assets such as cash or bank accounts, which are described as liquid assets. In most cases, only tangible assets are referred to as fixed.

IAS 16 (International Accounting Standard) defines Fixed Assets as assets whose future economic benefit is probable to flow into the entity, whose cost can be measured reliably. Fixed assets belong to one of 2 types: "Freehold Assets" - assets which are purchased with legal right of ownership and used, and "Leasehold Assets" - assets used by owner without legal right for a particular period of time.

Moreover, a fixed/non-current asset can also be defined as an asset not directly sold to a firm's consumers/end-users. As an example, a baking firm's current assets would be its inventory (in this case, flour, yeast, etc.), the value of sales owed to the firm via credit (i.e. debtors or accounts receivable), cash held in the bank, etc. Its non-current assets would be the oven used to bake bread, motor vehicles used to transport deliveries, cash registers used to handle cash payments, etc. While these non-current assets have value, they are not directly sold to consumers and cannot be easily converted to cash.

These are items of value that the organization has bought and will use for an extended period of time; fixed assets normally include items such as land and buildings, motor vehicles, furniture, office equipment, computers, fixtures and fittings, and plant and machinery. These often receive favorable tax treatment (depreciation allowance) over short-term assets.

It is pertinent to note that the cost of a fixed asset is its purchase price, including import duties and other deductible trade discounts and rebates. In addition, cost attributable to bringing and installing the asset in its needed location and the initial estimate of dismantling and removing the item if they are eventually no longer needed on the location.

The primary objective of a business entity is to make profit and increase the wealth of its owners. In the attainment of this objective it is required that the management will exercise due care and diligence in applying the basic accounting concept of "Matching Concept". Matching concept is simply matching the expenses of a period against the revenues of the same period.

The use of assets in the generation of revenue is usually more than a year, i.e. long term. It is therefore obligatory that in order to accurately determine the net income or profit for a period depreciation is charged on the total value of asset that contributed to the revenue for the period in consideration and charge against the same revenue of the same period. This is essential in the prudent reporting of the net revenue for the entity in the period.

Net book value of an asset is basically the difference between the historical cost of that asset and its associated depreciation. From the foregoing, it is apparent that in order to report a true and fair position of the financial jurisprudence of an entity it is relatable to record and report the value of fixed assets at its net book value. Apart from the fact that it is enshrined in Standard Accounting

Statement (SAS) 3 and IAS 16 that value of asset should be carried at the net book value, it is the best way of consciously presenting the value of assets to the owners of the business and potential investor.

Depreciating a Fixed Asset

Depreciation is, simply put, the expense generated by the uses of an asset. It is the wear and tear of an asset or diminution in the historical value owing to usage. Further to this; it is the cost of the asset less any salvage value over its estimated useful life. A fixed asset can be depreciated using the straight line method which is the most common form of depreciation.

Current Asset

In accounting, a current asset is any asset which can reasonably be expected to be sold, consumed, or exhausted through the normal operations of a business within the current fiscal year or operating cycle (whichever period is longer). Typical current assets include cash, cash equivalents, short-term investments (marketable securities), accounts receivable, stock inventory, supplies, and the portion of prepaid liabilities, sometimes referred to as prepaid expenses, which will be paid within a year.

On a balance sheet, assets will typically be classified into current assets and long-term assets.

The current ratio is calculated by dividing total current assets by total current liabilities. It is frequently used as an indicator of a company's liquidity, its ability to meet short-term obligations.

The quick ratio, or acid-test, measures the ability of a company to use its *near cash* or quick assets to extinguish or retire its current liabilities immediately. Quick assets are those that can be quickly turned into cash if necessary.

Investment (Macroeconomics)

In macroeconomics, investment is the amount purchased per unit time of goods which are not consumed at the present time. Types of investment include residential investment in housing that will provide a flow of housing services over an extended time, non-residential fixed investment in things such as new machinery or factories, human capital investment in workforce education, and inventory investment (the accumulation, intentional or unintentional, of goods inventories).

In measures of national income and output, "gross investment" (represented by the variable I) is a component of gross domestic product (GDP), given in the formula GDP = $C + I + G + NX$, where C is consumption, G is government spending, and NX is net exports, given by the difference between the exports and imports, $X - M$. Thus investment is everything that remains of total expenditure after consumption, government spending, and net exports are subtracted (i.e. I = GDP $- C - G - NX$).

"Net investment" deducts depreciation from gross investment. Net fixed investment is the value of the net increase in the capital stock per year.

Fixed investment, as expenditure over a period of time (e.g., "per year"), is not capital but rather leads to changes in the amount of capital. The time dimension of investment makes it a *flow*. By contrast, capital is a *stock*—that is, accumulated net investment up to a point in time.

Investment is often modeled as a function of income and interest rates, given by the relation $I = f(Y, r)$. An increase in income encourages higher investment, whereas a higher interest rate may discourage investment as it becomes more costly to borrow money. Even if a firm chooses to use its own funds in an investment, the interest rate represents an opportunity cost of investing those funds rather than lending out that amount of money for interest.

Liabilities

- A liability is a present obligation of the enterprise arising from past events, the settlement of which is expected to the result in an outflow of a resource embodying economic benefits.
- A liability is an existing obligation based on the evidence available on balance sheet date.
- A liability is recognised when outflow of economic resources in settlement of present obligation can be anticipated and the value of outflow can be reliably measured.

Long-Term Liabilities

- Long-term liabilities are a company's debts or obligations that are to be repaid or performed beyond one year.
  Source of fund
  Examples:
  - Bank Loan.
  - Loan from Financial Institution.
  - Debentures.

Current Liabilities

- Current liabilities are a company's debts or obligations that are to be repaid or performed within one year.
  - Emerge from normal business.
  - Examples:
    - Creditors (Accounts Payable).
    - Outstanding Expenses.
    - Interest accrued but not due on Loan.
    - Provision for Tax.
    - Bank Overdraft.

Provision

Provision means any amount retained by way of providing for any known liability of which amount can not be determined with substantial accuracy.

Provision refers to an amount set aside for meeting claims which are admissible but the amount whereof has not been confirmed.

Examples

- Provision for payment of electricity charges (but bill is not yet received).
- Provision for taxes (till final amount is assessed by authorities).
- Provision for bonus.
- Amount set aside for writing off bad debts.

Contingent Liability

Contingent liability can be defined as:

a. Apossible obligation that arises from past events and the existence of which will be confirmed only by occurrence or non-occurrence of one or more uncertain future events not wholly within the control of the enterprise.

b. Apresent obligation that arises from past events but is not recognised because:

   i. It is not probable that an outflow of resources consisting economic benefits will be required to settle the obligation.

   ii. Areliable estimate of the amount of the obligation cannot be made.

Owners Fund

Owners fund is defined as residual interest of an enterprises after deducting all its liabilities.

Owners fund is the excess of aggregate assets of an enterprises over its aggregate liabilities.

Balance Sheet Equation

Assets = Liabilities + Owners Fund

Therefore,

Owners Fund= Assets – Liabilities

Owners Fund= Capital + Retained Earnings

A = L + O

1. Company borrows from bank.

+	+		(+ Bank, + Bank Loan Payable)

1. Issue of shares by company.

+		+	(+ Bank, + Equity Shares)

a. Cash purchase of equipment.

b. Collection of debtors.

a.	+,–			(+ Equipment, – Bank)
b.	+,–			(+ Bank, – Debtors)

a. Company repays bank loan.

b. Payment of creditors / suppliers.

a.	–	–		(– Loan Payable, – Bank)
b.	–	–		(– Creditors, – Bank)

Company pays dividend to shareholders.

–		–	(– Bank, – Reserves)

Company purchases shares from shareholder, pays immediately (buy-back of shares).

–		–	(– Bank, – Equity Capital)

Liability is converted into equity shares e.g., loan is converted into equity shares.

–	+	(– Loan Payable, + Equity shares)

Company incurs new liability to pay existing liability, e.g., Creditors are converted into long-term loan.

	+,–		(– Creditors, + Loan Payable)

Company distributes stock dividend to stockholders (Bonus Shares).

		+,–	(+ Equity Capital, – Reserves)

Vertical Format of Balance Sheet

Sources of Funds	Rs.	Rs.
Owners Fund		XX
Borrowing Funds		
Secured Loan	XX	

Unsecured Loan	XX	XX
Total Capital Employed		XX

Application of Fund	Rs.	Rs.
Fixed Assets		XX
Investments		XX
Working Capital		
Current Assets	XX	
Current Liabilities	(XX)	
Net Working Capital		XX
Total Assets Employed		XX

Every company has to prepare balance sheet in the form set out in Part I of Schedule VI of Companies Act.

Exercise:

1. On January 2, owners invest Rs.15,000 in ShriRam Company to begin the business.
2. On January 3, ShriRam Company borrows Rs. 10,000 from DhanLakshmi Bank.
3. On January 5, ShriRam Company purchases Rs. 18,000 of inventory from suppliers. Payment due on Jan 8.
4. On January 9, ShriRam Company sells inventory that cost Rs. 6,000 for Rs. 8,000 in cash.
5. On January 10, ShriRam Company pays for inventory purchased on January 5.
6. On January 12, ShriRam Company sells inventory that cost Rs. 5,000 for Rs. 6,000, on account. Payment will be received on January 31.
7. On January 31, ShriRam Company collects the account receivable and puts in bank.

Prepare Balance sheet of the concern after each transaction.

1. On January 2, owners invest Rs.15,000 in ShriRam Company to begin the business.

ShriRam Company Balance Sheet January 2, Year 1			
Liabilities		Assets	
Capital	15,000	Bank	15,000
Total	15,000	Total	15,000

2. On January 3, ShriRam Company borrows Rs. 10,000 from DhanLakshmi Bank.

ShriRam Company Balance Sheet January 3, Year 1			
Liabilities		Assets	
Paid-up capital	15,000	Bank	25,000
DhanLakshmi Bank Loan	10,000		
Total	25,000	Total	25,000

3. On January 5, ShriRam Company purchases Rs. 18,000 of inventory from suppliers, on account Payment due on January 8.

ShriRam Company Balance Sheet January 5, Year 1			
Liabilities		Assets	
Paid-up capital	15,000	Bank	25,000
DhanLakshmi Bank Loan	10,000	Inventory	18,000
Accounts Payable/Creditors	18,000		
Total	43,000	Total	43,000

4. On January 9, ShriRam Company sells inventory that cost Rs. 6,000 for Rs. 8,000 in.

ShriRam Company Balance Sheet January 9, Year 1			
Liabilities		Assets	
Paid-up capital	15,000	Bank	33,000
Reserves	2,000	Inventory	12,000
DhanLakshmi Bank Loan	10,000		
Creditors	18,000		
Total	45,000	Total	45,000

5. On January 10, ShriRam Company pays for inventory purchased on January 5.

ShriRam Company Balance Sheet January 10, Year 1			
Liabilities		Assets	
Paid-up capital	15,000	Bank	15,000
Reserves	2,000	Inventory	12,000
DhanLakshmi Bank Loan	10,000		
Creditors	Nil		
Total	27,000	Total	27,00

6. On January 12, ShriRam Company sells inventory that cost Rs. 5,000 for Rs. 6,000, on account. Payment will be received on January 31.

ShriRam Company Balance Sheet January 12, Year 1			
Liabilities		Assets	
Paid-up capital	15,000	Bank	15,000
Reserves	3,000	Inventory	7,000
DhanLakshmi Bank Loan	10,000	Debtors	6,000
Total	28,000	Total	28,000

7. On January 31, ShriRam Company collects the debtors and puts in bank.

ShriRam Company Balance Sheet January 31, Year 1			
Liabilities		Assets	
Paid-up capital	15,000	Bank	21,000
Reserves	3,000	Inventory	7,000
DhanLakshmi Bank Loan	10,000	Debtors	Nil
Total	28,000	Total	28,000

Exercise:

Show the effect of each transaction on the balance sheet of M/s. Krishna Book Stores

- Shyam and Murlidhar set up a book stall M/s. Krishna Book Stores in their town. On 1 Jan 2010, Shyam opened new bank account in the name of their partnership by depositing Rs. 1,00,000 cash and Murlidhar brought his own shop worth Rs. 2,00,000 as capital.
- On 2 January 2010, store purchased book of Rs. 75,000 and Stationary of Rs. 10,000 on immediate payment from SK International.
- On 5 January 2010, Stores supplies books of Rs. 90,000 (costing 60,000) to Saraswati Highschool. School paid cheque Rs. 45,000 immediately and reaming amount will be paid on 10 January 2010.
- On 9 January 2010, books costing 47,000 purchased on credit from SSK and Associates.
- On 10 January 2010, Rs. 15,000 received from Saraswati Highschool.
- On 15 January 2010, cheque of Rs. 47,000 paid to creditors.

Balance Sheet as on 1 Jan 2010

Liabilities	Amount	Assets	Amount
Capital			
Shyam	1,00,000	Shop Premises	2,00,000
Murlidhar	2,00,000	Bank	1,00,000
	3,00,000		3,00,000

Balance Sheet as on 2 Jan 2010

Liabilities	Amount	Assets	Amount
Capital			
Shyam	1,00,000	Shop Premises	2,00,000
Murlidhar	2,00,000	Bank	15,000
		Inventory	85,000
	3,00,000		**3,00,000**

Balance Sheet as on 5 Jan 2010

Liabilities	Amount	Assets	Amount
Capital			
Shyam	1,00,000	Shop Premises	2,00,000
Murlidhar	2,00,000	Bank	60,000
Profit and Loss A/c	30,000	Sundry Debtors	45,000
		Inventory	25,000
	3,30,000		3,30,000

Balance Sheet as on 9 Jan 2010

Liabilities	Amount	Assets	Amount
Capital			
Shyam	1,00,000	Shop Premises	2,00,000
Murlidhar	2,00,000	Bank	60,000
Profit and Loss A/c	30,000	Inventory	72,000
Sundry Creditors	47,000	Sundry Debtors	45,000
	3,77,000		3,77,000

Balance Sheet as on 10 Jan 2010

Liabilities	Amount	Assets	Amount
Capital			
Shyam	1,00,000	Shop Premises	2,00,000
Murlidhar	2,00,000	Bank	75,000
Profit and Loss A/c	30,000	Inventory	72,000
Sundry Creditors	47,000	Sundry Debtors	30,000
	3,77,000		**3,77,000**

Balance Sheet as on 15 Jan 2010

Liabilities	Amount	Assets	Amount
Capital			
Shyam	1,00,000	Shop Premises	2,00,000
Murlidhar	2,00,000	Bank	28,000
Profit and Loss A/c	30,000	Inventory	72,000
		Sundry Debtors	30,000
	3,30,000		3,30,000

Income Statement

An income statement or profit and loss account (also referred to as a *profit and loss statement* (P&L), *statement of profit or loss, revenue statement, statement of financial performance, earnings statement, operating statement, or statement of operations*) is one of the financial statements of a company and shows the company's revenues and expenses during a particular period. It indicates how the revenues (money received from the sale of products and services before expenses are taken out, also known as the "top line") are transformed into the net income (the result after all revenues and expenses have been accounted for, also known as "net profit" or the "bottom line"). It displays the revenues recognized for a specific period, and the cost and expenses charged against these revenues, including write-offs (e.g., depreciation and amortization of various assets) and taxes. The purpose of the income statement is to show managers and investors whether the company made or lost money during the period being reported.

One important thing to remember about an income statement is that it represents a period of time like the cash flow statement. This contrasts with the balance sheet, which represents a single moment in time.

Charitable organizations that are required to publish financial statements do not produce an income statement. Instead, they produce a similar statement that reflects funding sources compared against program expenses, administrative costs, and other operating commitments. This statement is commonly referred to as the statement of activities. Revenues and expenses are further categorized in the statement of activities by the donor restrictions on the funds received and expended.

The income statement can be prepared in one of two methods. The Single Step income statement takes the simpler approach, totaling revenues and subtracting expenses to find the bottom line. The more complex Multi-Step income statement (as the name implies) takes several steps to find the bottom line, starting with the gross profit. It then calculates operating expenses and, when deducted from the gross profit, yields income from operations. Adding to income from operations is the difference of other revenues and other expenses. When combined with income from operations, this yields income before taxes. The final step is to deduct taxes, which finally produces the net income for the period measured.

Usefulness and Limitations of Income Statement

Income statements should help investors and creditors determine the past financial performance of the enterprise, predict future performance, and assess the capability of generating future cash flows through report of the income and expenses.

However, information of an income statement has several limitations:

- Items that might be relevant but cannot be reliably measured are not reported (*e.g.*, brand recognition and loyalty).
- Some numbers depend on accounting methods used (*e.g.*, using FIFO or LIFO accounting to measure inventory level).
- Some numbers depend on judgments and estimates (*e.g.*, depreciation expense depends on estimated useful life and salvage value).

INCOME STATEMENT GREENHARBOR LLC

For the year ended DECEMBER 31 2010

	€ Debit	€ Credit
Revenues		
GROSS REVENUES (including INTEREST income)		296,397

Expenses:		
ADVERTISING	6,300	
BANK & CREDIT CARD FEES	144	
BOOKKEEPING	2,350	
SUBCONTRACTORS	88,000	
ENTERTAINMENT	5,550	

INSURANCE	750	
LEGAL & PROFESSIONAL SERVICES	1,575	
LICENSES	632	
PRINTING, POSTAGE & STATIONERY	320	
RENT	13,000	
MATERIALS	74,400	
TELEPHONE	1,000	
UTILITIES	1,491	

TOTAL EXPENSES		(195,512)

NET INCOME		100,885

Guidelines for statements of comprehensive income and income statements of business entities are formulated by the International Accounting Standards Board and numerous country-specific organizations, for example the FASB in the U.S.

Names and usage of different accounts in the income statement depend on the type of organization, industry practices and the requirements of different jurisdictions.

If applicable to the business, summary values for the following items should be included in the income statement:

Operating Section

- Revenue - Cash inflows or other enhancements of assets (including accounts receivable) of an entity during a period from delivering or producing goods, rendering services, or other activities that constitute the entity's ongoing major operations. It is usually presented as sales minus sales discounts, returns, and allowances. Every time a business sells a product or performs a service, it obtains revenue. This often is referred to as gross revenue or sales revenue.
- Expenses - Cash outflows or other using-up of assets or incurrence of liabilities (including accounts payable) during a period from delivering or producing goods, rendering services, or carrying out other activities that constitute the entity's ongoing major operations.
    - Cost of Goods Sold (COGS) / Cost of Sales - represents the direct costs attributable to goods produced and sold by a business (manufacturing or merchandizing). It includes *material costs*, *direct labour*, and *overhead costs* (as in absorption costing), and excludes operating costs (period costs) such as selling, administrative, advertising or R&D, etc.
    - Selling, General and Administrative expenses (SG&A or SGA) - consist of the combined payroll costs. SGA is usually understood as a major portion of non-production related costs, in contrast to production costs such as direct labour.

- Selling expenses - represent expenses needed to sell products (e.g., *salaries of sales people, commissions and travel expenses, advertising, freight, shipping, depreciation of sales store buildings and equipment*, etc.).
- General and Administrative (G&A) expenses - represent expenses to manage the business (*salaries of officers / executives, legal and professional fees, utilities, insurance, depreciation of office building and equipment, office rents, office supplies*, etc.).
    - Depreciation / Amortization - the charge with respect to fixed assets / intangible assets that have been capitalised on the balance sheet for a specific (accounting) period. It is a systematic and rational allocation of cost rather than the recognition of market value decrement.
    - Research & Development (R&D) expenses - represent expenses included in research and development.

Expenses recognised in the income statement should be analysed either by nature (raw materials, transport costs, staffing costs, depreciation, employee benefit etc.) or by function (cost of sales, selling, administrative, etc.). (IAS 1.99) If an entity categorises by function, then additional information on the nature of expenses, at least, – depreciation, amortisation and employee benefits expense – must be disclosed. (IAS 1.104) The major exclusive of costs of goods sold, are classified as operating expenses. These represent the resources expended, except for inventory purchases, in generating the revenue for the period. Expenses often are divided into two broad sub classifications selling expenses and administrative expenses.

Non-operating Section

- Other revenues or gains - revenues and gains from other than primary business activities (e.g., *rent, income from patents*, goodwill). It also includes unusual gains that are either unusual or infrequent, but not both (e.g., *gain from sale of securities* or *gain from disposal of fixed assets*).
- Other expenses or losses - expenses or losses not related to primary business operations, (e.g., *foreign exchange loss*).
- Finance costs - costs of borrowing from various creditors (e.g., interest expenses, bank charges).
- Income tax expense - sum of the amount of tax payable to tax authorities in the current reporting period (current tax liabilities/ tax payable) and the amount of deferred tax liabilities (or assets).

Irregular Items

They are reported separately because this way users can better predict future cash flows - irregular items most likely will not recur. These are reported *net of taxes*.

- Discontinued operations is the most common type of irregular items. Shifting business location(s), stopping production temporarily, or changes due to technological improvement do **not** qualify as discontinued operations. Discontinued operations *must* be shown separately.

Cumulative effect of changes in accounting policies (principles) is the difference between the book value of the affected assets (or liabilities) under the old policy (principle) and what the book value would have been if the new principle had been applied in the prior periods. For example, valuation of inventories using LIFO instead of weighted average method. The changes should be applied retrospectively and shown as adjustments to the *beginning* balance of affected components in Equity. All comparative financial statements should be restated.

However, changes in estimates (e.g., estimated useful life of a fixed asset) only requires prospective changes.

No items may be presented in the income statement as extraordinary items under IFRS regulations, but are permissible under US GAAP. (IAS 1.87) *Extraordinary items* are both unusual (abnormal) and infrequent, for example, unexpected natural disaster, expropriation, prohibitions under new regulations. [Note: natural disaster might not qualify depending on location (e.g., frost damage would not qualify in Canada but would in the tropics)].

Additional items may be needed to fairly present the entity's results of operations.

Disclosures

Certain items must be disclosed separately in the notes (or the statement of comprehensive income), if material, including: (IAS 1.98)

- Write-downs of inventories to net realisable value or of property, plant and equipment to recoverable amount, as well as *reversals* of such write-downs.
- Restructurings of the activities of an entity and *reversals* of any provisions for the costs of restructuring.
- Disposals of items of property, plant and equipment.
- Disposals of investments.
- Discontinued operations.
- Litigation settlements.
- Other reversals of provisions.

Earnings Per Share

Because of its importance, earnings per share (EPS) are required to be disclosed on the face of the income statement. A company which reports any of the irregular items must also report EPS for these items either in the statement or in the notes.

$$\text{Earnings per share} = \frac{\text{Net income} - \text{Preferred stock dividends}}{\text{Weighted average of common stock shares outstanding}}$$

There are two forms of EPS reported:

- Basic: in this case "weighted average of shares outstanding" includes only actual stocks outstanding.
- Diluted: in this case "weighted average of shares outstanding" is calculated as if all stock options, warrants, convertible bonds, and other securities that could be transformed into shares are transformed. This increases the number of shares and so EPS decreases. Diluted EPS is considered to be a more reliable way to measure EPS.

Sample Income Statement

The following income statement is a very brief example prepared in accordance with IFRS. It does not show all possible kinds of accounts, but it shows the most usual ones. Please note the difference between IFRS and US GAAP when interpreting the following sample income statements.

Fitness Equipment Limited

INCOME STATEMENTS (in millions)

Year Ended March 31,	2009	2008	2007
Revenue	$14,580.2	$11,900.4	$8,290.3
Cost of sales	(6,740.2)	(5,650.1)	(4,524.2)
Gross profit	*7,840.0*	*6,250.3*	*3,766.1*
SGA expenses	(3,624.6)	(3,296.3	(3,034.0)
Operating profit	*$ 4,215.4*	*$ 2,954.0*	*$ 732.1*
Gains from disposal of fixed assets	46.3	-	-
Interest expense	(119.7)	(124.1)	(142.8)
Profit *before* tax	4,142.0	2,829.9	589.3
Income tax expense	(1,656.8)	(1,132.0)	(235.7)
Profit (or loss) for the year1	*$ 2,485.2*	*$ 1,697.9*	*$ 353.6*

DEXTERITY INC. AND SUBSIDIARIES

CONSOLIDATED STATEMENTS OF OPERATIONS (In millions)

Year Ended December 31,	2009	2008	2007
Revenue	$36,525.9	$29,827.6	$21,186.8
Cost of sales	(18,545.8)	(15,858.8)	(11,745.5)
Gross profit	*17,980.1*	*13,968.8*	*9,441.3*

Operating expenses:			
Selling, general and administrative expenses	(4,142.1)	(3,732.3)	(3,498.6)
Depreciation	(602.4)	(584.5)	(562.3)
Amortization	(209.9)	(141.9)	(111.8)
Impairment loss	(17,997.1)	—	—
Total operating expenses	(22,951.5)	(4,458.7)	(4,172.7)
Operating profit (or loss)	*$ (4,971.4)*	*$ 9,510.1*	*$ 5,268.6*
Interest income	25.3	11.7	12.0
Interest expense	(718.9)	(742.9)	(799.1)
Profit (or loss) from continuing operations *before* tax, share of profit (or loss) from associates and non-controlling interest	$ (5,665.0)	$ 8,778.9	$ 4,481.5
Income tax expense	(1,678.6)	(3,510.5)	(1,789.9)
Profit (or loss) from associates, *net of tax*	(20.8)	0.1	(37.3)
Profit (or loss) from non-controlling interest, *net of tax*	(5.1)	(4.7)	(3.3)
Profit (or loss) from continuing operations	*$ (3960.5)*	*$ 5,263.8*	*$ 2,651.0*
Profit (or loss) from discontinued operations,*net of tax*	(1,090.3)	(802.4)	164.6
Profit (or loss) for the year	*$ (2,870.2)*	*$ 4,461.4*	*$ 2,486.4*

Bottom Line

"Bottom line" is the net income that is calculated after subtracting the expenses from revenue. Since this forms the last line of the income statement, it is informally called "bottom line." It is important to investors as it represents the profit for the year attributable to the shareholders.

After revision to IAS 1 in 2003, the Standard is now using profit or loss for the year rather than *net profit or loss* or *net income* as the descriptive term for the bottom line of the income statement.

Requirements of IFRS

On 6 September 2007, the International Accounting Standards Board issued a revised *IAS 1: Presentation of Financial Statements*, which is effective for annual periods beginning on or after 1 January 2009.

A business entity adopting IFRS must include:

- A statement of comprehensive income.
- Two separate statements comprising:
    1. An income statement displaying components of profit or loss.
    2. A *statement of comprehensive income* that *begins* with profit or loss (bottom line of the income statement) and displays the items of other comprehensive income for the reporting period. (IAS1.81)

All non-owner changes in equity (i.e., *comprehensive income*) shall be presented in either in the statement of comprehensive income (or in a separate income statement and a statement of comprehensive income). Components of comprehensive income may not be presented in the statement of changes in equity.

Comprehensive income for a period includes profit or loss (net income) for that period and other comprehensive income recognised in that period.

All items of income and expense recognised in a period must be included in profit or loss unless a Standard or an Interpretation requires otherwise. (IAS 1.88) Some IFRSs require or permit that some components to be excluded from profit or loss and instead to be included in other comprehensive income.

Items and Disclosures

The statement of comprehensive income should include:

1. Revenue.
2. Finance costs (including interest expenses).
3. Share of the profit or loss of associates and joint ventures accounted for using the equity method.
4. Tax expense.
5. A *single* amount comprising the total of (1) the *post-tax* profit or loss of *discontinued operations* and (2) the *post-tax* gain or loss recognised on the disposal of the assets or disposal group(s) constituting the *discontinued operation.*
6. Profit or loss.
7. Each component of other comprehensive income classified by nature.
8. Share of the other comprehensive income of associates and joint ventures accounted for using the equity method.
9. Total comprehensive income.

The following items must also be disclosed in the statement of comprehensive income as allocations for the period:

- Profit or loss for the period attributable to non-controlling interests and owners of the parent.

- Total comprehensive income attributable to non-controlling interests and owners of the parent.

No items may be presented in the statement of comprehensive income (or in the income statement, if separately presented) or in the notes as *extraordinary items*.

Income

Income is the increase in economic benefits during the accounting period in the form of inflows or enhancement of asset or decreases of the liability. The definition of income encompasses revenue and gains.

- Revenue is an income that arises in the ordinary course of activities. e.g. sales.
- Gains are income, which may or may not arises in the ordinary course of activities. e.g. profit on sale of fixed asset.

Expenses

Expense is the decrease in economic benefits during the accounting period in the form of outflows or depletion of asset or incurrence of the liability.

- Expense arises in the ordinary course of activities. e.g. wages.
- Losses may or may not arises in the ordinary course of activities. e.g. loss on sale of fixed asset.

Entity Concept

In accounting, a business or an organization and its owners are treated as two separately identifiable parties. This is called the entity concept. The business stands apart from other organizations as a separate economic unit. It is necessary to record the business's transactions separately, to distinguish them from the owners' personal transactions. This helps to give a correct determination of the true financial condition of the business. This concept can be extended to accounting separately for the various divisions of a business in order to ascertain the financial results for each division.

"The entity view holds the business 'enterprise to be an institution in its own right separate and distinct from the parties who furnish the funds."

Proprietor

An example is a sole trader or one-man business(proprietorship): the sole trader takes money from the business by way of 'drawings': money for his own personal use. Despite it being his business and technically his money, there are still two aspects to the transaction: the business is 'giving' money and the individual is 'receiving' money. Even though there is no other legal distinction between the sole trader and the business, and the sole trader is liable for all of the debts of the business, business transactions will probably still be taxed separately from personal transactions, and the proprietor of the business may also find it useful to see the financial results of the business. For these reasons, the affairs of the individuals behind a business should be kept separate from the affairs of the business itself.

Example

Mr. Honey has three rooms in a house he has rented for $3,000 per month. He has set up a single-member accounting practice and uses one room for the purpose. Under the business entity concept, only 1/3 of the rent or $1,000 should be charged to business, because the other two rooms or $2,000 worth of rent are expended for personal purposes.

The Entity concept of an accounting practice states that the business enterprises is a separate identity apart from its owner.

- Business transaction are recorded in the books of business books of accounts and owners transaction in his personal books of accounts.
- This concept helps in keeping business affairs free from the influence of the personal affairs of the owner.
- Entity concept means that enterprises are liable to owner for capital investment made by the owner.
- Since the owner invested capital, which is also called risk capital he claim on the profit of the enterprise.

Basis of Accounting

A basis of accounting can be defined as the time various financial transactions are recorded. The cash basis (EU VAT vocabulary *Cash accounting*) and the accrual basis are the two primary methods of tracking income and expenses in accounting.

Both can be used in a range of situations, from the accounts of a whole country, a large corporation, a small business or an individual. In many cases, regulatory bodies require individuals, businesses or corporations to use one method or the other. When this is not the case, the choice of which to use is an important decision, as both methods have advantages and disadvantages.

Accrual Basis

The accrual method records income items when they are *earned* and records deductions when expenses are *incurred*. For a business invoicing for an item sold, or work done, the corresponding amount will appear in the books even though no payment has yet been received – and debts owed by the business show as they are incurred, even though they may not be paid until much later.

In the United States tax environment, the accrual basis has been an option since 1916. An "accrual basis taxpayer" looks to the "all-events test" and "earlier-of test" to determine when income is earned. Under the all-events test, an accrual basis taxpayer generally must include income "for the taxable year when all the events have occurred that fix the right to receive income and the amount of the income can be determined with reasonable accuracy." Under the "earlier-of test", an accrual basis taxpayer receives income when (1) the required performance occurs, (2) payment therefore is due, or (3) payment therefore is made, whichever happens earliest. Under the earlier of test outlined in Revenue Ruling 74-607, an accrual basis taxpayer may be treated as a cash basis taxpayer when payment is received before the required performance and before the payment is actually due. An accrual basis taxpayer generally can claim a deduction "in the taxable year in which all the events have occurred that establish the fact of the liability, the amount of the liability can be determined with reasonable accuracy, and economic performance has occurred with respect to the liability."

Similar definition of accrual basis accounting is true for financial accounting purposes, except that revenue can't be recognized until it is earned, even if a cash payment has already been received by the tax authorities.

Modified Accrual Basis

Also referred to as the Modified Cash Basis, combines elements of both accrual and cash basis accounting. The modified method records income when they are earned but deductions when expenses are paid out. The recording of income is then of accrual basis, while the recording of expenses is cash basis. The modified method does not conform to the GAAP.

Accrual Basis of Accounting

- Transaction are recognised as soon as they occur, whether or not cash is actually received or paid.
- Accrual basis ensures better matching between revenue and cost of the enterprise during an accounting period.
- Accrual means recognition of revenue and cost as they are earned or incurred and not as money is received or paid.
- Revenues may not be realised in cash.

Cash may be received simultaneously or before/after revenue is created.

Expense may not be paid in cash.

Cash may be paid simultaneously or before/after expense is made.

Matching Concept

The matching concept is an accounting practice whereby expenses are recognized in the same accounting period when the related revenues are recognized.

The matching concept thus helps avoid misstating earnings for a period. Reporting revenues for a period without reporting the costs of producing those revenues would result in overstated profits.

Prepaid and Outstanding Expenses

Matching concept is based on the accrual concept as it considers the occurrence of expenses and income and do not concentrate on actual inflow or outflow of cash. This leads to adjustment of items like prepaid and outstanding expenses.

Realisation Concept

Any change in the value of an asset is to be recorded only when the business realise it. When an asset is recorded at its cost of Rs. 15 Lakhs and even if its current cost is Rs. 45 Lakhs such change is not counted unless there is certainty that such change will materialise.

However, we follow a more conservative path. We try to cover all probable losses but do not count any probable gain. That is to say, if we anticipate decrease in value count it, but if there is increase in value ignore it until it is realised.

Profit & Loss A/c (Detailed Format)

Particulars	Amount
Sales	XX
Operating Expenses	(XX)
Operating Profit	XX
Non-Operating Income	XX
Non-Operating Expense	(XX)
Profit before Interest and Tax	XX
Interest	(XX)
Profit before Tax	XX
Tax	(XX)
Profit after Tax	XX

Earnings Before Interest and Taxes

In accounting and finance, earnings before interest and taxes (EBIT), is a measure of a firm's profit that includes all expenses except interest and income tax expenses. It is the difference between operating revenues and operating expenses. When a firm does not have non-operating income, then **operating *income*** is sometimes used as a synonym for **EBIT** and operating profit.

EBIT = revenue – operating expenses (OPEX)

Operating income = revenue – operating expenses

A professional investor contemplating a change to the capital structure of a firm (e.g., through a leveraged buyout) first evaluates a firm's fundamental earnings potential (reflected by earnings before interest, taxes, depreciation and amortization (EBITDA) and EBIT), and then determines the optimal use of debt vs. equity.

To calculate EBIT, expenses (e.g. the cost of goods sold, selling and administrative expenses) are subtracted from revenues. Net income is later obtained by subtracting interest and taxes from the result.

Example statement of income (figures in thousands)	
Revenue	
Sales revenue	$20,438
Operating expenses	
Cost of goods sold	$7,943
Selling, general and administrative expenses	$8,172
Depreciation and amortization	$960
Other expenses	$138
Total operating expenses	$17,213
Operating profit	**$3,225**
Non-operating income	$130
Earnings before Interest and taxes (EBIT)	**$3,355**
Financial income	$45
Income before interest expense (IBIE)	**$3,400**
Financial expense	$190
Earnings before income taxes (EBT)	**$3,210**
Income taxes	$1,027
Net income	**$2,183**

Operating Profit

Operating activities are principal revenue producing activities of the enterprise.

Operating profit is the figure obtained after subtracting personnel, depreciation and other expenses.

Operating profit is the surplus generated by the operations.

Profit Before Interest & Tax

The company irrespective of method of financing, earns this amount. The only other expense to be met at this stage, is the interest expense.

This is the measure of the operational efficiency of the company. This is usually referred as Earnings before Interest and Tax.

Profit Before Tax

Profit before Tax is the surplus after meeting all expenses, including interest.

This is the profit available to company as a result of both its operating as well as financing performance.

Profit After Tax

Profit after Tax is the net amount of surplus earned by the company during the accounting period.

This is the amount available to the company for appropriation. This amount can either distributed to owners or retained in the business as retained earning. Not distributing the profit to owners increases the owners investment in the business.

Exercise 1

In Padmanabham and co. following transaction took place during year 2009-10.

- Goods costing Rs. 1,40,000 purchased for cash.
- Padmanabham paid General expenses of Rs. 4,800.
- Salaries of Rs. 25,500 paid to office staff.
- Padmanabham sales on credit for two month. Total credit sales during year is Rs. 1,40,500 (cost: 90,000) and remaining goods were sold at cash to retail traders for cash at Rs. 69,000.
- Printing and stationary expense were Rs. 5,000 and Telephone expenses were Rs. 18,000.
- Padmanabham paid salary of Apr 2010, Rs. 2,000 in advance to one employee.
- Padmanabham paid Rs. 50,000 towards Bank of Baroda loan, of which Rs. 5,000 was interest component.
- Rs. 3,000 paid as tax.

Prepare profit and loss A/c from the given information of year 2009-10.

Profit and Loss A/c for year ended 31 March 2010	
Particulars	**Amount**
Cash Sales	69,000
Credit Sales	1,40,500
Total Sales	2,09,500
Cost of goods sold	(1,40,000)
Operating Profit	69,500
General Expenses	(4,800)
Salary Expenses	(25,500)
Printing and Stationary Expenses	(5,000)

Telephone Expenses	(18,000)
Profit Before Interest and Tax	16,200
Interest	(5,000)
Profit Before Tax	11,200
Tax	(3,000)
Net profit after Tax	**8,200**

References

- Warren, Carl (2008). Survey of Accounting. Cincinnati: South-Western College Pub. pp. 128–132. ISBN 978-0-324-65826-2
- "What are Accruals and the Meaning of Accrued in Accounting?". Simplestudies LLC. 25 February 2010. Retrieved 11, March 2020
- "US Small Business Administration sample spreadsheet for a small business". Archived from the original on 2007-07-15. Retrieved 08, April 2020
- "Balance sheet comparing two year-end balance sheets". Archived from the original on 2007-10-19. Retrieved 19, February 2020
- Williams, Jan R.; Susan F. Haka; Mark S. Bettner; Joseph V. Carcello (2008). Financial & Managerial Accounting. McGraw-Hill Irwin. p. 40. ISBN 978-0-07-299650-0
- Ernst, James. "3 Methods of HOA Accounting and How They Effect Financial Statements". www.echo-ca.org. ECHO. Retrieved 23, July 2020
- Epstein, Barry J.; Eva K. Jermakowicz (2007). Interpretation and Application of International Financial Reporting Standards. John Wiley & Sons. p. 931. ISBN 978-0-471-79823-1

5

Types of Auditing

Auditing refers to the independent examination or inspection of financial information of an organization in order to ascertain the accuracy of its financial statements and can be either internal or external. Financial audit, internal audit, cost auditing, continuous auditing, etc. are different types of auditing. This chapter discusses auditing and its various aspects in a comprehensive manner.

Financial auditing is the process of examining an organization's (or individual's) financial records to determine if they are accurate and in accordance with any applicable rules (including accepted accounting standards), regulations, and laws.

External auditors come in from outside the organization to examine accounting and financial records and provide an independent opinion on these records. Law requires that all public companies have their financial statements externally audited.

Internal auditors work for the organization as internal employees to examine records and help improve internal processes such as operations, internal controls, risk management, and governance.

Auditing Standards

The Public Company Accounting Oversight Board (PCAOB) maintains external auditing standards for public companies (issuers) registered with the Securities and Exchange Commission (SEC).

As of 2012, PCAOB has 15 permanent standards approved by the SEC and a number of interim standards that reflect generally accepted auditing standards, as described in standards issued by the Auditing Standards Board (ASB), which is part of the American Institute of CPAs (AICPA).

The ASB also issues Statements on Auditing Standards (SASs) that apply to preparing and releasing audit reports for nonissuers (companies not required to register with the SEC). AICPA members who audit a nonissuer are required by the AICPA Code of Professional Conduct to comply with these standards. As of 2012, there are more than 60 active standards.

For internal auditing, the Institute of Internal Auditors provides a conceptual framework called the International Professional Practices Framework (IPPF) that provides guidance for internal audits. Some of the guidance is mandatory, while others are considered strongly recommended, but not required by law.

Audit Planning

Audit planning includes deciding on the overall audit strategy and developing an audit plan.

Auditing Standard No. 9 from the PCAOB describes an external auditor's responsibility and the requirements for planning an audit. According to standard No. 9, an audit plan is expected to describe the planned nature, extent, and timing of the procedures for risk assessment and the tests to be done on the controls and substantive procedures, along with a description of other audit procedures planned to ensure the audit meets PCAOB standards.

For internal auditing, the Institute of Internal Auditors provides guidance for audit planning. Planning starts with determining the scope and objectives of the audit.

Internal auditors need to understand the business, operations, and unique characteristics of the department/unit being audited and to develop an audit plan that defines the procedures needed to do an efficient and effective audit.

Information Technology Audit

An information technology audit, or information systems audit, is an examination of the management controls within an Information technology (IT) infrastructure. The evaluation of obtained evidence determines if the information systems are safeguarding assets, maintaining data integrity, and operating effectively to achieve the organization's goals or objectives. These reviews may be performed in conjunction with a financial statement audit, internal audit, or other form of attestation engagement.

Accounting

Due to strong incentives (including taxation, misselling and other forms of fraud) to misstate financial information, auditing has become a legal requirement for many entities who have the power to exploit financial information for personal gain. Traditionally, audits were mainly associated with gaining information about financial systems and the financial records of a company or a business.

Financial audits are performed to ascertain the validity and reliability of information, as well as to provide an assessment of a system's internal control. As a result of this, a third party can express an opinion of the person/organisation/system (etc.) in question. The opinion given on financial statements will depend on the audit evidence obtained.

Due to constraints, an audit seeks to provide only reasonable assurance that the statements are free from material error. Hence, statistical sampling is often adopted in audits. In the case of financial audits, a set of financial statements are said to be true and fair when they are free of material misstatements – a concept influenced by both quantitative (numerical) and qualitative factors. But recently, the argument that auditing should go beyond just true and fair is gaining momentum. And the US Public Company Accounting Oversight Board has come out with a concept release on the same.

Cost accounting is a process for verifying the cost of manufacturing or producing of any article, on the basis of accounts measuring the use of material, labor or other items of cost. In simple words, the term, *cost audit* means a systematic and accurate verification of the cost accounts and records, and checking for adherence to the cost accounting objectives. According to the Institute of Cost and Management Accountants, cost audit is "an examination of cost accounting records and verification of facts to ascertain that the cost of the product has been arrived at, in accordance with principles of cost accounting."

In most nations, an audit must adhere to generally accepted standards established by governing bodies. These standards assure third parties or external users that they can rely upon the auditor's opinion on the fairness of financial statements or other subjects on which the auditor expresses an opinion. The audit must therefore be precise and accurate, containing no additional misstatements or errors.

Integrated Audits

In the US, audits of publicly traded companies are governed by rules laid down by the Public Company Accounting Oversight Board (PCAOB), which was established by Section 404 of the Sarbanes–Oxley Act of 2002. Such an audit is called an integrated audit, where auditors, in addition to an opinion on the financial statements, must also express an opinion on the *effectiveness* of a company's *internal control* over financial reporting, in accordance with PCAOB Auditing Standard No. 5.

There are also new types of integrated auditing becoming available that use unified compliance material. Due to the increasing number of regulations and need for operational transparency, organizations are adopting risk-based audits that can cover multiple regulations and standards from a single audit event. This is a very new but necessary approach in some sectors to ensure that all the necessary governance requirements can be met without duplicating effort from both audit and audit hosting resources.

Assessments

The purpose of an assessment is to measure something or calculate a value for it. Although the process of producing an assessment may involve an audit by an independent professional, its purpose is to provide a measurement rather than to express an opinion about the fairness of statements or quality of performance.

Auditors

Auditors of financial statements & non-financial information (including compliance audit) can be classified into three categories:

- External auditor/Statutory auditor is an independent firm engaged by the client subject to the audit to express an opinion on whether the company's financial statements are free of material misstatements, whether due to fraud or error. For publicly traded companies, external auditors may also be required to express an opinion on the effectiveness of internal controls over financial reporting. External auditors may also be engaged to perform other agreed-upon procedures, related or unrelated to financial statements. Most importantly, external auditors, though engaged and paid by the company being audited, should be regarded as independent.
- Cost auditor/Statutory cost auditor is an independent firm engaged by the client subject to the cost audit to express an opinion on whether the company's cost statements and cost sheet are free of material misstatements, whether due to fraud or error. For publicly traded companies, external auditors may also be required to express an opinion on the effectiveness of internal controls over cost reporting. These are Specialised Persons called Cost Accountants in India & CMA globally either Cost & Management Accountants or Certified Management Accountants.

  Government Auditors review the finances and practices of federal agencies. These auditors report their finds to congress, which uses them to create and manage policies and budgets. Government auditors work for the U.S. Government Accountability Office, and most state governments have similar departments to audit state and municipal agencies.
- Secretarial auditor/Statutory secretarial auditor is an independent firm engaged by the client subject to the audit of secretarial and applicable laws/compliances of other applicable laws to express an opinion on whether the company's secretarial records and compliance of applicable laws are free of material misstatements, whether due to fraud or error and inviting heavy fines or penalties. For bigger public companies, external secretarial auditors may also be required to express an opinion on the effectiveness of internal controls over compliances system management of the company. These are Specialized

Persons called Company Secretaries in India who are the members of Institute of Company Secretaries of India and holding Certificate of Practice.

The most commonly used external audit standards are the US GAAS of the American Institute of Certified Public Accountants and the International Standards on Auditing (ISA) developed by the International Auditing and Assurance Standard.

- Internal auditors are employed by the organisations they audit. They work for government agencies (federal, state and local); for publicly traded companies; and for non-profit companies across all industries. The internationally recognised standard setting body for the profession is the Institute of Internal Auditors - IIA. The IIA has defined internal auditing as follows: "Internal auditing is an independent, objective assurance and consulting activity designed to add value and improve an organisation's operations. It helps an organisation accomplish its objectives by bringing a systematic, disciplined approach to evaluate and improve the effectiveness of risk management, control, and governance processes". Thus professional internal auditors provide independent and objective audit and consulting services focused on evaluating whether the board of directors, shareholders, stakeholders, and corporate executives have reasonable assurance that the organization's governance, risk management, and control processes are designed adequately and function effectively. Internal audit professionals (Certified Internal Auditors - CIAs) are governed by the international professional standards and code of conduct of the Institute of Internal Auditors. While internal auditors are not independent of the companies that employ them, independence and objectivity are a cornerstone of the IIA professional standards; and are discussed at length in the standards and the supporting practice guides and practice advisories. Professional internal auditors are mandated by the IIA standards to be independent of the business activities they audit. This independence and objectivity are achieved through the organizational placement and reporting lines of the internal audit department. Internal auditors of publicly traded companies in the United States are required to report functionally to the board of directors directly, or a sub-committee of the board of directors (typically the audit committee), and not to management except for administrative purposes. As described often in the professional literature for the practice of internal auditing (such as Internal Auditor, the journal of the IIA) -, or other similar and generally recognized frameworks for management control when evaluating an entity's governance and control practices; and apply COSO's "Enterprise Risk Management-Integrated Framework" or other similar and generally recognized frameworks for entity-wide risk management when evaluating an organization's entity-wide risk management practices. Professional internal auditors also use control self-assessment (CSA) as an effective process for performing their work.
- Consultant auditors are external personnel contracted by the firm to perform

an audit following the firm's auditing standards. This differs from the external auditor, who follows their own auditing standards. The level of independence is therefore somewhere between the internal auditor and the external auditor. The consultant auditor may work independently, or as part of the audit team that includes internal auditors. Consultant auditors are used when the firm lacks sufficient expertise to audit certain areas, or simply for staff augmentation when staff are not available.

Performance Audits

Performance audit refers to an independent examination of a program, function, operation or the management systems and procedures of a governmental or non-profit entity to assess whether the entity is achieving economy, efficiency and effectiveness in the employment of available resources. Safety, security, information systems performance, and environmental concerns are increasingly the subject of audits. There are now audit professionals who specialize in security audits and information systems audits. With nonprofit organisations and government agencies, there has been an increasing need for performance audits, examining their success in satisfying mission objectives.

Quality Audits

Quality audits are performed to verify conformance to standards through review of objective evidence. A system of quality audits may verify the effectiveness of a quality management system. This is part of certifications such as ISO 9001. Quality audits are essential to verify the existence of objective evidence showing conformance to required processes, to assess how successfully processes have been implemented, and to judge the effectiveness of achieving any defined target levels. Quality audits are also necessary to provide evidence concerning reduction and elimination of problem areas, and they are a hands-on management tool for achieving continual improvement in an organization.

To benefit the organisation, quality auditing should not only report non-conformance and corrective actions but also highlight areas of good practice and provide evidence of conformance. In this way, other departments may share information and amend their working practices as a result, also enhancing continual improvement.

Project Management

A project audit provides an opportunity to uncover issues, concerns and challenges encountered during the project lifecycle. Conducted midway through the project, an audit affords the project manager, project sponsor and project team an interim view of what has gone well, as well as what needs to be improved to successfully complete the project. If done at the close of a project, the audit can be used to develop success criteria for future projects by providing a forensic review. This review identifies which elements of the project were successfully managed and which ones presented challenges. As a result, the review will help the organisation identify what it needs to do to avoid repeating the same mistakes on future projects.

Projects can undergo 2 types of Project audits:

- Regular Health Check Audits: The aim of a regular health check audit is to understand the current state of a project in order to increase project success.
- Regulatory Audits: The aim of a regulatory audit is to verify that a project is compliant with regulations and standards. Best practices of NEMEA Compliance Centre describe that, the regulatory audit must be accurate, objective, and independent while providing oversight and assurance to the organisation.

Other forms of Project audits:

Formal: Applies when the project is in trouble, sponsor agrees that the audit is needed, sensitivities are high, and need to be able prove conclusions via sustainable evidence.

Informal: Apply when a new project manager is provided, there is no indication the projects in trouble and there is a need to report whether the project is as opposed to where its supposed to Informal audits can apply the same criteria as formal audit but there is no need for such a in depth report or formal report.

Energy Audits

An energy audit is an inspection, survey and analysis of energy flows for energy conservation in a building, process or system to reduce the amount of energy input into the system without negatively affecting the output(s).

Operations Audits

An operations audit is an examination of the operations of the client's business. In this audit the auditor thoroughly examines the efficiency, effectiveness and economy of the operations with which the management of the entity (client) is achieving its objective. The operational audit goes beyond the internal controls issues since management does not achieve its objectives merely by compliance of satisfactory system of internal controls. Operational audits cover any matters which may be commercially unsound. The objective of operational audit is to examine Three E's, namely: Effectiveness – doing the right things with least wastage of resources. Efficiency – performing work in least possible time. Economy – balance between benefits and costs to run the operations.

A control self-assessment is a commonly used tool for completing an operations audit.

Forensic Audits

Also refer to forensic accountancy, forensic accountant or forensic accounting. It refers to an investigative audit in which accountants with specialised on both accounting and investigation seek to uncover frauds, missing money and negligences.

Audit Management

Audit management can be defined as a set of tools; techniques and planning that enable an organized examination of whether an object meets the predefined requirements. To put it more simply, audit management helps in the better organization of the workflow and collaborative process of audit reporting. It is an eclectic management of auditing involving the preparation of a detailed question list and evaluating the results and documents. Auditing management broadly involves the process of recruiting, training and overseeing the audit staff (internal and external) and running the auditing program.

Some of the important elements that make audit management successful are proactive and strong leadership, cohesion within the team, intricate planning, controls and a well-defined methodology. The process of managing an audit comprises of three dimensions, namely internal auditing, external auditing and third-party auditing.

Internal audit management: It refers to a set of auditing processes which the organization sets up in order to protect it from fraudulent activities and ensure that the organization's management and control are running at their optimum. The role of internal auditors is to be objective, neutral and report any issues only to the highest executive in the organization.

External audit management: It is the organization of auditing processes in order to determine whether the documentations filed are accurate and meet the required standards set by the organization or meets the government laid rules and regulations. The external auditor is independent of the firm is able to provide a more objective report and use the discretion in reporting to the concerned authorities in case of a breach.

Third party auditing: The question of third-party auditing arises only when the company intends to run a *quality management* system to meet or qualify for the desired certification.

Internal Audit

Internal audit is a function setup within the organisation to reduce the risk of fraud in the organisation and runs according to the management commands. This is the main difference between internal and external audit where external auditors are independent of management and hence external auditors give an opinion on the financial statements as presented by the management of the organisation. This is performed by the companies internal auditing team, this can help companies improve because strengths and weaknesses are identified. Senior internal audit managers need to manage the responsibilities of what different people want.

Like all supervisor that are part of the business there is a need to:

- Understand what a person with an interest or concern in the business and customers want.
- Agree aim and priorities.
- Plan activities.
- Establish resources and processes.
- Record performance, making changes to keep things on track if required.

External Audit

The objectives of an external audit or audits being conducted by someone not part of the business, is when one business audits a different business to determine if the accounting records are complete and correctly prepared according to GAAP (GAAP is the highest U.S. power on accounting standards and they must be followed by jurisprudence when preparing financial information for businesses) provisions. The organisations have a formal agreement for the supply of goods and services. External audits make good business exercise.

Smaller businesses benefit from external audit because it can act as a education for small business owners, as many small business owners don't have an in-depth understanding of accounting. Businesses can use external auditor to spot mistakes that might have occurred and went noticed. Errors that occur in accounting statements can lead to businesses making bad decisions. For larger corporation audit provide confidence to the shareholder and investors that the figures shown in the books is reliable. Audit management for external auditors might be surpass than the businesses they work with because they are likely to be investing in the best software possible and are a specialist for that particular area.

Companies have to appoint an auditor to do an annual external audit on your accounts if your business is:

- An authorised professional firm.
- A BIPRU investment firm.
- An insurance intermediary.
- An investment management firm.

- A mortgage administrator
- A mortgage intermediary
- A mortgage lender
- A personal investment firm
- A securities and futures firm
- A service company

Third Party Audit

A third party audit gives feedback to important documents and processes including quality manuals or performance development plan, records including instructing, organisational charts, and examination of the processes within the extent of the audit. A third party audit is conducted by an audit organisation that doesn't have the traditional customer-supplier relationship and does not carry any conflict of interest. Institutions such as registrars (certification bodies) or legislature are usually the types of organisations that perform these types of audit.

Managing an Audit

To manage an audit team in a manner to achieve good results, it is important that audit managers have strong leadership skills, workers want to work for someone that has moved up the ranks which shows that the manager they work with has experience doing the job team members are doing. It is important that the teams works efficiently, carrying out audit can be time consuming so being organised and managing different information helps with the productiveness. Auditing involves planning, method, facts, procedures, controls, risk, and management. Communication skills is key to many successful auditors, as you develop through your career getting you message across in your unique way clearly helps project your professionalism. Auditors from different countries may work with each other to help the same client, it is common for auditors to work directly at their client company in their offices.

Audit Directive and Regulation

It is important that the United Kingdom economy has organised and effective capital markets and there is self-assurance in the business framework through greater transparency. Offering reliable and informative reporting supplies to this pledge. It includes the application of global accounting principles and global principles on auditing and requires an ongoing conversation with UK stakeholders and EU or international law makers on measures to encourage market firmness. Companies that are publicly traded may be required to submit an audit.

Financial Audit

Financial auditing refers to an accounting process applied in business. The process involves using an individual body for evaluating the financial transactions and statements of a business. The ultimate purpose of financial audit is presenting an accurate amount of the business transactions of a company. Besides, it ensures that the accounts presented to the public and shareholders are accurate and justified.

This examination by a knowledgeable outsider is needed to provide credibility to an organization's financial statements. If an auditor does not find any issues, then he or she issues an audit opinion, which accompanies the certified financial statements when they are issued. Lenders, creditors, and investors want to see an audit opinion, as proof that the financial statements are correct.

An auditor will conduct a variety of tests to verify that the financial records are complete, and fairly represent the financial results and condition of an organization. These tests may include tests of controls, tests of transactions, analytical procedures, and tests of balances. Financial audits are most commonly conducted for the financial statements of a firm, but may be targeted at more specific areas, such as tax records.

Financial audits dig deep into a company's financial situation, probing accounting records, internal controls policies, cash holdings and other sensitive financial areas. Publicly-traded corporations are subject to external financial audits on a regular basis, and even privately owned small businesses can be subjected to an external financial audit by the IRS or other government authority. Knowing how to perform a financial audit on your own books can help you to prepare for a possible external audit, keep your accounting system in order and discourage internal fraud and theft.

The Big Four

Greenwood et al. (1990) defined the audit firm as professional partnership which has a decentralized organization relationship between the national head office and local offices. Local offices can make most decision except for the drawing up professional standard and maintaining it.

The Big Four are the four largest international professional services networks, offering audit, assurance, tax, consulting, advisory, actuarial, corporate finance, and legal services. They handle the vast majority of audits for publicly traded companies as well as many private companies, creating an oligopoly in auditing large companies. It is reported that the Big Four audit 99% of the companies in the FTSE 100, and 96% of the companies in the FTSE 250 Index, an index of the leading mid-cap listing companies. The Big Four firms are shown below, with their latest publicly available data. None of the Big Four firms is a single firm; rather, they are professional services networks. Each is a network of firms, owned and managed independently, which have entered into agreements with other member firms in the network to share a common name, brand and quality standards. Each network has established an entity to co-ordinate the activities of the network. In one case (KPMG), the co-ordinating entity is Swiss, and in three cases (Deloitte Touche Tohmatsu, PricewaterhouseCoopers and Ernst & Young) the co-ordinating entity is a UK limited company. Those entities do not themselves perform external professional services, and do not own or control the member firms. They are similar to law firm networks found in the legal profession. In many cases each member firm practises in a single country, and is structured to comply with the regulatory environment in that country. In 2007 KPMG announced a merger of four member firms (in the United Kingdom, Germany, Switzerland and Liechtenstein) to form a single firm. Ernst & Young also includes separate legal entities which manage three of its four areas: Americas, EMEIA (Europe, The Middle East, India and Africa), and Asia-Pacific. (Note: the Japan area does not have a separate area management entity). These firms coordinate services performed by local firms within their respective areas but do not perform services or hold ownership in the local entities. This group was once known as the "Big Eight", and was reduced to the "Big Six" and then "Big Five" by a series of mergers. The Big Five became the Big Four after the demise of Arthur Andersen in 2002, following its involvement in the Enron scandal.

Costs

Costs of audit services can vary greatly dependent upon the nature of the entity, its transactions, industry, the condition of the financial records and financial statements, and the fee rates of the CPA firm. A commercial decision such as the setting of audit fees is handled by companies and their auditors. Directors are responsible for setting the overall fee as well as the audit committee. The fees are set at a level that could not lead to audit quality being compromised. The scarcity of staffs and the lower audit fee lead to very low billing realization rates. As a result, accounting firms, such as KPMG, PricewaterhouseCoopers and Deloitte who used to have very low technical inefficiency, have started to use AI tools.

Governance and Oversight

Seal of the United States Government Accountability Office.

In the United States, the SEC has generally deferred to the accounting industry (acting through various organisations throughout the years) as to the accounting standards for financial reporting, and the U.S. Congress has deferred to the SEC.

This is also typically the case in other developed economies. In the UK, auditing guidelines are set by the institutes (including ACCA, ICAEW, ICAS and ICAI) of which auditing firms and individual auditors are members. While in Australia, the rules and professional code of ethics are set by The Institute of Chartered Accountants Australia (ICAA), CPA Australia (CPA) and The National Institute of Accountants (NIA).

Accordingly, financial auditing standards and methods have tended to change significantly only after auditing failures. The most recent and familiar case is that of Enron. The company succeeded in hiding some important facts, such as off-book liabilities, from banks and shareholders. Eventually, Enron filed for bankruptcy, and (as of 2006) is in the process of being dissolved. One result of this scandal was that Arthur Andersen, then one of the five largest accountancy firms worldwide, lost their ability to audit public companies, essentially killing off the firm.

A recent trend in audits (spurred on by such accounting scandals as Enron and Worldcom) has been an increased focus on internal control procedures, which aim to ensure the completeness, accuracy and validity of items in the accounts, and restricted access to financial systems. This emphasis on the internal control environment is now a mandatory part of the audit of SEC-listed companies, under the auditing standards of the Public Company Accounting Oversight Board (PCAOB) set up by the Sarbanes-Oxley Act.

Many countries have government sponsored or mandated organizations who develop and maintain auditing standards, commonly referred to generally accepted auditing standards or GAAS. These standards prescribe different aspects of auditing such as the opinion, stages of an audit, and controls over work product (*i.e.*, working papers).

Some oversight organisations require auditors and audit firms to undergo a third-party quality review periodically to ensure the applicable GAAS is followed.

Stages of an Audit

The following are the stages of a typical audit:

Phase I: plan and Design an Audit Approach

- Accept Client and Perform Initial Planning.
- Understand the Client's Business and Industry.
  - o What should auditors understand?
    - ◇ The relevant industry, regulatory, and other external factors including the applicable financial reporting framework.

◇ The nature of the entity.

◇ The entity's selection and application of accounting policies.

◇ The entity's objectives and strategies, and the related business risks that may result in material misstatement of the financial statements.

◇ The measurement and review of the entity's financial performance.

◇ Internal control relevant to the audit.

- Assess Client's Business Risk.
- Set Materiality and Assess Accepted Audit Risk (AAR) and Inherent Risk (IR).
- Understand Internal Control and Assess Control Risk (CR).
- Develop Overall Audit Plan and Audit Program.

Phase II: Perform test of Controls and Substantive Test of Transactions

- Test of Control: if the auditor plans to reduce the determined control risk, then the auditor should perform the test of control, to assess the operating effectiveness of internal controls (e.g. authorisation of transactions, account reconciliations, segregation of duties) including IT General Controls. If internal controls are assessed as effective, this will reduce (but not entirely eliminate) the amount of 'substantive' work the auditor needs to do.
- Substantive test of transactions: evaluate the client's recording of transactions by verifying the monetary amounts of transactions, a process called substantive tests of transactions. For example, the auditor might use computer software to compare the unit selling price on duplicate sales invoices with an electronic file of approved prices as a test of the accuracy objective for sales transactions. Like the test of control in the preceding paragraph, this test satisfies the accuracy transaction-related audit objective for sales. For the sake of efficiency, auditors often perform tests of controls and substantive tests of transactions at the same time.
- Assess Likelihood of Misstatement in Financial Statement.

Notes:

- At this stage, if the auditor accept the CR that has been set at the phase I and does not want to reduce the controls risk, then the auditor may not perform test of control. If so, then the auditor perform substantive test of transactions.
- This test determines the amount of work to be performed i.e. substantive testing or test of details.

Phase III: Perform Analytical Procedures And Tests of Details Of Balances

- Where internal controls are strong, auditors typically rely more on Substantive Analytical Procedures (the comparison of sets of financial information, and financial with non-financial information, to see if the numbers 'make sense' and that unexpected movements can be explained).
- Where internal controls are weak, auditors typically rely more on Substantive Tests of Detail of Balance (selecting a sample of items from the major account balances, and finding hard evidence (e.g. invoices, bank statements) for those items).

Notes:

- Some audits involve a 'hard close' or 'fast close' whereby certain substantive procedures can be performed before year-end. For example, if the year-end is 31 December, the hard close may provide the auditors with figures as at 30 November. The auditors would audit income/expense movements between 1 January and 30 November, so that after year end, it is only necessary for them to audit the December income/expense movements and 31 December balance sheet. In some countries and accountancy firms these are known as 'rollforward' procedures.

Phase IV: Complete the Audit and Issue an Audit Report

After the auditor has completed all procedures for each audit objective and for each financial statement account and related disclosures, it is necessary to combine the information obtained to reach an overall conclusion as to whether the financial statements are fairly presented. This highly subjective process relies heavily on the auditor's professional judgment. When the audit is completed, the CPA must issue an audit report to accompany the client's published financial statements.

Responsibilities of an Auditor

Corporations Act 2001 requires the auditor to:

- Gives a true and fair view about whether the financial report complies with the accounting standards.
- Conduct their audit in accordance with auditing standards.
- Give the directors and auditor's independence declaration and meet independence requirements.
- Report certain suspected contraventions to ASIC.

Commercial Relationships Versus Objectivity

One of the major issues faced by private auditing firms is the need to provide independent auditing services while maintaining a business relationship with the audited company.

The auditing firm's responsibility to check and confirm the reliability of financial statements may be limited by pressure from the audited company, who pays the auditing firm for the service. The auditing firm's need to maintain a viable business through auditing revenue may be weighed against its duty to examine and verify the accuracy, relevancy, and completeness of the company's financial statements. This is done by auditor.

Numerous proposals are made to revise the current system to provide better economic incentives to auditors to perform the auditing function without having their commercial interests compromised by client relationships. Examples are more direct incentive compensation awards and financial statement insurance approaches. See, respectively, Incentive Systems to Promote Capital Market Gatekeeper Effectiveness and Financial Statement Insurance.

Auditors and Technology

Currently, many entities being audited are using information systems, which generate information electronically. For the audit evidences, auditors get dynamic information generated from the information systems in real time. There are less paper documents and pre-numbered audit evidences available, which leads a revolution to audit mythology.

Internal Audit

An internal audit (IA) is an organizational initiative to monitor and analyze its own business operations in order to determine how well it conforms to a set of specific criteria.

In the enterprise, an internal audit can focus on enterprise risk management functions, security processes or maintaining regulatory compliance, as well as many other business departments and activities. As part of the internal audit plan, auditors try to find discrepancies between operational processes and what those processes are designed to do. If internal auditors do find discrepancies, these issues are included in the final report issued to company leadership so the processes can be improved.

Internal audit plans are often designed as a pre-emptive maneuver to maintain operational efficiency and financial reliability, as well as to safeguard assets.

Reasons why Internal Audits Matter

Regular internal audits assess a company's controls and help uncover evidence of fraud, waste or abuse. The frequency of internal audits will depend on the department or process being examined. Some types of manufacturing may require daily audits for quality control, while a department such as human resources may require only an annual audit of records.

Unlike an external auditor that primarily considers financial risk, the internal auditor examines issues relating to wide-ranging risks to the organization's reputation and growth. For example, an internal audit can uncover threats to the organization's reputation if it finds employee safety violations or instances where employees are treated unfairly. One of the internal auditor's primary goals is to assess the management of risk and to ensure that risk management processes are efficient, effective, secure and compliant.

Once the internal audits are completed, auditors issue a final audit report outlining how well the systems and processes are working. This report is often provided first to the most senior levels of executive management, as well as to its internal audit committee. When required, internal auditors offer consulting help to improve areas in which systems and processes are lacking and conduct a follow-up audit to determine how well the improvements are working.

Information provided by internal auditors can help the company thrive in a competitive business environment and inform new initiatives to help it continue to prosper.

Organizational Independence

While internal auditors are not independent of the companies that employ them, independence and objectivity are a cornerstone of the IIA professional standards; and are discussed at length in the standards and the supporting practice guides and practice advisories. Professional internal auditors are mandated by the IIA standards to be independent of the business activities they audit. This independence and objectivity are achieved through the organizational placement and reporting lines of the internal audit department. Internal auditors of publicly traded companies in the United States are required to report functionally to the board of directors directly, or a sub-committee of the board of directors (typically the audit committee), and not to management except for administrative purposes.

The required organizational independence from management enables unrestricted evaluation of management activities and personnel and allows internal auditors to perform their role effectively. Although internal auditors are part of company management and paid by the company, the primary customer of internal audit activity is the entity charged with oversight of management's activities. This is typically the Audit Committee, a sub-committee of the Board of Directors. Organizational independence is effectively achieved when the chief audit executive reports functionally to the board. Examples of functional reporting to the board involve the board: Approving the internal audit charter; Approving the risk based internal audit plan; Approving the internal audit budget and resource plan; Receiving communications from the chief audit executive on the internal audit activity's performance relative to its plan and other matters; Approving decisions regarding the appointment and removal of the chief audit executive; Approving the remuneration of the chief audit executive; and Making appropriate inquiries of management and the chief audit executive to determine whether there are inappropriate scope or resource limitations.

Role in Internal Control

Internal auditing activity is primarily directed at evaluating internal control. Under the COSO Framework, internal control is broadly defined as a process, effected by an entity's board of directors, management, and other personnel, designed to provide reasonable assurance regarding the achievement of the following core objectives for which all businesses strive:

- Effectiveness and efficiency of operations.
- Reliability of financial and management reporting.
- Compliance with laws and regulations.
- Safeguarding of Assets.

Management is responsible for internal control, which comprises five critical components: the control environment; risk assessment; risk focused control activities; information and communication; and monitoring activities. Managers establish policies, processes, and practices in these five components of management control to help the organization achieve the four specific objectives listed above. Internal auditors perform audits to evaluate whether the five components of management control are present and operating effectively, and if not, provide recommendations for improvement.

In the United States, internal auditors may assist management with compliance with the Sarbanes-Oxley Act (SOX).

Role in Risk Management

Internal auditing professional standards require the function to evaluate the effectiveness of the organization's Risk management activities. Risk management is the process by which an organization identifies, analyzes, responds, gathers information about, and monitors strategic risks that could actually or potentially impact the organization's ability to achieve its mission and objectives.

Under the COSO enterprise risk management (ERM) Framework, an organization's strategy, operations, reporting, and compliance objectives all have associated strategic business risks - the negative outcomes resulting from internal and external events that inhibit the organization's ability to achieve its objectives. Management assesses risk as part of the ordinary course of business activities such as strategic planning, marketing planning, capital planning, budgeting, hedging, incentive payout structure, credit/lending practices, mergers and acquisitions, strategic partnerships, legislative changes, conducting business abroad, etc. Sarbanes-Oxley regulations require extensive risk assessment of financial reporting processes. Corporate legal counsel often prepares comprehensive assessments of the current and potential litigation a company faces. Internal auditors may evaluate each of these activities, or focus on the overarching process used to manage risks entity-wide. For example, internal auditors can advise management regarding the reporting of forward-looking operating measures to the Board, to help identify emerging risks; or internal auditors can evaluate and report on whether the board and other stakeholders can have reasonable assurance the organization's management team has implemented an effective enterprise risk management program.

In larger organizations, major strategic initiatives are implemented to achieve objectives and drive changes. As a member of senior management, the Chief Audit Executive (CAE) may participate in status updates on these major initiatives. This places the CAE in the position to report on many of the major risks the organization faces to the Audit Committee, or ensure management's reporting is effective for that purpose.

The internal audit function may help the organization address its risk of fraud via a fraud risk assessment, using principles of fraud deterrence. Internal auditors may help companies establish and maintain Enterprise Risk Management processes. This process is highly valued by many businesses for establishing and implementing effective management systems and ensuring quality is maintained & professional standards are met Internal auditors also play an important role in helping companies execute a SOX 404 top-down risk assessment. In these latter two areas, internal auditors typically are part of the risk assessment team in an advisory role.

Role in Corporate Governance

Internal auditing activity as it relates to corporate governance has in the past been generally informal, accomplished primarily through participation in meetings and discussions with members of the Board of Directors. According to COSO's ERM framework, governance is the policies, processes and structures used by the organization's leadership to direct activities, achieve objectives, and protect the interests of diverse stakeholder groups in a manner consistent with ethical standards. The internal auditor is often considered one of the "four pillars" of corporate governance, the other pillars being the Board of Directors, management, and the external auditor.

A primary focus area of internal auditing as it relates to corporate governance is helping the Audit Committee of the Board of Directors (or equivalent) perform its responsibilities effectively. This may include reporting critical management control issues, suggesting questions or topics for the Audit Committee's meeting agendas, and coordinating with the external auditor and management to ensure the Committee receives effective information. In recent years, the IIA has advocated more formal evaluation of Corporate governance, particularly in the areas of board oversight of enterprise risk, corporate ethics, and fraud.

Audit Project Selection or "Annual Audit Plan"

Based on the risk assessment of the organization, internal auditors, management and oversight boards determine where to focus internal auditing efforts. This focus or prioritization is part of the annual/ multi-year Annual Audit Plan. The Audit Plan is typically proposed by the CAE (sometimes with several options or alternatives) for the review and approval of the Audit Committee or the Board of Directors. Internal Auditing activity is generally conducted as one or more discrete assignments.

Internal Audit Execution

A typical Internal Audit Assignment involves the following steps:

1. Establishing and communicating the scope and objectives of the Audit to appropriate members of management.
2. Developing an understanding of the business area under review - this includes objectives, measurements & key transaction types and involves interviews and a review of documents - flowcharts and narratives may be created, if necessary.
3. Describing the key risks facing the business activities within the scope of the Audit.
4. Identifying management practices in the five components of control used to ensure that each key risk is properly controlled and monitored. Internal Audit Checklist can be a helpful tool to identify common risks and desired controls in the specific process or specific industry being audited.
5. Developing and executing a risk-based sampling and testing approach to determine whether the most important management controls are operating as intended.
6. Reporting issues and challenges identified and negotiating action plans with the management to address these problems.
7. Following-up on reported findings at appropriate intervals. Internal Audit Departments maintain a follow-up database for this purpose.

Audit Assignment length varies based on the complexity of the activity being audited and Internal Audit resources available. Many of the above steps are iterative and may not all occur in the sequence indicated.

In addition to assessing business processes, specialists called Information Technology (IT) Auditors review Information technology controls.

Internal Audit Reports

Internal auditors typically issue reports at the end of each audit that summarize their findings, recommendations, and any responses or action plans from management. An audit report may have an executive summary—a body that includes the specific issues or findings identified and related recommendations or action plans, and appendix information such as detailed graphs and charts or process information. Each audit finding within the body of the report may contain five elements, sometimes called the "5 C's":

1. Condition: What is the particular problem identified?
2. Criteria: What is the standard that was not met? The standard may be a company policy or other benchmark.
3. Cause: Why did the problem occur?
4. Consequence: What is the risk/negative outcome (or opportunity foregone) because of the finding?
5. Corrective action: What should management do about the finding? What have they agreed to do and by when?

The recommendations in an internal audit report are designed to help the organization achieve effective and efficient governance, risk and control processes associated with operations objectives, financial and management reporting objectives; and legal/regulatory compliance objectives.

Audit findings and recommendations may also relate to particular assertions about transactions, such as whether the transactions audited were valid or authorized, completely processed, accurately valued, processed in the correct time period, and properly disclosed in financial or operational reporting, among other elements.

Under the IIA standards, a critical component of the audit process is the preparation of a balanced report that provides executives and the board with the opportunity to evaluate and weigh the issues being reported in the proper context and perspective. In providing perspective, analysis and workable recommendations for business improvements in critical areas, auditors help the organization meet its objectives.

Quality of Internal Audit Report

- Objectivity - The comments and opinions expressed in the Report should be objective and unbiased.
- Clarity - The language used should be simple and straightforward.
- Accuracy - The information contained in the report should be accurate.
- Brevity - The report should be concise.
- Timeliness - The report should be released promptly immediately after the audit is concluded, within a month.

Strategy

Internal audit functions may also develop functional strategies described in multi-year strategic plans. Professional guidance on building an Internal Audit strategic plan was issued by the *Institute of Internal Auditors* in July 2012 via a Practice Guide called *Developing the Internal Audit Strategic Plan*. A key aspect of developing IA strategy is understanding the expectations of stakeholders, such as the Audit Committee and top management. This helps guide the IA function in its mission of helping the organization address the risks it faces. Specific topics considered in IA strategic planning include:

- Scope and emphasis: An IA function may be involved in addressing risks related to financial reporting, operations, legal and regulatory compliance, and the company strategy. There may also be special topics of interest to stakeholders that change considerably year-to-year.
- Portfolio of services: IA functions may provide traditional audit assurance across the risk spectrum as well as consulting project support in a variety of areas such as project management, data analysis, and monitoring of major company initiatives. Larger audit functions may establish specialty areas to handle their service portfolio.
- Competency development: The stakeholder expectations around scope and service portfolio determine what competencies the function needs, which drives decisions regarding hiring of specific skills and training programs. The internal audit function is often used as a "management training ground" to provide employees with a deeper knowledge of the company's operations before they are rotated into a management position.
- Technology: IA functions use a variety of technology tools/software to support audit process workflow, statistical analysis, and obtaining data from systems.

Building the IA strategy may involve a variety of strategic management concepts and frameworks, such as strategic planning, strategic thinking, and SWOT analysis.

Measuring the Internal Audit Function

The measurement of the internal audit function can involve a balanced scorecard approach. Internal audit functions are primarily evaluated based on the quality of counsel and information provided to the Audit Committee and top management. However, this is primarily qualitative and therefore difficult to measure. "Customer surveys" sent to key managers after each audit engagement or report can be used to measure performance, with an annual survey to the Audit Committee. Scoring on dimensions such as professionalism, quality of counsel, timeliness of work product, utility of meetings, and quality of status updates are typical with such surveys. Understanding the expectations of senior management and the audit committee represent important steps in developing a performance measurement process, as well as how such measures help align the audit function with organizational priorities. Independent peer reviews are part of the quality assurance process for many internal audit groups as they are often required by standards. The resulting peer review report is made available to the Audit Committee.

Reporting of Critical Findings

The Chief Audit Executive (CAE) typically reports the most critical issues to the Audit Committee quarterly, along with management's progress towards resolving them. Critical issues typically have a reasonable likelihood of causing substantial financial or reputational damage to the company. For particularly complex issues, the responsible manager may participate in the discussion. Such reporting is critical to ensure the function is respected, that the proper "tone at the top" exists in the organization, and to expedite resolution of such issues. It is a matter of considerable judgment to select appropriate issues for the Audit Committee's attention and to describe them in the proper context.

Operational Auditing

Operational auditing is a comprehensive and constructive review of organisational structure or components thereof, i.e. method of operation and use of physical facilities'. Operational Auditing is essentially a frame of mind, a method of approach; one can approach any area from a financial or accounting point of view or from operating or management point of view.

A control system via appraisal system to keep the management informed of 'opportunities gained' and 'opportunities lost' is Operation Audit or Operational Auditing. Federal Financial Officers' Institute in Canada defines Operational Audit as a systematic independent appraisal activity within an organisation for a review of the entire departmental operations as a service to management.

The overall objective of operational auditing is to assist all levels of management in the effective discharge of their responsibilities by furnishing them with objective analyses, appraisals, recommendations and pertinent comments concerning the activities reviewed.

This definition does not specifically mention about financial and accounting areas of the operation but a careful review of the use of the words 'entire departmental operations' in the definition characterizes the inclusion of both financial and operational areas.

Thus operational audit may be conceived of as a body of knowledge which seeks to:

(a) Determine effectiveness of performance in each delegated functional area.

(b) Establish potential impact of successes and failures (especially, failures) in the specialised functional areas of operation.

Objectives of Operation Audit:

The objectives of any company are:

Productivity, profitability, market expansion, innovation, efficient managerial performance, upgrading the employees attitude and work performance and discharging social responsibilities. The operational audit may serve the business in discharging these objectives.

The objectives of the operational auditing may, therefore, be stated as below:

i. Appraisal of company's objectives,

ii. Evaluation of company's policies,

iii. Evaluation of company's plans,

iv. Evaluation of the structure of organisation,

v. Evaluation of controls,

vi. Appraisal of performance, which involves examination of work flow, determination of work force, performance of work load, measurement of productivity, measurement of profitability, performance of job, and appraisal of costs,

vii. Evaluation of company's social responsibilities, e.g. extent of benefits passed on to the consumers, creation of employment opportunities, etc.

Advantages and Disadvantages

Going through the operational audit process provides a company with objective opinions. Those opinions often generate quicker production or sales turnaround, better allocation of costs, improved control systems, the location of areas of delay and an overall streamlined workflow. However, similar to any audit, operational audits cost money to perform. Those involved in the audit cannot be engaged in other operational processes when they are meeting with the auditor or gathering data for the auditor to use. Additionally, operational audits take considerable time to complete, and it can be harder to determine exactly what is causing problems the more complex operations are. Additionally, even though overhauling operations based on audit results may save the business money in the long run, doing so can rattle employees, cause initial confusion and necessitate increased training or significant staffing alterations.

Cost Auditing

Cost Audit is a critical review undertaken to verify the correctness of Cost Accounts and to check that cost accounting principles and planning have been efficiently followed. It is noteworthy that India is the only country which has introduced statutory cost audit to regulate about 45 vital industries of the country. Cost Audit has been defined by the Chartered Institute of Management Accountants (CIMA) of Landon as "the verification of cost accounts and a check on the adherence to the cost accounting plan."

This implies the following:

(i) The objects of cost accounting with reference to which the cost accounting plan must have been drawn up have to be kept in mind to see whether or not the plan itself and the figures collected will lead to the achievement of the goal or objective set. For instance, if the objective is to achieve maximum efficiency, the plan and the analysis of data will be different from the case where the only objective is to fix prices.

(ii) It has to be examined whether the methods laid down for ascertaining costs and other relevant decisions are being implemented. Treatment and determination of abnormal losses of gains or treatment of certain expenses as direct or indirect are cases in point.

(iii) The correctness of the figures has to be vouched.

The concept of cost audit has been elaborated by ICWA as 'an audit of efficiency of minute details of expenditure, while the work is in progress and not a post mortem examination. Financial audit is a 'fait accompli', cost audit is mainly a preventive measure, a guide for management policy and decision in addition, to being a barometer of performance'.

Cost Audit can be called efficiency audit. It is evidenced by amendment in section 209 which reads. 'The object of the amendment of the section is to ensure specified company proper records relating to utilisation of material labour are available which would make efficiency audit (cost- audit) possible'.

Advantages of Cost Audit

(i) A close check will be maintained on all wastages—materials in store, labour, etc.—and they will be promptly located and reported.

(ii) Inefficiencies in production (or efficiencies) will be located and converted into monetary terms.

(iii) Through fixation of individual responsibility, management by exception will be possible.

(iv) The system of budgetary control and standard costing will be greatly facilitated with cost audit at the hands of a qualified cost accountant.

(v) Records will be up-to-date and information for various purposes will be available.

(vi) Cost audit may unearth a number of errors and frauds which may not be revealed otherwise. This is because a cost auditor examines expenditure minutely and compares it with standards and ascertains exact reasons for discrepancy.

Cost audit offers many advantages to management, cost accountant, shareholders, statutory auditor, consumers and the government.

Advantages to Management:

(i) Errors in following costing principles and techniques are detected. Inconsistencies and frauds can also be detected. This keeps everyone alert and promotes efficiency.

(ii) Cost audit can serve to measure performance of managers and better performance can be rewarded.

(iii) It helps to prepare accurate cost reports and this business planning can be more accurate.

(iv) Inter-firm comparisons can be made with ease and this might be a very useful proposition if industrial intelligence is good.

(v) Cost audit can give an idea about the comparative operational efficiency of each department of division; and may thus pin-point deficiencies and also encourage to operate in a competitive spirit.

Advantages to Management/Cost Accountant:

Important advantages are:

(i) His task is facilitated since errors, deficiencies, etc., are pointed out. Costing plans can be prepared to take care of these things.

(ii) Cost audit may help in easier reconciliation of cost and financial accounts.

(iii) If the cost auditor is an outsider and is an expert, he can certainly give some practical and sound advice to streamline costing systems and organisation.

(iv) Cost audit helps to focus attention of management on the problems faced by the cost accountant. This helps him to realize his goals and objectives with ease.

Advantages to Statutory Auditor:

(i) Audited cost data helps him to determine the value of stocks, remuneration of managerial personnel, etc., with ease and accuracy.

(ii) Data and statements of cost audit help him to prepare his audit programme and plan so that he concentrates more on those aspects which have not been adequately covered by cost audit.

Advantages to Consumers:

(i) The direct benefit accrues where a statutory cost audit has been done to fix a reasonable price for the consumers.

(ii) Since cost audit aims at ensuring efficiency in the organisation, this may also get reflected in reduced prices to the consumers.

Advantages to Labour:

(i) If cost audit is done thoroughly labour also stands to gain through increased profitability in the shape of bonus and other benefits.

(ii) Also it brings into focus the role of labour in improving efficiency in term of increased productivity.

Advantages to Shareholders:

(i) There is correct valuation of all kinds of inventories. This may project a true picture of the organisation before shareholders and other investors and help them to assess its performance.

(ii) External cost audit highlights efficiency or inefficiency, utilisation of manpower and other resources, adequacy of return, etc.

Advantages to Government and Economy:

(i) It helps the government to settle accounts where cost-plus contracts have been made.

(ii) The government can intervene to protect the interests of the consumers, labour, shareholders and investors from exploit-age or inefficient managements.

(iii) At the national level, cost audit promotes cost consciousness and overall efficiency. This means that every rupee invested produces the maximum quantity of goods and services.

Types of Cost Audit:

(i) Cost Audit as an Aid to Management:

The aim is to see that all information placed before management is relevant, reliable and prompt so that management can discharge its duties well. It must also be seen that no relevant or pertinent information is suppressed.

(ii) Cost Audit on Behalf of a Customer:

Often contracts are placed on "Cost Plus" basis. In other words, the customer will determine the final price to be paid on the basis of exact cost plus an agreed margin of profit. The customer, in such a case, usually gets cost accounts of the product concerned audited to establish correct cost and, therefore, price.

(iii) Cost Audit on Behalf of Government:

Sometimes the Government is approached with request for financial help or protection. Before taking a decision on the request, the Government may choose to get cost accounts of the applicant audited to establish whether the need for help is genuine or is a result of mere inefficiency.

(iv) Cost Audit under Statute:

The Amendment Act of 1965 has inserted a new section, 233B, in the Companies Act, 1956 whereby the Central Government may order that certain classes of companies will get their cost accounts audited by a member of the Institute of Cost and Works Accounts of India. Only such companies as are required to maintain proper records regarding materials consumed, labour and other expenses under Section 209 (as amended to date) and may be required to get their cost accounts audited.

The powers and duties and manner of appointment of the cost auditor are the same as that of external financial auditor and the same disqualifications will apply. The cost auditor will submit his report to the Company Law Board with a copy to the company. The right to investigate all aspects of cost accounts is presumably granted to the cost auditor.

The aim of cost audit under statute seems to be that the Government wishes to know, as an instrument of control, the costs of various goods. Government has the power to prescribe the forms in which cost audit reports are to be made out. These are designed not only to verify information, but also to convey good deal of information to Government.

(v) Cost Audit on Behalf of the Trade Association:

Sometimes trade associations seek to maintain prices at a certain level. For this purpose, the accuracy of costing information submitted by various concerns has to be checked. The trade associations may seek to have full information about production capacity and the relative efficiency of productive processes.

Objectives of Cost Auditor

1. Prospective Objective: Under which cost audit aims to identify the undue wastage or losses and ensure that costing system determines the correct and realistic cost of production.
2. Constructive Objectives: Cost audit provides useful information to the management regarding regulating production, economical method of operation, reducing cost of operation and reformulating Cost accounting plans.

Continuous Auditing

Continuous auditing has been defined as a methodology or framework that enables auditors to present written results on the subject matter by means of one or a series of reports issued at the same time. The ability to report on events in a concurrent environment can provide important benefits to the users of audit reports. Continuous auditing is consequently designed to enable auditors to report on subject matter in a much shorter timeframe than under the conventional model. In theory, in some environments it should be probable to reduce the reporting timeframe to provide auditing on almost an instantaneous basis. The article focuses on the reliability of continuous auditing, applicability of continuous auditing to organizations and relevance of continuous auditing to auditors.

Reliability of Continuous Auditing

While there has been noteworthy academic research on continuous auditing, as well as numerous efforts by professional standard setting bodies the world over, there has been little, if any, reporting on a constant basis. This is a consequence of a number of factors, which are inclusive of such things as demand, cost vs. benefit and technological issues. While the notion of continuous auditing has been around for many years the real practice and demand for this service has been low. At least from the external audit viewpoint, this is a consequence of the perceived cost outweighing the perceived benefit in continuous auditing. This perspective is a straight result of focusing on continuous auditing only from the financial reporting perspective.

Indisputably, the price of issuing an audit report on a complete set of financial statements each week, month or quarter would be significant and would exceed its value. Nevertheless, if the audit report only addressed definite types of related data in the financial or non-financial category, performance measures or some other information that was of significance to users and could be audited at a rational cost, then the benefits of this type of reporting may be in excess of its cost. If continuous auditing is needed to be established, organizations and auditors must start small. They should start with effortlessly auditable data that has important value to users, such as investors and the equity markets, and structure an obligation to permit an auditor to report within a timeframe that provides value to users of the data.

Applicability of Continuous Auditing to Organizations

Many organizations are not ready for continuous auditing from either a maturity level or a technological level. This is a factor concerning the maturity of their processes, systems and controls. The cost and time required to execute a continuous auditing exercise increases as the strength of an organization's processes and controls decreases. It is observed that organizations with strong processes and controls and mature systems are better suited to a continuous auditing engagement since the auditor can place greater reliance on the processes, controls and systems to lessen the degree, nature and timing of testing to provide support to a continuous auditing opinion. For example, if an organization wanted to make public audited monthly sales and production information two days after month end, the auditor must execute all audit procedures within two days to meet the reporting deadline. On the contrary, the auditor could place dependence on the processes and controls over the systems that process monthly sales and production data and test those processes.

Relevance of Continuous Auditing to Auditors

The special skills and knowledge that auditors have are necessary for the assessment of these controls and for the performance of these engagements related to continuous auditing. This means that auditors are the solution to the issuance of any continuous auditing report; in spite its subject matter. Organizations with superior internal control environments and well-controlled information systems were well-matched for the process of continuous auditing. This conclusion was founded on the assumption that, to make continuous auditing achievable and gainful, important dependence on controls was required. The study noted that auditors would have a vital involvement in continuous auditing engagements as it was projected that many of the controls would be IT controls.

Components

Continuous auditing is made up of three main parts: continuous data assurance (CDA), continuous controls monitoring (CCM), and continuous risk monitoring and assessment (CRMA).

Continuous Data Assurance

Continuous data assurance verifies the integrity of data flowing through the information systems. Continuous data assurance uses software to extract data from IT systems for analysis at the transactional level to provide more detailed assurance. CDA systems provide the ability to design expectation models for analytical procedures at the business-process level, as opposed to the current practice of relying on ratio or trend analysis at higher levels of data aggregation. CDA software can continuously and automatically monitor transactions, comparing their generic characteristics with predetermined benchmarks, thereby identifying anomalous situations. When significant discrepancies occur, alarms are triggered and routed to appropriate stakeholders and auditors.

Continuous Controls Monitoring

Continuous controls monitoring consists of a set of procedures used for monitoring the functionality of internal controls. CCM relies on automatic procedures, presuming that both the controls themselves and the monitoring procedures are formal or able to be formalized. CCM can be used for monitoring access control and authorizations, system configurations, and business process settings. CDA and CCM are complementary processes. Neither process is self-sufficient or comprehensive. Even if no data faults are found it cannot be concluded that controls are fail-safe. Further, even if controls are being implemented, data integrity cannot be assumed. When combined, however, these monitoring approaches present a more complete reliance picture.

Continuous Risk Monitoring and Assessment

Continuous risk monitoring and assessment is used to dynamically measure risk and provide input for audit planning. CRMA is a real-time integrated risk assessment approach, aggregating data across different functional tasks in organizations to assess risk exposures and provide reasonable assurance on the firms' risk assessments.

Black Box Logging

In addition to the aforementioned three components, the black box audit log file is also an important part of continuous auditing. This file can be viewed as an extension of the existing practice of documenting audit activities in manual or automated work papers. A black box log file is a read-only, third-party controlled record of the actions of auditors. The objective of black box logging is to protect a continuous auditing system against auditor and management manipulations.

Continuous Reporting

Continuous reporting is the release of financial and non-financial information on a real-time or near real-time basis. The purpose of continuous reporting is to allow external parties access to information as underlying events take place, rather than waiting for end-of-period reports. The adoption of XBRL by companies makes the release of continuous reporting information more feasible. Continuous reporting also benefits users under Regulation Fair Disclosure. Continuous reporting is a point of constant debate. Some parties, including analysts and investors, are interested in knowing how a company is doing at a given point in time. They argue that near real-time information would provide them with the ability to take advantage of important business moves as they happen. However, opponents are skeptical of how the raw information can be useful and fear information overload, or that there would be too much irrelevant information out there. Additionally, some companies are fearful that continuously reported financial information would give away important strategic moves and undermine competitive advantage.

Implementation

Generally, the implementation of continuous auditing consists of six procedural steps, which are usually administered by a continuous audit manager. Knowing about these steps will enable auditors to better monitor the continuous audit process and provide recommendations for its improvement, if needed. These steps include:

- Establishing priority areas.

This entails choosing which organizational areas to audit. When performing the actions listed above, auditors need to consider the key objectives from each audit procedure. Objectives can be classified as one of four types: detective, deterrent (also known as preventive), financial, and compliance. A particular audit priority area may satisfy any one of these four objectives.

- Identifying monitoring and continuous audit rules.

The second step consists of determining the rules or analytics that will guide the continuous audit activity, which need to be programmed, repeated frequently, and reconfigured when needed. In addition, monitoring and audit rules must take into consideration legal and environmental issues, as well as the objectives of the particular process.

- Determining the process' frequency.

Continuous auditing need not be literally continuous. Auditors need to consider the natural rhythm of the process being audited, including the timing of computer and business processes as well as the timing and availability of auditors trained or with experience in continuous auditing.

- Configuring continuous audit parameters.

Rules used in each audit area need to be configured before the continuous audit procedure (CAP) is implemented. In addition, the frequency of each parameter might need to be changed after its initial setup based on changes stemming from the activity being audited. When defining a CAP, auditors should consider the costs and benefits of error detection as well as audit and management follow-up activities.

- Following up.

Another type of parameter relates to the treatment of alarms and detected errors. Questions such as who will receive the alarm (e.g., line managers, internal auditors, or both – usually the alarm is sent to the process manager, the manager's immediate supervisor, or the auditor in charge of that CAP) and when the follow-up activity must be completed, need to be addressed when establishing the continuous audit process.

- Communicating results.

A final item to be considered is how to communicate with auditees. When informing auditees of continuous audit activity results, it is important for the exchange to be independent and consistent.

Demand

Demand for continuous auditing has come from a variety of sources, primarily user-driven requirements. External disclosure, internal drivers, laws and regulation, and technology all play important roles in pushing up demand.

External Disclosure

More frequent disclosure will drive the nature of the audit process. This increase improves the quality of earnings while reducing manager aggressiveness and decreasing stock market volatility.

Internal Drivers

As companies have become more integrated within their own departments and with other companies, such as suppliers and retailers, a desire for data integrity throughout the electronic data exchange process is also driving demand for continuous auditing.

Laws and Regulation

Laws and regulation require activities and ways a company followed in order to achieve a specific goal to be monitored. Under such laws and regulation company commenced for continuous auditing.

Technology

XBRL

XBRL facilitates the development of continuous auditing modules by providing a way for systems to understand the meaning of tagged data. Proper use of XBRL assures that relevant data gathered from multiple sources is easily comparable and analyzable. XBRL is a derivative of the XML file format, which tags data with contextual and hierarchical information. It is expected that many enterprise resource planning systems will provide data in the XBRL-GL format to facilitate machine readability.

Security

Because of the nature of the information passing through continuous auditing systems, security and privacy issues are also being addressed. Data assurance techniques, as well as access control mechanisms and policies are being implemented into CA systems to prevent unauthorized access and manipulation, and CCM can help test these controls.

Challenges

For many organizations, there are a number of challenges to implementing a continuous auditing approach. The following are some common challenges with associated recommendations.

- Accessing Complex, Diverse System Environment

Few organizations have a completely homogenous, seamless system environment. There is typically a mix of ERPs or multiple instances of one ERP, mainframe systems, off-the-shelf applications, and legacy systems—all of which may contain valuable data. Technology is available to access all of this data to gain a complete picture.

- Reluctance to Expand the use of Technology

Technology may be viewed as a threat to those who perceive that automation might replace jobs. A benefit of continuous auditing is that it performs routine, repetitive tasks and provides the opportunity for the more interesting exploratory work that adds far more value to the organization.

- Overwhelming Results

When not properly implemented, continuous auditing can result in hundreds—even thousands—of false positives and wasted effort. Many companies that have experienced success with continuous auditing recommend that you start small. Select which area of the company poses the greatest risk and where its transactions and control systems are most important to the company for your initial foray into continuous auditing. Automate a small number of key initial tests, such as comparing your accounts payable vendor master file with the employee address file, to uncover potential policy violations or fraud. Moving forward, increase the tests and gradually expand into other business processes in stages.

- Training

Training is essential for optimum results. A number of institutions, including ACL Services Ltd., offer training on computer-aided audit techniques including continuous auditing through automation. Training can be conducted either on-site or remotely, depending on the need of companies.

Comparison to Computer-aided Auditing

Continuous auditing is often confused with computer-aided auditing. The purpose and scope of the two techniques, however, are quite different. Computer-aided auditing employs end user technology including spreadsheet software, such as Microsoft Excel, to allow traditional auditors to run audit-specific analyses as they conduct the periodic audit. Continuous auditing, on the other hand, involves advanced analytical tools that automate a majority of the auditing plan. Where auditors manually extract data and run their own analyses in computer-aided auditing during the course of their traditional audit, high-powered servers automatically extract and analyze data at specified intervals as a part of continuous auditing.

Auditor's Report

An auditor's report provides an opinion on the validity and reliability of a company's financial statements.

When financial statements are finalised, they usually must contain an evaluation – an auditor's report - from a licensed accountant or auditor. This report provides an overview of the evaluation of the validity and reliability of a company or organization's financial statements.

The goal of an auditor's report is to document reasonable assurance that a company's financial statements are free from error.

Along with balance sheets, profit & loss statements, and directors reports, auditor's reports make up part of a company's statutory accounts.

Preparation of the Report

An audit of a company's financial statements should result in a report wherein the accountant or auditor is free to share their opinion about the validity and reliability of a company's financial statements.

In this report, the auditor should provide an accurate picture of the company and their financial statements. The auditor should also state whether they are externally or internally connected to the company.

Within the report, the auditor can share any reservations about the condition of the company's finances or relevant additional information. Reservations could arise if the auditor disagrees with something found in the financial statements, e.g. if the auditor disagrees with management about the valuation of an asset because they believe that this has a more significant impact on the financial statements.

In the Report

There are rules concerning what an auditor's report should include and the order in which various items should be reported.

Auditor's reports must adhere to accepted standards established by governing bodies. Standards such as those set by the UK Generally Accepted Accounting Practice (UK GAAP) help to assure external users that the auditor's opinion on the fairness of financial statements is based on a commonly accepted framework.

A typical auditor's report will state:

1. The company that has been audited and what their accounting method is.
2. The responsibility of the auditor and their report.
3. Reservations (if any).
4. Conclusion.
5. Any additional information.
6. A management report.
7. The date and auditor's signature.

Types of Auditor's Report

There are four common types of auditor's reports, each one presenting a different situation encountered during the auditor's work. The four reports are as follows:

Unqualified Opinion

An opinion is said to be unqualified when he or she does not have any significant reservation in respect of matters contained in the Financial Statements. The most frequent type of report is referred to as the "Unqualified Opinion", and is regarded by many as the equivalent of a "clean bill of health" to a patient, which has led many to call it the "Clean Opinion", but in reality it is not a clean bill of health, because the Auditor can only provide reasonable assurance regarding the Financial Statements, not the health of the company itself, or the integrity of company records not part of the foundation of the Financial Statements. This type of report is issued by an auditor when the financial statements are free of material misstatements and are presented fairly in accordance with the Generally Accepted Accounting Principles (GAAP), which in other words means that the company's financial condition, position, and operations are fairly presented in the financial statements. It is the best type of report an auditee may receive from an external auditor.

An Unqualified Opinion indicates the following:

(1) The Financial Statements have been prepared using the Generally Accepted Accounting Principles which have been consistently applied.

(2) The Financial Statements comply with relevant statutory requirements and regulations.

(3) There is adequate disclosure of all material matters relevant to the proper presentation of the financial information subject to statutory requirements, where applicable.

(4) Any changes in the accounting principles or in the method of their application and the effects thereof have been properly determined and disclosed in the Financial Statements.

The report consists of a title and header, a main body, the auditor's signature and address, and the report's issuance date. US auditing standards require that the title includes "independent" to convey to the user that the report was unbiased in all respects. Traditionally, the main body of the unqualified report consists of three main paragraphs, each with distinct standard wording and individual purpose. Nonetheless, certain auditors have since modified the arrangement of the main body (but not the wording) in order to differentiate themselves from other audit firms, even though such modification is contrary to the clarified US AICPA standards on auditing.

The first paragraph (commonly referred to as the introductory paragraph) states the audit work performed and identifies the responsibilities of the auditor and the auditee in relation to the financial statements. The second paragraph (commonly referred to as the scope paragraph) details the scope of audit work, provides a general description of the nature of the work, examples of procedures performed, and any limitations the audit faced based on the nature of the work. This paragraph also states that the audit was performed in accordance with the country's prevailing generally accepted auditing standards and regulations. The third paragraph (commonly referred to as the opinion paragraph) simply states the auditor's opinion on the financial statements and whether they are in accordance with generally accepted accounting principles.

Qualified Opinion Report

Qualified report is given by the auditor in either of these two cases:

- When the financial statements are materially misstated due to misstatement in one particular account balance, class of transaction or disclosure that does not have pervasive effect on the financial statements.

- When the auditor is unable to obtain audit evidence regarding particular account balance, class of transaction or disclosure that does not have pervasive effcct on the financial statements.

The report is mostly like a Clear Opinion Report and only includes a paragraph viz. Basis for Qualification after Scope paragraph and before Opinion paragraph. Opinion paragraph in addition to its standard wording includes "except for the matter described in Basis for Qualification paragraph the financial statements give true and fair view."

Detailed below:

A Qualified Opinion report is issued when the auditor encountered one of the two types of situations which do not comply with generally accepted accounting principles, however the rest of the financial statements are fairly presented. This type of opinion is very similar to an unqualified or "clean opinion", but the report states that the financial statements are fairly presented with a certain exception which is otherwise misstated. The two types of situations which would cause an auditor to issue this opinion over the Unqualified opinion are:

- Single deviation from GAAP – this type of qualification occurs when one or more areas of the financial statements do not conform with GAAP (e.g. are misstated), but do not affect the rest of the financial statements from being fairly presented when taken as a whole. Examples of this include a company dedicated to a retail business that did not correctly calculate the depreciation expense of its building. Even if this expense is considered material, since the rest of the financial statements do conform with gaap, then the auditor qualifies the opinion by describing the depreciation misstatement in the report and continues to issue a clean opinion on the rest of the financial statements.
- Limitation of scope – this type of qualification occurs when the auditor could not audit one or more areas of the financial statements, and although they could not be verified, the rest of the financial statements were audited and they conform to GAAP. Examples of this include an auditor not being able to observe and test a company's inventory of goods. If the auditor audited the rest of the financial statements and is reasonably sure that they conform with GAAP, then the auditor simply states that the financial statements are fairly presented, with the exception of the inventory which could not be audited.

The wording of the qualified report is very similar to the Unqualified opinion, but an explanatory paragraph is added to explain the reasons for the qualification after the scope paragraph but before the opinion paragraph. The introductory paragraph is left exactly the same as in the unqualified opinion, while the scope and the opinion paragraphs receive a slight modification in line with the qualification in the explanatory paragraph.

The scope paragraph is edited to include the following phrase in the first sentence, so that the user may be immediately aware of the qualification. This placement also informs the user that, except for the qualification, the rest of the audit was performed without qualifications:

> "*Except as discussed in the following paragraph,* we conducted our audit..."

The opinion paragraph is also edited to include an additional phrase in the first sentence, so that the user is reminded that the auditor's opinion explicitly excludes the qualification expressed. Depending on the type of qualification, the phrase is edited to either state the qualification and the adjustments needed to correct it, or state the scope limitation and that adjustments could have but not necessarily been required in order to correct it.

For a qualification arising from a deviation from GAAP, the following phrase is added to the opinion paragraph:

> "In our opinion, *except for the effects of the Company's incorrect determination of depreciation expense,* the financial statement referred to in the first paragraph presents fairly, in all material respects, the financial position of..."

For a qualification arising from a scope of limitation, the following phrase is added to the opinion paragraph:

> "In our opinion, *except for the effects of such adjustments, if any, as might have been determined to be necessary had we been able to perform proper tests and procedures on the Company's inventory,* the financial statement referred to in the first paragraph presents fairly, in all material respects, the financial position of."

Adverse Opinion Report

An Adverse Opinion Report is issued on the financial statements of a company when the financial statements are materially misstated and such misstatements have pervasive effect on the financial statements.

In Audit Report after Scope paragraph but before Opinion paragraph, Basis for Adverse Opinion paragraph is added. In Opinion paragraph the wording changes to, "Because of situations mentioned in Basis for Adverse Opinion paragraph, in our opinion the financial statements of XYZ Co. Ltd. as mentioned in first paragraph does not give true and fair view/are not free from material misstatements."

An Adverse Opinion is issued when the auditor determines that the financial statements of an auditee are materially misstated and, when considered as a whole, do not conform with GAAP. It is considered the opposite of an unqualified or clean opinion, essentially stating that the information contained is materially incorrect, unreliable, and inaccurate in order to assess the auditee's financial position and results of operations. Investors, lending institutions, and governments very rarely accept an auditee's financial statements if the auditor issued an adverse opinion, and usually request the auditee to correct the financial statements and obtain another audit report.

Generally, an adverse opinion is only given if the financial statements pervasively differ from GAAP. An example of such a situation would be failure of a company to consolidate a material subsidiary.

The wording of the adverse report is similar to the qualified report. The scope paragraph is modified accordingly and an explanatory paragraph is added to explain the reason for the adverse opinion after the scope paragraph but before the opinion paragraph. However, the most significant change in the adverse report from the qualified report is in the opinion paragraph, where the auditor clearly states that the financial statements are not in accordance with GAAP, which means that they, as a whole, are unreliable, inaccurate, and do not present a fair view of the auditee's position and operations.

> "In our opinion, *because of the situations mentioned above* (in the explanatory paragraph), the financial statements referred to in the first paragraph *do not* present fairly, in all material respects, the financial position of."

Disclaimer of Opinion Report

A Disclaimer of Opinion is issued in either of the following cases:

- When the auditor is not independent or when there is conflict of interest.
- When the limitation on scope is imposed by client, as a result the auditor is unable to obtain sufficient appropriate audit evidence.
- When there are significant uncertainties in the business of client.

The audit report changes significantly when there is Disclaimer of opinion. An additional paragraph "Basis for Disclaimer" is added in audit report which is placed after Scope paragraph and before Opinion paragraph. In Scope paragraph the wording changes to "We were engaged to audit the financial statements of XYZ Co. Ltd." from "We have audited the financial statements of XYZ Co. Ltd." In Opinion paragraph wording changes to "We do not express an opinion on the financial statements of XYZ Co. Ltd. due to situations explained in Basis for Disclaimer paragraph".

A Disclaimer of Opinion, commonly referred to simply as a Disclaimer, is issued when the auditor could not form and consequently refuses to present an opinion on the financial statements. This type of report is issued when the auditor tried to audit an entity but could not complete the work due to various reasons and does not issue an opinion. The disclaimer of opinion report can be traced back to 1949, when the Statement on Auditing Procedure No. 23: *Recommendation Made To Clarify Accountant's Representations When Opinion Is Not Expressed* was published in order to provide guidance to auditors in presenting a disclaimer.

Statements on Auditing Standards (SAS) provide certain situations where a disclaimer of opinion may be appropriate:

- A lack of independence, or material conflict(s) of interest, exist between the auditor and the auditee (SAS No. 26).
- There are significant scope limitations, whether intentional or not, which hinder the auditor's work in obtaining evidence and performing procedures (SAS No. 58).
- There is a substantial doubt about the auditee's ability to continue as a going concern or, in other words, continue operating (SAS No. 59).
- There are significant uncertainties within the auditee (SAS No. 79).

Although this type of opinion is rarely used, the most common examples where disclaimers are issued include audits where the auditee willfully hides or refuses to provide evidence and information to the auditor in significant areas of the financial statements, where the auditee is facing significant legal and litigation issues in which the outcome is uncertain (usually government investigations), and where the auditee has going concern issues (the auditee may not continue operating in the near future). Investors, lending institutions, and governments typically reject an auditee's financial statements if the auditor disclaimed an opinion, and will request the auditee to correct the situations the auditor mentioned and obtain another audit report.

A disclaimer of opinion differs substantially from the rest of the auditor's reports because it provides very little information regarding the audit itself, and includes an explanatory paragraph stating the reasons for the disclaimer. Although the report still contains the letterhead, the auditee's name and address, the auditor's signature and address, and the report's issuance date, every other paragraph is modified extensively, and the scope paragraph is entirely omitted since the auditor is basically stating that an audit could not be realized.

In the introductory paragraph, the first phrase changes from "We have audited" to "We were engaged to audit" in order to let the user know that the auditee commissioned an audit, but does not mention that the auditor necessarily completed the audit. Additionally, since the audit was not completely and/or adequately performed, the auditor refuses to accept any responsibility by omitting the last sentence of the paragraph. The scope paragraph is omitted in its entirety since, effectively, no audit was performed.

Similar to the qualified and the adverse opinions, the auditor must briefly discuss the situations for the disclaimer in an explanatory paragraph.

Auditor's Report on Internal Controls of Public Companies

Following the enactment of the Sarbanes-Oxley Act of 2002, the Public Company Accounting Oversight Board (PCAOB) was established in order to monitor, regulate, inspect, and discipline audit and public accounting firms of public companies. The PCAOB Auditing Standards No. 2 now requires auditors of public companies to include an additional disclosure in the opinion report regarding the auditee's internal controls, and to opine about the company's and auditor's assessment on the company's internal controls over financial reporting. These new requirements are commonly referred to as the COSO Opinion.

The auditor's report is modified to include all necessary disclosures by either presenting the report subsequent to the report on the financial statements, or combining both reports into one auditor's report.

Going Concern

Going concern is a term which means that an entity will continue to operate in the near future which is generally more than next 12 months, so long as it generates or obtains enough resources to operate. If the auditee is not a going concern, it means that the entity might not be able to sustain itself within the next twelve months. Auditors are required to consider the going concern of an auditee before issuing a report. If the auditee is a going concern, the auditor does not modify his/her report in any way. However, if the auditor considers that the auditee is not a going concern, or will not be a going concern in the near future, then the auditor is required to include an explanatory paragraph before the opinion paragraph or following the opinion papragraph, in the audit report explaining the situation, which is commonly referred to as the going concern disclosure. Such an opinion is called an "unqualified modified opinion".

Unfortunately, many auditors are increasingly reluctant to include this disclosure in their opinions, since it is considered a "self-fulfilling prophecy" by some. This is because a disclosure for a lack of going concern is viewed negatively by investors, lending institutions, and credit agencies, and therefore reduces the chance that the auditee may obtain the capital or borrowing it needs to survive once the disclosure is made. If this situation occurs, the auditee is more likely to stop being a going concern while the auditor loses potential future audit engagements, and so the auditor may be pressured to avoid including a going concern disclosure. In a study performed on 2001 bankruptcies, nearly half (48%) of selected public companies who faced bankruptcy in 2001 did not have a "going concern disclosure" in the previous auditor's reports. Additionally, 12 of the 20 largest bankruptcies in U.S. history occurred between 2001 and 2002 and none of them had a "going concern disclosure" in their previous auditor's report.

As for the actual wording of the auditor's report, when a lack of going concern is determined by the auditor, the disclosure paragraph should state the situation, state the auditor's determination, and state the auditee's plan to correct the situation. The disclosure paragraph should immediately follow the opinion paragraph.

Other Explanatory Information and Paragraphs

Although the auditor reports are the standard reports for financial statement audits, the auditor may add additional information to the report if it is deemed necessary without changing the overall opinion of the report. Usually, this additional information is included after the opinion paragraph, although some situations require that the additional information be included in paragraphs before the opinion paragraph. The most frequent paragraphs include:

- Limiting distribution of the report – In some occasions, the audit report is restricted to a specified user and the auditor includes this restriction in the report, such as a report for financial statements made in cash basis which are prepared for tax purposes only, financial statements for a wholly owned subsidiary whose sole user of its financial statements is its parent company, etc.
- Additional or supplemental information – Certain auditees include additional and/or supplemental information with their financial statements which is not directly related to the financial statements. Examples due to size, time, location, and/or technical constraints. When the main auditor has to rely on another auditor's work, the main auditor may either accept responsibility for the component's information and not modify the audit report, or may chose to disclaim the audit on the specific component, stating that the main auditor did not audit the component, that another auditor audited the component, that the component's audited information is therefore the responsibility of another auditor, and that the main auditor is simply including it in the original auditee's information. If used, this disclaimer is usually included in the introductory paragraph.

Auditor's Reports on Financial Statements in Different Countries

The auditor's report usually does not vary from country to country, although some countries do require either additional or less wording. In the United States, auditors are required to include in the scope paragraphs a phrase stating that they conducted their audit "in accordance with generally accepted auditing standards in the United States of America", and, in the opinion paragraph, state whether the financial statements are presented "in conformity with generally accepted accounting principles in the United States of America". Some countries, such as the Philippines, use similar reports to those issued in the United States, with the exception that second paragraph would state that the audit was conducted in accordance with Philippine Standards on Auditing, and that the financial statements are in accordance with Philippine Financial Reporting Standards.

Opinion Shopping

Opinion shopping is a term used by external auditors and, after the Enron and Arthur Andersen accounting scandals, the media and general public refer to auditees who contract or reject auditors based on the type of opinion report they will issue on the auditee. The underlying principles of this concept are that auditees determine the compensation to auditors for their work (called "audit fees") as well as awarding future audit engagements; that such fees are the auditor's main source of income; that certain auditees may try to contract auditors that will issue audit opinions based on the auditees' needs; and that certain auditors are willing to comply with such demands so long as they are assured future audit engagements.

The most common example is an auditee that knows that the current auditor is going to issue a qualified, adverse, or disclaimer of opinion report, who then rescinds the audit engagement before the opinion is issued, and subsequently "shops" for another auditor who is willing to issue an "unqualified" opinion, regardless of any qualifying situations mentioned in the previous sections. However, opinion shopping is not limited to auditees contracting auditors based on issuing opinions. It also includes auditors who are over-pleasing to auditees by issuing unqualified reports without properly auditing, or by simply overlooking material issues affecting the audit. These auditors' objective is to appear much more attractive and easy-going than other auditors in order to secure future audit engagements and fees.

Although the great majority of auditors are not willing to jeopardize their profession and reputation for guaranteed audit fees, there are some that will issue opinions solely based on obtaining or maintaining audit engagements. This includes auditors who knowingly emit unmodified unqualified opinions for auditees who are engaged in illegal activities, auditees who have caused a material limitation of scope, auditees that have a lack of going concern, or auditees who present fraudulent financial statements (e.g. Enron and Arthur Andersen). This situation is a clear conflict of interest which should hinder an auditor's independence and the ability to audit (AICPA Code of Ethics), but some auditors willingly ignore this statute.

Recent laws and industry standards have been implemented in order to correct this situation, which include the Sarbanes-Oxley Act and the AICPA's practice-monitoring program and Peer Review Program, which are in some cases voluntary, and in other cases, required.

Other Engagements and Reports

There are various other audits and evaluations which an external auditor performs in addition to the engagements mentioned in the previous sections, each with their respective standard report(s):

- Certification audit reports (for example, an ISO 9000 audit report).
- Compilations (not an audit, but requires a report).
- Due Diligence.
- Environmental audit report.
- Financial forecasts.
- Filing of a public company's Form 10-Q and Form 10-K.
- Agreed Upon Procedures.
- Internal audit reports.
- Regulatory inspection reports.
- Review of financial statements (an overview with very limited auditing procedures).
- Fraud & Materiality Memo.
- Second opinion.
- XBRL assurance.
- Information security audit information technology audit or information technology security audit.

Internal Control

Internal control is an interlocking set of activities that are layered onto the normal operating procedures of an organization, with the intent of safeguarding assets, minimizing errors, and ensuring that operations are conducted in an approved manner. Another way of looking at internal controls is that these activities are needed to mitigate the amount and types of risk to which a firm is subjected.

Internal control comes at a price, which is that control activities frequently slow down the natural process flow of a business, which can reduce its overall efficiency. Consequently, the development of a system of internal control requires management to balance risk reduction with efficiency. This process can sometimes result in management accepting a certain amount of risk in order to create a strategic profile that allows a company to compete more effectively, even if it suffers occasional losses because controls have been deliberately reduced.

A system of internal controls tends to increase in comprehensiveness as a firm increases in size. This is needed, because the original founders do not have the time to maintain complete oversight when there are many employees and/or locations. Further, when a company goes public, there are additional financial control requirements that must be implemented, especially if the firm's shares are to be listed for sale on a stock exchange. Thus, the cost of controls tends to increase with size.

Internal control comes in many forms, which include the following:

- A board of directors oversees the entire organization, providing governance over the management team.
- Internal auditors routinely examine all processes, looking for failings that can be corrected with either new controls or tweaks of existing controls.
- Processes are altered so that more than one person is involved in each one; this is done so that people can cross-check each other, reducing fraud incidents and the likelihood of errors.
- Access to computer records is restricted, so that information is only made available to those people who need it to conduct specific tasks. Doing so reduces the risk of information theft and the risk of asset theft through the modification of ownership records.
- Assets are locked up when not in use, making it more difficult to steal them.

A key concept is that even the most comprehensive system of internal control will not entirely eliminate the risk of fraud or error. There will always be a few incidents, typically due to unforeseen circumstances or an exceedingly determined effort by someone who wants to commit fraud.

Preventative vs. Detective Controls

Internal controls are typically comprised of control activities such as authorization, documentation, reconciliation, security and the separation of duties. And they are broadly divided into preventative and detective activities.

Preventive control activities aim to deter the errors or fraud from happening in the first place, and include thorough documentation and authorization practices. And the separation of duties ensures that no single individual is in a position to authorize, record and be in custody of a financial transaction and the resulting asset. Authorization of invoices and verification of expenses are internal controls. In addition, preventative internal controls include limiting physical access to equipment, inventory, cash and other assets.

Detective controls are backup procedures that are designed to catch items or events that have been missed by the first line of defense. Here the most important activity is reconciliation, used to compare data sets, and corrective action is taken upon material differences. Other detective controls include external audits from accounting firms and internal audits of assets such as inventory.

Limitations of Internal Controls

Regardless of the policies and procedures established by an organization, only reasonable assurance may be provided that internal controls are effective and financial information is correct. The effectiveness of internal controls is limited by human judgment. A business will often give high-level personnel the ability to override internal controls for operational efficiency reasons, and internal controls can be circumvented through collusion.

References

- Auditing and Assurance Vol.1. The Institute of Chartered Accountants of India. 2011. p. 3.4. ISBN 978-81-8441-135-5
- Gilbert W. Joseph and Terry J. Engle (December 2005). "The Use of Control Self-Assessment by Independent Auditors". The CPA Journal. Retrieved 05, April 2020
- Sawyer, Lawrence (2003). Sawyer›s Internal Auditing 5th Edition. Institute of Internal Auditors. ISBN 978-0894135095
- "Internal Audit Checklists of various processes". Internal Audit Expert. internalauditexpert.in. Archived from the original on 13 December 2013. Retrieved 19, May 2020
- Pathak, Jagdish; Lind, Mary R. (November 2003). "Audit Risk, Complex Technology, and Auditing Processes". EDPACS. 31 (5): 1–9. doi:10.1201/1079/43853.31.5.20031101/78844.1

Permissions

All chapters in this book are published with permission under the Creative Commons Attribution Share Alike License or equivalent. Every chapter published in this book has been scrutinized by our experts. Their significance has been extensively debated. The topics covered herein carry significant information for a comprehensive understanding. They may even be implemented as practical applications or may be referred to as a beginning point for further studies.

We would like to thank the editorial team for lending their expertise to make the book truly unique. They have played a crucial role in the development of this book. Without their invaluable contributions this book wouldn't have been possible. They have made vital efforts to compile up to date information on the varied aspects of this subject to make this book a valuable addition to the collection of many professionals and students.

This book was conceptualized with the vision of imparting up-to-date and integrated information in this field. To ensure the same, a matchless editorial board was set up. Every individual on the board went through rigorous rounds of assessment to prove their worth. After which they invested a large part of their time researching and compiling the most relevant data for our readers.

The editorial board has been involved in producing this book since its inception. They have spent rigorous hours researching and exploring the diverse topics which have resulted in the successful publishing of this book. They have passed on their knowledge of decades through this book. To expedite this challenging task, the publisher supported the team at every step. A small team of assistant editors was also appointed to further simplify the editing procedure and attain best results for the readers.

Apart from the editorial board, the designing team has also invested a significant amount of their time in understanding the subject and creating the most relevant covers. They scrutinized every image to scout for the most suitable representation of the subject and create an appropriate cover for the book.

The publishing team has been an ardent support to the editorial, designing and production team. Their endless efforts to recruit the best for this project, has resulted in the accomplishment of this book. They are a veteran in the field of academics and their pool of knowledge is as vast as their experience in printing. Their expertise and guidance has proved useful at every step. Their uncompromising quality standards have made this book an exceptional effort. Their encouragement from time to time has been an inspiration for everyone.

The publisher and the editorial board hope that this book will prove to be a valuable piece of knowledge for students, practitioners and scholars across the globe.

Index

www.ingramcontent.com/pod-product-compliance
Lightning Source LLC
LaVergne TN
LVHW080716210926
848485LV00003B/475